MASTERING KNOWLEDGE IN MODERN TIMES

Fethullah Gülen as an Islamic Scholar

MASTERING KNOWLEDGE
IN MODERN TIMES

Fethullah Gülen as an Islamic Scholar

Edited by
İsmail Albayrak

BLUE DOME

Published by Blue Dome Press
244 Fifth Avenue #2HS
New York, NY 10001

www.bluedomepress.com

Library of Congress Cataloging-in-Publication Data Available

ISBN: 978-1-935295-10-5

Printed by
Çağlayan A.Ş., Izmir - Turkey

CONTENTS

LIST OF CONTRIBUTORS

İsmail Acar has recently been appointed as an Assistant Professor of Islamic Law, Dokuz Eylul University, Turkey. Before this appointment he taught Islam at Bard College, NY for four years 2006–2010; did research at ILSP of Harvard Law School as research fellow in fall 2008; joined Lutheran School of Theology as a visiting scholar of Christian-Muslim relations in 2004–2006; studied at CNES of UCLA as recipient of the Turkish Academy of Science Scholarship in 2002–2004. He received his PhD in Islamic Law from Dokuz Eylul University in 1999. His main research focuses on both classical and contemporary Islamic law.

İsmail Albayrak received his PhD degree from Leeds University and then took up a position at Sakarya University in Turkey, where he taught and wrote on Qur'anic studies, classical exegesis, contemporary approaches to the Qur'an and orientalism. He is currently Professor of Islamic Studies at the Australian Catholic University. He is co-editor of *Oryantalizmi Yeniden Okumak: Batı'da İslam Çalışmalar* (Re-Reading Orientalism: Islamic Studies in the West), and author of *Klasik Modernizm'de Kur'an'a Yeni Yaklaşımlar* (Approaches to the Qur'an in Classic Modernism) and *Fethullah Gülen Hocaefendi'nin Tefsir Anlayışı* (Fethullah Gülen's Approaches to the Qur'anic Exegesis). He also has research interests concerning interfaith dialogue together with the place of Muslim communities and their activities in a globalizing world.

Halim Çalış received an MA in Islamic systematic theology from Marmara University in 1999. He completed another MA at the Lutheran School of Theology in Chicago, USA in 2006 on the subject of world religions and is currently a PhD candidate at the University of Chicago. He has written several articles in various journals and magazines such as *The Fountain*, *Yağmur* (Rain), and *Yeni Ümit* (New Hope). Some of his important papers deal with the notion of allegory, figurative speech, sacred sources of human dignity, and many other religio–ethical issues. His research interests also include comparative religion, interfaith dialogue, and the Gülen Movement (Hizmet Movement) associated with Fethullah Gülen.

Ergün Çapan, PhD, is the General Coordinator of *Yeni Ümit*, a quarterly periodical of Islamic disciplines published in Turkey. He graduated from the Faculty of Divinity, Atatürk University in Erzurum, and obtained his MA degree and PhD in Qur'anic studies from Marmara University in Istanbul. In addition to his academic studies at the school of divinity, Çapan also attended Fethullah Gülen's private study group to master in various classical Islamic disciplines. In his MA thesis Çapan analyzed the Surah Ahzab of the Qur'an in relation to Islamic family structure. The title of his PhD thesis was "The Companions of the Prophet in the Qur'an" which was later published as *Kur'an'da Sahabe* in Turkish. Çapan is also the editor of *Terror and Suicide Attacks: An Islamic Perspective* published in many world languages. He recently convened two major international symposiums in Istanbul: "Kur'an ve Bilimsel Hakikatler" (The Qur'an and Scientific Truths) in June 2010, "Peygamber Yolu" (The Prophet's Way) in October 2010. He is also lecturer in newly established Divinity Faculty in Fatih University, Turkey.

Zeki Sarıtoprak holds a PhD in Islamic systematic theology from the University of Marmara, Turkey. He has been the head of the Nursi Chair in Islamic Studies at John Carroll University since 2003. He is the author of several books and articles in Turkish, English and Arabic. His publications include *The Antichrist (al-Dajjal) in Islamic Theology* and *Fundamentals of Rumi's Thought: A Mawlawi Sufi Perspective* (editor and translator). He also edited *The Muslim World*'s Special Issue on Fethullah Gülen (July 2005). His research interests concentrate on the study of Islamic eschatology, Islamic theology, Said Nursi's work, the Gülen Movement, Islamic ethics, interfaith dialogue, and Muslims in the modern world.

Mehmet Yavuz Şeker received his MA degree from Sakarya University, Turkey. He is currently a PhD candidate at the Australian Catholic University in Melbourne and is examining the topic of the role and concept of the heart according to Sufi tradition with special reference to the works of Fethullah Gülen. He is the author of *Beware! Satan: Strategies of Defense*, *Melekler ve Cinler* (Angels and the Jinn), *Müspet Hareket* (Positive Action), *Kullukta Dört Esas* (Four Fundamentals in Servanthood), and *Zühd* (Renunciation). Şeker's most recent work on sending salutations to the Prophet Muhammad, peace be upon him, is currently in the process of publication. He is also a regular presenter at both national and international panels, conferences and workshops.

INTRODUCTION

İsmail Albayrak

Although a number of conferences have been organized in recent years emphasizing the social, civic, and educational activities of the Gülen Movement (aka Hizmet), as well as Gülen's contribution to interreligious dialogue, very little attention has been paid to his formal and informal education, his scholarly works, and his interpretation of basic Islamic sources and disciplines in the modern period. In fact, his expertise goes beyond the limitations of modern academic compartmentalization of Islamic studies. This edited book aims to explore Gülen's personal and theological profile in relation to Qur'anic exegesis (*tafsīr*), Prophetic tradition (*hadith*), Islamic law (*fiqh*), Islamic systematic theology (*kalam*), and Islamic mysticism or Sufism (*tasawwuf*).

Before we move on to the chapters and their contributors, it is appropriate to provide some brief biographical information about Fethullah Gülen. Gülen is a Muslim intellectual, thinker and religious scholar. He was born in Erzurum, eastern Turkey, in 1941, and grew up in a very religious environment, his first teachers being his parents. He mastered the Qur'an at a very early age, learning Arabic from his father, and continued his traditional education in different village institutions of his hometown. The spiritual and religious training that began at home continued under the tutoring of various famous religious scholars of the time. When Gülen was still a young man he met students of Bediüzzaman Said Nursi and was introduced to the *Risale-i Nur* collections, which in some respects could be considered a "complete" and "contemporary" Islamic school that contributed a great deal to his intellectual and spiritual formation. Meanwhile, he privately continued his "modern" education in science, philosophy, literature, and history.

In 1959, when he was about twenty years old, Gülen moved to Edirne, an old Turkish city on the Balkan border, to work as an official imam. After military service and following his years in Edirne he was appointed, in 1966, as a Qur'anic teacher to Izmir, the third largest city in Turkey. Besides teaching the Qur'an and Arabic, he travelled a great deal in the Aegean part of Turkey delivering speeches concerning religious, social, and ethical issues. He went on *hajj* (pilgrimage) in 1968. In the 1970s he became a very well known preacher and respected scholar in Turkey. After the military coup of 12 March 1971, Gülen was arrested unjustly under suspicion of trying to undermine the social, political, and economic foundations of the secularist regime in Turkey, and of founding an association and secret community for this purpose, thus taking advantage of people's religious feelings. Six months later he was released of all charges and returned to his official position. He was then assigned as a preacher to different cities and finally to Bornova, Izmir, where he worked until 1980. He retired in 1981, re-started his regular sermons in an emeritus capacity in 1986, and continued giving sermons until the beginning of the 1990s. In 1994, he established the Journalists and Writers Foundation to promote dialogue and tolerance among all social strata and has received a warm welcome from people from all walks of life. He visited the Vatican and had a meeting with the late Pope, John Paul II in 1998. In 1999 he went to the United States of America for medical treatment and has lived there ever since.

Shaped by his opinions a small group came into being in Izmir, Turkey, during the late 1960s and commenced activities involving service to others based on Gülen's teachings. Currently, many people from all walks of life continue these activities, serving without thought of material reward. They preach, teach, and establish private educational institutions and intercultural dialogue centers all over the world. They also publish books and magazines, as well as daily and weekly newspapers, participate in television and radio broadcasts, and fund scholarships for poor students. The companies and foundations set up by people of different worldviews who agree about the need to serve humanity, especially in the field of education, have founded and are operating hundreds of schools and many universities based in more than 120 countries. Gülen's notion of service permits no expectation of material or political gain.[1] This picture indicates that with thousands of followers inside and outside Turkey, the Gülen Movement is a global one.

---

[1] http://en.fgülen.com/content/category/148/160/10/.

As mentioned earlier, Gülen is first and foremost an Islamic scholar. He taught and still teaches privately and informally many divinity graduates in various Islamic disciplines. However, with the exception of *Kalbin Zümrüt Tepeleri* (published in English as *Emerald Hills of the Heart*),[2] he has not written any work that is specifically dedicated to any of the Islamic disciplines as we know them in the academia. His works like *Kur'an'dan İdrake Yansıyanlar* (Reflections on the Qur'an), *Kur'an'ın Altın İkliminde* (In the Golden Clime of the Qur'an) – which will be published in English within the next few years – touches upon selected verses from the Qur'an and provide some unique commentary that opens up new gateways for researchers to take on further. Gülen has not written theological treatises or a complete exegesis on the Qur'an. Nonetheless, in his various books and speeches, he deals with these issues extensively. The authors of this volume base their research on Gülen's various texts.

In the first chapter İsmail Albayrak focuses on Gülen's exegetical works. Although Gülen has not written a complete exegesis on the Qur'an, Albayrak will refer to his important exegetical works to show where Gülen stands in relation to diverse modern Muslim scholarship on the Qur'an. Albayrak's chapter examines Gülen's re-reading of Qur'anic text, his approach to the nature and status of the Qur'an as divine revelation, the notions of abrogation, the thematic unity of the Qur'an, verses that are explicit in meaning (*muhkam*) and allegorical or ambiguous (*mutashābih*), Qur'anic narratives and the occasion of revelation. The main questions that Albayrak tackles are: What is the difference between Gülen's reading of the Qur'an and that of his counterparts who follow both classical and modern approaches? Does Gülen offer a new reading differing from others or does he follow very well-established exegetical traditions? How does he deal with modern sciences and ongoing scientific developments in relation to Qur'anic verses and do Muslims need a new type of hermeneutics in their interpretation of the Qur'an?

According to Albayrak, some might see Gülen as a stereotypical traditionalist who embellishes his exegesis with a few modern discourses while for others, who approach him more sympathetically, he is a progres-

---

2   *The Essentials of the Islamic Faith* by Gülen can be considered a volume on systematic theology but that book does not cover all issues of theology. Furthermore, he has also written about the life of the Prophet Muhammad, peace be upon him, and the importance of Prophetic tradition, however, these are not complete texts on these issues.

sive Muslim intellectual who has sufficient religious and scientific background to offer changes to the interpretation of various Islamic disciplines. Albayrak, however, thinks that Gülen is actually a representative of
Ottoman exegetical tradition. He is well-acquainted with classical and
modern commentaries and is also familiar with contemporary issues and
scientific developments. In addition, Gülen is a man of action; therefore
Albayrak says that it is inappropriate to view his exegetical efforts from the
perspective of mere intellectualism.

Concerning the methodology of the exegesis, Albayrak holds the view
that Gülen is a representative of *via media*. He uses reports on "the occasions
of revelations" while sometimes criticizing these reports. His approach to
the notion of *isrāīliyyāt*[3] follows a similar pattern. Observing his analysis of
the notion of *naskh* (abrogation) and *muhkam* and *mutashābih*, Albayrak
notices his broader understanding of the issues. Thus, Albayrak situates
Gülen somewhere between traditionalist and modernist scholars in his evaluation of these hermeneutical devices. Similarly, Albayrak considers Gülen
as a representative of the middle ground when he is interpreting the nature
of the Qur'an, looking at the relationship between scientific developments
and Qur'anic verses etc. Gülen argues against the wholesale adoption of a
scientific, literary or classical approach. Instead, he suggests that Muslim
scholars and interpreters of the Qur'an should use an approach that is rooted in Islamic tradition and experience, without neglecting modern developments. With regard to mystical, theological and legal interpretation of the
Qur'an, Albayrak sees his style as being a moderate one which follows traditional literature, while giving credit to modern interpretations and scientific
explorations.

Halim Çalış explores Gülen's thought regarding the Prophetic tradition
of Islam known as *hadith*. Having summarized Gülen's ideas on the subject
through examples taken from his works, Çalış presents brief discussions on
various specific matters to cover everything under the title of *hadith* such as
information about *hadith*, the chain of *isnad* (transmitters) and *matn* (texts)
and their criticism, the types of *hadith* collections, the status of *hadith* (the

---

3   In a restricted sense, *isra'iliyyat* applies to the traditions and reports that contain elements
    of the legendary and religious Jewish and Christian literature, but more inclusively and
    more commonly it also refers to Zoroastrian and other Near Eastern elements including
    folklore.

second source of Islam), the importance of the Prophet in Islam, the function of *hadith*, criticism of Western scholarship of *hadith*, the notion of sola scriptura, some information about Gülen's early *hadith* studies, and Gülen's expertise on *ilm al-rijal* (*hadith* narrators).

Çalış deals with these various issues from three dimensions notably, how Gülen uses and interprets *hadith* in his works as a "commentator," what contribution he makes as a "teacher," and finally what point of view he holds in the face of contemporary debates over *hadith*. Çalış depicts Gülen as an intellectual *ālim*-type scholar who is well-acquainted with various Islamic and modern sciences and finds Gülen's re-reading of *hadith* very rich. He draws attention to Gülen's interpretation of *hadith* in the light of the Qur'an. Though Gülen follows the Sunni paradigm closely, he always seeks a middle way to combine *hadith* with mainstream understanding. Thus, it has been frequently observed that Gülen, instead of denying the authenticity of reports concerning traditions such as the creation of Eve from Adam's rib, the runaway camel's creation from Satan or many other ambiguous *hadith* prefers to explain them allegorically. For Çalış, at the heart of Gülen's approach to *hadith* (in the light of mainstream Islam) is his intention to solve the problems of modern times by using the flexibility that already exists in the essence of religion and being respectful of Sufism.

Çalış also focuses on another aspect of Gülen's expertise on *hadith*, namely modern discussions about *hadith* and science. According to Çalış, Gülen is able to derive original answers to the questions raised in modern times using *hadith* material. In doing so, he reminds the reader that Gülen maintains a balance and never takes modern sciences as the only criteria for the interpretation of *hadith*. Human reason and scientific facts are welcome as long as they assist but do not determine the process of interpretation. Çalış places great emphasis on Gülen's defense of *hadith* in the modern period. As is seen frequently, not only does Gülen narrate *hadith* in his preaching and public lectures but he also comments on them and teaches subjects related to them. Gülen, in his evaluation of *hadith*, criticizes seriously both those who try to minimize or completely ignore the theological and jurisprudential effectiveness of the *sunnah*, and those who assess it as a purely blind imitation of the Prophet. Although Gülen attaches himself very tightly to the classical view, he also develops a modern interpretative methodology. According to Çalış, first Gülen recognizes the historical and cultural

xiv   *Mastering Knowledge in Modern Times*

background of the Prophet's actions and statements and makes distinctions between personal and universal characteristics of the *sunnah*. Second, Gülen emphasizes the "spirit" of the *sunnah* which has priority to be observed, in his understanding. This approach allows Gülen to recognize the authority of the *sunnah* on the one hand, and to interpret this source to meet the needs of contemporary Muslims on the other.

One can also find in Çalış's analysis Gülen's extensive information in relation to the peoples and events that take place in a given *hadith*. In addition, Gülen produces a response against those who criticize some famous narrators of *hadith* and their recording of *hadith*. Thus this chapter can be considered a concise summary of Gülen's thought on *hadith*.

İsmail Acar tries to situate Gülen's legal methodology within contemporary Islamic legal and intellectual discourse. He argues that Gülen transforms contemporary Islamic thinking intellectually through his active engagement with Islamic learning and the current questions that many Muslims face today; he produces *fatwa*s (legal rulings) and juristic interpretations in the light of both classical sources and modern conditions. One of the crucial questions for Acar is whether Gülen is a qualified independent jurist or not. To answer such an important query requires investigation into Gülen's competence in his various *ijtihad*s. According to Acar, there are two important points to tackle before answering this question. The first is to look at the circumstances of Gülen's life and the second is to consider the conditions for *ijtihad*. Concerning the first point, Acar reminds us of some turning points in Gülen's life. A major change was his re-location from his very conservative hometown to modern cities where religious observances did not seem to be followed so well, in particular, his migration to the USA and his stay there for over a decade. For Acar, these circumstances equipped Gülen with an understanding of the needs of modern people and instilled in him a desire to explain and preserve the core values of Islamic law.

Regarding the second point, Acar uses the argument of the great Muslim scholar Ghazzali. Acar is very confident in approving Gülen's qualifications for independent *ijtihad*. Moreover, Acar believes that Gülen's extensive familiarity with classical sources allows him to bring new perspectives and critical thinking to Islamic jurisprudence. It is also important to note that Gülen, as a preacher by profession, demonstrates a good balance between theoretical and practical application of the law. Nonetheless, Gülen never disregards firmly established Islamic legal thought. According to Acar, Gülen generally works in line with the Hanafi-Maturidi school with special emphasis on the re-examination of all juristic interpretations based on tradition and custom. For Acar, this is the new perspective which Gülen tries to bring into the modern life of contemporary Muslims. He also adds that Gülen holds the view that this important mission can only be carried out by a qualified committee.

Acar gives a number of examples from Gülen's *ijtihad* to show how he deals with various issues. Moreover, Gülen makes a clear distinction between issues that can be re-evaluated and others that cannot. Acar also mentions Bediüzzaman's influence on Gülen concerning his approach to Islamic law. Finally, Acar draws attention to the notion of *maslaha* (public interest) and the role it plays in Gülen's legal reasoning. This very insightful chapter sheds light on a considerably neglected area of Gülen's scholarship.

Zeki Sarıtoprak is trying to find an answer to the question of whether it is possible to talk about a contemporary Islamic theology of social responsibility. To do so, he briefly provides a background to theological discourse in Islam as well as discussing an Islamic theology of social responsibility and its possibility in present time. The first question Sarıtoprak has tackled is the definition of *iman* (belief) and its relation to *amal* (action) in Muslim theological tradition. He argues that although the lack of action may not be considered the same as a lack of faith, action is a great sign of the strength or weakness of one's faith. Furthermore, he draws attention to the difference between theology (mere intellectual) and jurisprudence (praxis) in Islamic studies. According to Sarıtoprak, Muslim theologians developed intellectual and theoretical aspects of Islamic theology and left the action aspect of it to the science of *fiqh*, which deals with a believer's daily activities including daily prayers, social interactions, charities, marriages, trades, etc. In the modern period there are some attempts to develop a social theology of Islam but the majority of these endeavors focus on the idea of sociology rather than the Qur'an. Having based his approach on Dermot A. Lane's book, *Foundations for a Social Theology*, Sarıtoprak argues that there is no classical or modern scholar of Islam who places greater stress on the importance of praxis in theology (*kalam*) than Gülen.

Then, Sarıtoprak moves to the core of his argument and introduces Gülen to the reader as an exceptional voice in an Islamic theology of social responsibility. For Sarıtoprak, Gülen is not satisfied with the traditionally established task of *kalam* (defending the Islamic creed against intellectual attacks) but adds that one of the important dimensions of modern Muslim *kalam* is its inclusion of praxis. In this regard, *kalam* will not only respond to the challenges that come from a Western critical approach to religion, but will also provide a solid ground for some social activists. Gülen, with his active endeavors, represents this aspect of the science of *kalam*. Similar to social theology in the West, Gülen's theology of social responsibility contains a collective approach to the spiritual and social problems of modern times through the lenses of many social sciences. Sarıtoprak says that Gülen finds the roots of social theology in the practices of the Prophet. Furthermore, the concept of love plays a significant role in the determination of his approach to theology. The believer should "hasten to stop cries and respond to grievances, should treat pains with antidotes, and transform the cries of people to laughter."

Positive action is another notion in Gülen's notion of a theology of social responsibility. Every individual is capable of contributing to the community. One way of doing this is to participate actively in the social life of institutions, and with individual piety guide others to perfection and maturity, not only in their personal lives but in their social lives. According to Sarıtoprak, Gülen's approach, as distinct to that of other imams, lies in this. Gülen has also developed analytical approaches to the social realities of our time and how problems can be cured through positive action. There are two dimensions to positive action, one is education and the other is interreligious dialogue. Clearly, Gülen's theology of social responsibility embraces all humanity. It is also important to note that Sarıtoprak points out various aspects of Gülen-inspired activities. Though education and interfaith activities are the backbone, Gülen's theology of social responsibility goes beyond works in schools and gatherings for mere dialogue. Sarıtoprak summarizes why his understanding of theology is so important: "Gülen successfully managed to combine the values of Islam with contemporary life through educational, social, and public health institutions, a combination which has few precedents in the history of Islam."

Mehmet Y. Şeker discusses the Sufi dimension of Gülen's scholarship. Şeker begins by giving information about *tasawwuf* (Sufism) from a Sunni Muslim perspective. The first topic he dwells on is the aim of Sufism. Briefly, he considers *tasawwuf* as an original property of Islam, as it is simply first and foremost a way of life. Before focusing on Gülen's approach to Sufism, he follows the standard division of *tasawwuf* and provides the essential features of each period in history. The first period is called *zuhd* (renunciation and piety) and it is very plain when it is compared with the complex development of the following centuries. Referring to several sources, Şeker notes that during this period the generic name of *tasawwuf* is still unknown to many and there is no rule or principle outside the primary sources of Islam. A Sufi's only desire is to imitate the life of the Prophet and the Companions. In the second period of Sufism, many Sufis develop a method of *riyadah* (austerity) and *mujahadah* (striving). It is also observed that there are great stresses placed on the notion of spiritual states of learning and knowledge, *ma'rifah*. This period has seen the emergence of many distinguished mystics, and Sufism becomes a real Islamic discipline. The final stage is the period of *tariqah*. In this period Sufism is institutionalized and many powerful Sufi orders are established. After this introduction to the development of Sufism, Şeker summarizes numerous technical Sufi terms, eloquently describing the spiritual journey of Sufis, in order to pave the way to a clear understanding of Gülen's approach to Islamic mysticism. This journey is an inner trip of the heart to end up with one's beloved, God Almighty.

In his rich and beneficial summary, Şeker then concentrates on Gülen's family and his social and educational milieu. Clearly, his family from early childhood, and some local scholars and mystics had a great influence on his adoption of the Sufi lifestyle. Nonetheless, the prime place concerning Sufism must be given to Bediüzzaman Said Nursi. According to Şeker, though neither Gülen nor Nursi have been engaged in any formal Sufi order, they both laid enormous stress on the inner and personal dimension of Sufism. Therefore Şeker frequently repeats that Gülen never sees himself as a Sufi master, a shaykh. Equally, it is important to note the main Sufi concepts (earnestness, suffering, sorrow, worship) that Gülen uses frequently in his speeches and writing. Şeker also tries to find traces of earlier Sufis in shaping Gülen's understanding of Sufism.

Having inspired a global movement of education, philanthropy, and dialogue, Gülen stresses active practice of Sufi life and guides himself and others. According to Şeker, Gülen considers such a life to be the vocation of the Prophet and his Companions. Finally, Şeker draws attention to Gülen's masterpiece on Sufism, *Emerald Hills of the Heart*. According to Şeker, despite the commonality of these concepts with traditional sources, their presentations and contents are quite different from their classical counterparts. Şeker holds the view that this new attempt by Gülen gives Sufism dynamism. His focus on the path of *ajz*, *faqr*, *shawq*, and *shukr*, together with his emphasis on the balance of the inner and outer world, resonate with Nursi's work.

The last chapter is written by **Ergün Çapan**, who is an expert in Qur'anic studies in Turkey. Çapan's article draws attention to an aspect of Gülen that has not been discussed before. In the beginning of his work, Çapan specifically focuses on the environment, sources, and teaching style which Gülen has grown with. He has found an opportunity to seek education from teachers or imams who were educated under the traditional Ottoman education system, during a period which can be considered as a period of drought for Islamic learning. Çapan explains that Gülen received an education from the period's most important and most influential teachers or imams and studied their books, alongside his own personal perseverance and study of Arabic textbooks that were taught throughout classic Ottoman schools. Çapan's most interesting analysis is perhaps his explanation that Gülen, through his own personal persistence and endeavor, benefited from modern texts that would be hard to think of in the framework of classic religious educational circles. Gülen, who has read some of the most famous works of the East and West, has also studied literature, philosophy, sociology, psychology, and scientific works of his time

This chapter, which provides a real contribution to the Gülen's scholarly profile, also contains important information regarding Gülen's private study circle and the texts and style of education that Gülen has taught. The list provided by Çapan shows that the works taught by Gülen are quite extensive and sizeable. From exegesis to Islamic mysticism, from law to *hadith* and theology, from Arabic and eloquence to the life of the Prophet, Gülen has read an extensive range of classic and modern works with his students, some of which he has read and taught more than once, and if we take this into consideration, enough information can be given to us regarding classic excerpts of benefit. It is mentioned that sometimes 50–60 pages of a book is read after morning prayers or a whole collection of books are completed during the month of Ramadan. Gülen who desires for his students to attend class prepared, often provides comments and assessments on texts studied, which Çapan states as the most pleasurable and satisfying moments of the class. For this reason, Çapan's article does not only focus on Gülen's expertise on the topic of basic Islamic disciplines, but deals with Gülen's expertise as a whole in general Islamic studies, the way he teaches in the class. In addition, the article is written by one of the pupils of Gülen himself, which is why this article is an important contribution in defining Gülen's mastership in Islamic disciplines.

It is my primary duty to express my sincere thanks to the contributors who enriched this volume by each of them covering a different aspect of Fethullah Gülen's Islamic scholarship, thus making this book – the first of its kind – possible. I am also grateful to colleagues who have offered generous and constructive criticism. Pride of place belongs to Dr. İsmail Acar, Prof. Raymond Canning, Dr. İhsan Yılmaz and Hakan Yeşilova. Maryna Mews and Derya İner edited the manuscript and made some helpful suggestions. Finally, this book could not have been written without the constant support and encouragement of my wife, Fatma Albayrak.

CHAPTER ONE

Fethullah Gülen's Approach to Qur'anic Exegesis

İsmail Albayrak

1. INTRODUCTION

Muslim exegetical endeavor in the modern period is a most interesting topic. The last two centuries have witnessed a period of great effort in scrutinizing new attitudes towards the interpretation of the Qur'an among contemporary Muslim intellectuals. Nonetheless, we must admit that many of these works do not cover the exegetical literature in various vernacular languages. Turkish exegesis of the Qur'an constitutes one of the most important missing parts of this literature.[4] In this chapter, we will focus on the exegetical works of Fethullah Gülen, one of the most influential Turkish scholars of recent times. Although Gülen has not written a complete exegesis on the Qur'an, we will refer to his important exegetical works to show where he stands in relation to diverse modern Muslim scholarship on the Qur'an. This chapter will examine Gülen's re-reading of the Qur'anic text, his approach to the nature and status of the Qur'an as divine revelation, the notions of abrogation, clear (*muhkam*) and allegorical (*mutashābih*) verses, thematic unity among the chapters and verses of the Qur'an, Qur'anic narratives and the occasion of revelation. The main questions that we will tackle in this context are: what is the difference between Gülen's reading of the Qur'an and that of his counterparts adhering to both classical and modern approaches? Does Gülen offer a new reading differing from others, or does he follow very well established exegetical traditions?

---

[4]   For instance, J. M. S. Baljon regrets in his *Modern Muslim Koran Interpretation (1880–1960)* that he is unable to cover the commentaries of Turkish exegetes (p. vii).

How does he deal with modern sciences and ongoing scientific developments in relation to Qur'anic verses? Do Muslims need a new type of hermeneutics in their interpretation of the Qur'an?

2. GÜLEN'S VIEW OF THE NATURE AND STATUS OF THE QUR'AN

In order to properly evaluate Gülen's exegetical approach, it is important to look at his general opinions on the nature and status of the Qur'an. We primarily focus here on his opinions about the nature of the Qur'an, the notion of revelation, its place in primordial existence, the epistemic value of the Qur'an, its universality, its authority or power in forming Muslim societies, and the role played by the Qur'an in defining the relationship between God and the creation, and as a consequence, the relationship between human beings and the universe.

There are significant similarities between Gülen's approaches to the above-mentioned issues and the approach of classical and modern Muslim scholars. Despite these similarities, the discourse produced by Gülen is quite different from both his modern and classical counterparts. Moreover, we come across a variety of additional information in Gülen's accounts. First of all, Gülen states that the Qur'an is a unique book that preserves its divine origin. It comes directly from the everlasting "Speech" attribute (*kalam*) of God and therefore, the Qur'an is the eternal Word of God. Nonetheless, Gülen notes that God's speech is different from the speech of His creatures, and human beings are not able to comprehend all dimensions of His speech. Following the *Maturidi* school of thought, he provides detailed information about inner speech (*kalam al-nafsī*) and outer speech (*kalam al-lafzī*). In normal speech we see letters, words, sentences etc. This speech is channeled into letters, words, and sentences and becomes spoken words, the *kalam al-lafzī*. There is another type of speech that is not spoken with sound but is spoken as inner speech to oneself; this is called *kalam al-nafsī*.[5] Gülen gives many examples of inner speech from the Qur'an such as the Prophet Joseph's speech about his brothers in verse 12:77. "They said: If he has stolen – well, a brother of his stole before. But Joseph (endured their false accusation in silence and) held it secret in his soul and did not disclose it them. He said (to himself): 'You are indeed

---

5   Gülen 1997a, p. 22.

in a bad situation (now and say so). God has full knowledge of what you allege.'"[6] Gülen believes that whenever the Qur'an is heard, listened to, recited or written down, Muslims understand the inner meanings in the outer words and sentences. For instance, when a Muslim reads the verse *inna alladhīna kafarū* (those who disbelieve ...), the expression *inna* is composed of a *hamza* and a *nūn*. When we state or write them, we simultaneously see the existence of this *kalam al-nafsī* (inner speech) in the *kalam al-lafzī* format, and feel the weight of the Divine Word.[7] Therefore, Muslims never tire of repeating the Qur'an. Even if they get bored with the literal word and meaning of the Qur'an, they never become tired of its inner meaning. In short, we may not be able to point to this indefinite nature of the inner speech (the meaning), but we always sense it.

According to Gülen, one cannot express pleasure with this inner meaning, whatever is said can only be amazement or astonishment.[8] Gülen's explanation of the nature of the Qur'an is worth examining. Clearly, he considers the inner meaning, which is embedded in the letters and words of the Qur'an, as essential. He also puts great emphasis on the incomprehensible nature of this meaning.[9] With this approach he raises his objection to two schools of thought. On the one hand, he criticizes the Mu'tazilites who hold that the speaker is the creator of the word; on the other hand, he rejects the idea of the Kharijites who claim that the Word of God is composed of letters and sounds. In conclusion Gülen considers the Qur'an as the most precious eternal diamond of the *lawh al-mahfūz* (Guarded Tablets).[10]

Another important topic relating to the nature of the Qur'an is the notion of *wahy* (revelation). Gülen is very cautious about several issues relating to the Qur'anic revelation such as the way in which the Prophet received the revelation, the difference between revelation and inspiration, the effects of the revelation on him, recording of the revelation, etc. Gülen states that the manifestation of revelation in the form of Qur'anic scripture is the most suitable way to convey the message of God. He also adds that this type of revelation corresponds to the level of human understanding.[11]

---

6   See also the verse 7:205; Gülen 1997a, pp. 22–23.
7   Ibid, p. 23.
8   Ibid, p. 23.
9   Ibid, p. 24.
10 Gülen 1989, p. 3.
11 Gülen 2004a, p. 20.

Having followed the classical definition of the term *wahy* (revelation), Gülen points out the richness of the meaning of this term in Arabic. Moreover, he frequently draws attention to the Prophet's reception of the revelation. Although the Qur'an and Prophetic traditions give extensive information about the difficult nature of this process, Gülen claims that because the Prophet is the only person who has experienced the revelation, he is the one who knows the exact details of this difficult experience. Revelation's unique association with the Prophet makes its detailed comprehension impossible for others.[12] Nevertheless, Gülen cautiously explains the process of revelation with an example:

> For instance, receptors transfer the signal of the alphabets of Morse into everyday letters and words. Every signal is equal to the specific letter. A person who uses this receptor knows which sign is equal to which letter. In order to make the process of revelation understandable, we can use this comparison. Briefly, (may God forgive my analogy) God puts thousands of the spiritual receptors inside the nature of the Prophet to allow him to receive every divine signal as a specific word.[13]

In addition, Gülen argues that it is not wise to claim that revelation came to the Prophet as meaning and the Prophet himself put these meanings into the form of letters (words).[14] Furthermore, Gülen adds to the discussion by saying that because of the complete match between the receiver and the received, there is no single anecdote in the Qur'an and traditions recorded of the Prophet asking God to repeat verses while receiving them from Him. In short, denying the Divine origin of the Qur'an and reducing revelation to the limits of human understanding is an alien notion, in Gülen's understanding.[15] On the basis of the verse (42:51) "It is not fitting for a man that God should speak to him except by inspiration or from behind a veil, or by the sending of a messenger to reveal, with God's permission, what God wills: for He is Most High, Most Wise," Gülen also argues that all the Prophets before the Prophet Muhammad, peace be upon him, received their messages in a similar way. According to him, the word *wahy* connotes objectivity and this is the main difference between revelation (*wahy*) and inspira-

---

[12] Ibid, pp. 19–20.
[13] Ibid, p. 20.
[14] See the discussion of the late Fazlur Rahman in his *Islam*, p. 31.
[15] Gülen 2004a, pp. 19–20.

tion (*ilhām*). In other words, inspiration is subjective, open to interpretation, without witnesses, and not binding; whereas revelation is subjective but binding and confirmed by witnesses. Although both revelation and inspiration come from God, the receiver of the inspiration never communicates with the Angel Gabriel.[16]

It is also noteworthy that Gülen frequently uses two important Qur'anic concepts to show the distinct nature of Qur'anic revelation. The first one is the word *furqān*, which signifies the difference, uniqueness, and exceptional status of the Qur'an. In Gülen's theology, this means that human beings are not the Creator or sender of the revelation; therefore, they are supposed to serve their Lord.[17] The second Qur'anic term is *qarin* (the close one). Gülen explains that this term identifies the relationship between God and human beings through the Qur'an. To put it another way, believers will come close to God via the Qur'an and when they come close to God, their knowledge and wisdom will automatically increase.[18]

Because of the strong association of Qur'anic revelation with the speech of God, Gülen constantly asserts that the Qur'an itself is a blessing. Like Bediüzzaman Said Nursi, Gülen reiterates that the Qur'an is a book of wisdom, ritual, law, prayer, contemplation, reflection, etc.[19] Because the Qur'an is a divine manifestation, Gülen considers the Qur'an extremely important within the circular and interdependent relationship of the universe, human beings, and the Qur'an. Gülen points out that the universe is the universe of God (*kāināt Allah*), the Qur'an is the Book of God (*kitāb Allah*), and a human being is the servant of God (*ibād Allah*). One of the common themes among these three entities is God (*Allah*) who manifested Himself in the Qur'an.[20] The attributes of God can only be known fully through this eternal speech of God. For Gülen, the Qur'an is the brightest and most enduring miracle of the Prophet. Its language and style are beyond any description and any rules of ethics, morality, social relations and law that contain the basis of modern disciplines and sciences. Strictly speaking, Gülen considers the Qur'an to be the shortest way to God. It is an endless source of solutions

---

[16] Gülen 2005a, pp. 110–111.
[17] Gülen 1997a, p. 56.
[18] Ibid, p. 55.
[19] Ibid, pp. 47–48.
[20] Ibid, p. 25.

to many modern problems. So Gülen holds the view that it is the Book from which one cannot stay away.[21]

Gülen's approach to the Qur'an might be reminiscent of a kind of traditional reading of the Qur'an, but in fact it is not. He simply refers to various dimensions that we can reach via the Qur'an. For a sound and authentic communication, Gülen points out the necessity for a strong connection between the sender and receiver of the message. If there is no harmony between them, there is no relationship.[22] In various places Gülen states that the Qur'an is a very jealous text, if you do not hold it firmly or open yourself to it completely, it is quite difficult to benefit from it.[23] The crux of the matter, according to Gülen, lies in the correct understanding of the Qur'anic status that facilitates a relationship between human beings and God. Gülen never sees the Qur'an as a neutral, theoretical or descriptive book, but a way of life and a prescriptive text that shapes individuals and societies. Gülen expresses dissatisfaction with the kind of analysis that deals with the Qur'an solely on an epistemological basis. He argues that there are various levels of relationship between human beings and the Qur'an. One of them is the notion of guidance. He believes that the Qur'an is primarily a book of guidance. It is the determiner while the human, as its object, is the determined one. This perception indicates that if we accept the Qur'an as the Word of God, it means that we automatically accept that its messages are contemporary.

This point brings us to another notion, namely the universality of the Qur'an. Although the Qur'an is revealed within a known historical context, it is generally considered both as a historical and an unhistorical oral text. Gülen thinks that if there was no Qur'an, there would be no real and valid judgments for eternity.[24] From this one should not conclude that Gülen thinks that the Qur'an provides a legal rule for every single event or conveys a general law applicable to all local issues. For him, one of the faults of this approach is making the Qur'an solely an ethical book or a judicial book. Gülen's emphasis on the universality of the Qur'an is far removed from this kind of reductionism. For instance, when Gülen comments on the verse 21:30:

21 Gülen 2005c, pp. 4–5.
22 Gülen 1997b, p. 155.
23 Gülen 1997a, p. 7.
24 Ibid, p. 54.

"Do not the unbelievers see that the heavens and the earth were joined together (as one unit of creation), before We clove them asunder? We made from water every living thing. Will they not then believe?" He reiterates that the Qur'an uses the expression *kafarū* (who did not believe) not only to describe Bedouins who tried to understand the stars with their naked eyes but also to address modern faithless human beings who close their eyes to the truth.[25]

Gülen's frequent emphasis on the status of the Qur'an goes even further as he says that every Muslim should consider the Qur'an as if it is being revealed to him or her unceasingly. This is the first step for understanding the universality of the Qur'an.[26] Gülen considers memorization a superficial act if the Qur'an does not allow the person who committed it to memory to re-think and re-shape his life.[27] Thus, one should read the Qur'an as if one is listening to it from God, the Angel Gabriel, and the Messenger of God.[28] As well as stressing the external dynamics of the Qur'anic recitation (competence with the language of the Qur'an, recitation in accordance with the rules of *tajwīd* etc.), Gülen regularly emphasizes the necessity of serious engagement with the Qur'an, entering the mysterious world of the verses, and internalizing their meanings from the bottom of one's heart. He also draws attention to the importance of reciting the Qur'an with immense sensitivity and humility.[29]

3. GENERAL APPROACH TO EXEGESIS

In this section we are going to analyze Gülen's general attitude towards exegesis. His evaluation of traditional and rational exegesis and the issue of Qur'anic translation will also be discussed. Finally we will focus on the notion of *tanāsub* (harmony among the verses and chapters of the Qur'an).

3.1. Gülen's evaluation of exegesis

Gülen frequently states that being the word of God does not contradict the Qur'an's revelation in Arabic. The Qur'an itself refers to this fact several

---

[25] Ibid, pp. 41–42.
[26] Gülen 2002, p. 97.
[27] Gülen 1997b, p. 155.
[28] Gülen 1997a, p. 14.
[29] Gülen 1995a, p. 195.

times. Two broad approaches to exegesis have been adopted by many commentators, namely textual and historical analysis of the Qur'an since the formative period of exegesis. Gülen summarizes his own understanding of exegesis as follows:

> Exegesis is produced in order to understand a text. From the Qur'anic perspective,
> this task is carried out via linguistic and literary analysis together with intertextual-
> ity, Prophetic traditions, and exegetical reports. In addition to all these, one also
> needs the light of the heart and the mind (faith) in his interpretation of the Qur'an.
> If the exegetes place stress on historical analysis, it is described as traditional
> (*riwāyah*), if priority is given to linguistic analysis, it is called rational exegesis
> (*dirāyah*).[30]

Gülen discusses various exegetes whose works are classified under
above stated categories. He mentions, for example, Tabarī, Samarqandī,
Zamakhsharī, Rāzī, Baydāwī, Ibn Kathīr, Suyūtī, Ālūsī and some Ottoman
commentators such as Abu al-Suūd, Kamalpashazādah, Muhammad Hamdi
Yazır and Konyalı Vehbi.[31] While referring to continuous exegetical traditions, he also draws attention to some exegetical schools. Be that as it may,
Gülen, as a man of *via media*, always keeps the balance between *dirāyah* and
riwāyah in his exegesis. In contrast to some modern thinkers who criticize
the insistence of the classical exegetical works on many reports, textual analysis and specific references to detailed linguistic information, Gülen unhesi-
tatingly borrows methodologies from this classical heritage. For instance, we
come across references in Gülen's Qur'anic interpretation dealing with
whether a word has a definite article or not, whether the objects are priori-
tized or delayed, whether the verb is transitive or intransitive (i.e., the structure of the verb) as well as the meaning of the conjunctions, derivations, and
many other linguistic issues. The verb *ihdinā* (guide us to the right path) in
verse 1:5 is a good example of his methodology. Gülen states that the verb
hidāyah is mentioned in both transitive and intransitive forms. Therefore the
meaning of the word changes according to its usage. Briefly, for Gülen there
are two types of guidance: with an intermediary and without an intermediary (without any means). Gülen says that despite the presence of every possible intermediary, one cannot obtain guidance, whereas sometimes one can
be guided without any assistance. Gülen derives this interpretation from the

---

[30] Gülen 2005c, pp. 5–6.
[31] Ibid.

linguistic nature of the word which is both transitive and intransitive according to its usage.[32]

Gülen is not a simple imitator of past exegeses. He sometimes criticizes these exegetes, offering alternative interpretations.[33] According to Gülen, there are three levels of meaning in the text: *lafzī* (literal meaning), *aqlī* (to understand some realities in the text intellectually), and finally *dhawqī* (goes beyond the text so as to understand, experience or to "taste" the meaning).[34] Elsewhere Gülen explains that the Qur'an addresses people's straightforward understanding, their minds as well as their hearts, and their inner spiritual faculties such as *sirr, khafa,* and *akhfa*.[35] If there is no contradiction in the text in relation to these levels of understanding, this text is a complete text. Gülen argues that since the Qur'anic text is an accurate text, its interpretation should also be carried out properly.[36] At this point it is worth mentioning that unlike many modern thinkers, Gülen lays down an undisputed condition for the correct understanding of the Qur'an, namely powerful faith in God. In order to feel every level of Qur'anic meaning, this essential element is a *sine qua non* of the exegetes.[37] Moreover, he also suggests that currently the interpretation of the Qur'an is beyond the skills of individuals and that it requires the collective effort of experts from various sciences.[38]

3.2. Translation of the Qur'an

Another important issue regarding the Qur'an in the modern era is the translation of the Qur'an into various vernaculars. Gülen's thinking on the translation of the Qur'an is full of insight. If someone studies Gülen's partial translation of the Qur'an in his written and oral works, one will see the significance of his approach to the subject matter. Bearing in mind the notion of *i'jāz* (inimitability) and *ījāz* (precision), Gülen sees the Qur'an as a unique text. He claims that not only the content, but also the style of the Qur'an is a miracle. Using classical arguments Gülen explains that the Qur'an is a miracle from three perspectives: *nazm* (composition), *jazālah*

---

[32] Gülen 1997a, pp. 196–97.
[33] Gülen 2000a, pp. 47, 93; 2000b, p. 347.
[34] Gülen 1997a, pp. 97–98.
[35] Gülen 2000a, p. 30.
[36] Ibid, pp. 30–31.
[37] Gülen, 2000c, p. 3.
[38] Gülen 1992a, p. 2.

(beauty of diction – purity of speech) and *tanāsub* (harmony among the chapters and verses of the Qur'an).[39] On the basis of these notions Gülen considers the Qur'an as the easiest book to read, even though it is absolutely impossible to produce anything similar to Qur'anic text.[40] Thus Gülen believes that it is almost impossible to translate such a multi-dimensional text. Gülen also argues that translation does not do justice to the Qur'anic text because a perfect translation should simultaneously include clarity (*sarāhat*) and inference (*dalālah*), summary (*ijmāl*) and detailed explanation (*tafsīl*), particular (*khusūs*) and general (*umūm*) meanings, unconditional (*itlāq*) and restricted (*muqayyad*) implications.[41] In fact, it is impossible to achieve everything in a translation.

Gülen's skepticism concerning the translation of the Qur'an is not limited to the above-mentioned arguments. Today, deficiencies introduced from various perspectives in the translations show that an exact translation of the Qur'an is impossible. Because of this limitation Gülen insists on reading some kind of explanatory translation rather than literal translations. He also strongly advises that these explanatory translations should be carried out by experts who are familiar with the literary eloquence of the Arabic language. In addition, Gülen explains that every translation should pass through the filters of major Islamic disciplines such as exegesis, Islamic jurisprudence, theology, and Prophetic tradition.[42] Moreover, he suggests translators benefit from cultural, sociological, psychological, anthropological, and communications research. These sciences can make important contributions to achieving a complementary meaning. Gülen also argues that Muslims who are knowledgeable in Arabic and Islamic sciences should read some explanatory translations but ordinary Muslims should be directed to the exegetical works rather than studying the Qur'an from mere translations. The reason for Gülen's disapproval is quite clear since there are many mistakes in current translations. Gülen draws attention to some dogmatic and literary mistakes in modern Turkish translations.[43] He also criticizes many Turkish translations in terms of their poor language. This is quite a complicated

---

39 Gülen 1997a, pp. 52–53.
40 Gülen 2000a, p. 21.
41 Gülen 2005c, p. 4.
42 Ibid.
43 Gülen 2000a, p. 199.

issue, but many Arabic words are already used in Turkish and it is difficult to translate some common Qur'anic terms into pure Turkish.[44] Gülen also expresses his dissatisfaction with the translations of some specific names such as *al-rahman* and *al-rahim* as well as other names of God.[45]

3.3. The notion of *tanāsub*

There is another important issue that comes to fore in modern exegesis, the notion of *tanāsub* (harmony among the verses and chapters of the Qur'an). According to classical exegetes, this is the most prestigious science in Qur'anic exegesis although very few commentators have paid it sufficient attention.[46] Bearing in mind that the Qur'an was revealed over a period of twenty-three years, some scholars have questioned the existence of the notion of *tanāsub* in the Qur'an, while others have praised it as an important exegetical device. However, Western scholars' criticism of Qur'anic text from the point of view of thematic and chronological order in particular, have recently encouraged a great number of modern Muslims to look at this issue in detail. Gülen, like many modern commentators, uses this exegetical device frequently, but not as a reaction to the Western scholars or classical scholars. In his article entitled "Eternal Music," Gülen explains why he concentrates on the notion of *tanāsub*: "The Qur'anic verses and chapters are not collected randomly; they are arranged according to Prophetic order, *tawqīfī*."[47] This approach lets Gülen explore the Qur'an to find the strong relationship between the verses and chapters as if they were all revealed at the same time and were concerned with one specific topic.[48] Thus, according to Gülen, reading the Qur'an without referring to the previous and following sections or passages, but concentrating on similar narratives located in different chapters leads the reader to error.[49] While explaining the relationship between the opening chapter and the following chapters of the Qur'an Gülen states that:

---

[44] Gülen 1997a, pp. 173, 196.
[45] Ibid, p. 90.
[46] Zarkashī 1990, pp. 130–32; Suyūtī 1993, pp. 976–77.
[47] Gülen 1997a, pp. 20–21.
[48] Ibid, p. 98.
[49] Gülen 1995a. p. 185.

> The relationship between Sūrah Fātiha and other Sūrahs is very interesting. On the one hand Fātiha stands in the Qur'an like a lonely star in the sky which has no connection with other stars and planets; on the other hand, it looks like a sun which has a strong relationship with the other stars and planets. Stars look like Qur'anic chapters and verses because one of the meanings of the verses of the Qur'an is *najm* (star). Like the stars of the sky which have close but different relationships among them, Qur'anic verses also have very strong, but at the same time different connections with each other.[50]

Gülen focuses on not only the relationship between verses and chapters but also the relationship between words and letters. In addition, he sometimes gives detailed information about the ending of verses that are called *fawāsil*.[51] In conclusion, Gülen finds a very interesting affiliation between verses and chapters. The reason for his concentration on the notion of *tanāsub* can be associated with his theological understanding of Qur'anic text, and to some extent, his relationship to Muslim exegetical traditions.

4. ISSUES RELATED TO THE METHODOLOGY OF EXEGESIS

In this subheading we will focus on some methodological issues related to Gülen's understanding of exegesis. First of all, we will deal with the notion of *asbāb al-nuzūl* (occasions of revelation), and then we will discuss the status of Qur'anic narratives and *isrā'īliyyāt* (non-Islamic materials in Qur'anic exegesis) reports. We will also concentrate on very important hermeneutical devices in Muslim exegetical traditions, namely the notion of *naskh* (abrogation), *muhkam* and *mutashābih* (clear and allegorical verses of the Qur'an).

4.1. *Asbāb al-nuzūl* (occasions of revelation)

For classical exegesis, various reports of the occasion of revelation are very important hermeneutical devices for the interpretation of the Qur'an. Despite the high esteem with which these reports are held by classical scholars, pre-modern Muslim intellectuals have criticized them and argued that they are the main hindrance to understanding the Qur'an. Thus they express skepticism about the origin and authenticity of these reports. One of the leading thinkers to first raise the issue in the pre-modern period is Sir Sayy-

---

[50] Gülen 1997a. pp. 94, 109.
[51] See verses 9:111 and 14:5. Gülen 2000a, p. 182.

id Ahmad Khan. He complained that the majority of the reports[52] are weak or inauthentic, and many are not directly related to the interpretation of the subject matter of the verse. He insisted on deriving the historical context of the verse directly from Qur'anic presentation, *qarīna haliyyah*.[53] Recently, modern Muslim Qur'anic scholarship has rediscovered the importance of these reports. The motives for such an interest stem from different aims. In particular, because of the influence of Western historical criticism, they have developed new approaches in defining the relationship between revelation and the events that occurred during the twenty-three-year period of the revelation. First of all, they generally argue that the Companions never perceived the Qur'an as a book, even though it was written down though not compiled as an ordered text. Furthermore, the dialogue between God and man during the period of revelation was so lively and immediate that people were mostly aware of the occasions of revelation. To put it another way, the Companions did not try to understand the Qur'an on the basis of textual analysis, but followed Qur'anic teachings and put what they had learnt into practice immediately. Modern Muslims asked whether the instructions that are provided in the Qur'an should be followed regardless of time, place, and circumstances. Because many of these scholars reduced the Qur'an to being only an essential religious and ethical Scripture, they claimed that if the real purpose (or cause/*illah*) of the verse(s) was found, one might be justified in going beyond its literal meaning.[54]

According to Gülen, reports of the occasions of revelation are also important, but he finds the modernists' frequent emphasis on the reports of the occasions of revelation exaggerated, and consequently he tries to limit the role of occasion in understanding the Qur'an. Gülen does not consider the occasion of revelation (*sabab nuzūl*) as the occasion of existence (*sabab wujūd*).[55] The connection between condition (*sabab*) and revelation (*nuzūl*) is not a *sine qua non* relation. According to Gülen, it is incorrect to argue that if there is no occasion (*sabab*) there will be no revelation (*musabbab*).[56] In fact, due to its considerable theological connotation,

---

[52] He names *asbāb al-nuzūl* (occasion of revelation) as the *sha'n al-nuzūl*.
[53] Rahbar 1956, p. 324.
[54] Albayrak 2006, pp. 457−69.
[55] Çapan 2002, p. 38.
[56] Gülen 2000b, pp. 180−81.

instead of using the expression *sabab al-nuzūl*, Gülen, prefers to use *sabab al-iqtirān*, which means that although God will send the verse(s), because of His divine wisdom, His revelation comes down in connection to a particular point in time.[57] Nonetheless, he sees the relationship between occasion and revelation from a hermeneutical point of view; namely, the occasion of revelation is an auxiliary means in the interpretation of Qur'anic verses.[58] Furthermore, Gülen highlights the fact that many verses in the Qur'an were revealed on no specific occasion. This clearly indicates that events (conditions) in seventh-century Arabia did not determine the incidence of revelation; but on the contrary, revelation determined or shaped events. In addition, those verses that came as a direct response to specific questions should not be considered as answers to those specific queries. We can state this issue in the famous technical formula: the specific nature of the *sabab* (occasion) does not hinder the generality of the rule. Gülen frequently uses this rule in his exegesis. He believes in this rule's dynamism and that it conveys the message of the Qur'an in a timeless manner. For instance, regarding the interpretation of the verse 2:114 "And who is more unjust than he who forbids that in places for the worship of God, His name should be celebrated? ..." Gülen comments that:

> Considering the occasion of revelation of this verse, it is generally stated that the verse targets those who prevented the Jewish people from reaching the temple in Jerusalem for prayer. However, if adhered to strictly, this interpretation narrows the scope of the verse. Once, Meccan pagans tortured and prohibited the Prophet Muhammad, peace be upon him, from praying at the Ka'bah. Consequently, this verse addresses every tyrant who hinders or impedes believers from praying in their places for worship.[59]

Although there are many other relevant examples, the limitations of space require us to focus on Gülen's understanding of other important features of the occasion of revelation. One of the significant aspects of these reports is to demonstrate to believers to what extent the combination of theory and praxis is important in Islam.[60] In addition, Gülen considers these reports as databases for understanding the background of some verses. He explains that, just as

---

Gülen 1995b, pp. 180–81.
Görgün 1998, p. 149.
Gülen 2000a, p. 66.
Gülen 2000b, p. 182.

with those who first heard the Qur'an, these reports provide later generations of Muslims with the means to grasp the meaning of the verse with vivid understanding of the context of the event.[61] Moreover, he regards the verses which begin with the formula "if they ask you, say ..." as the most important evidence of the vitality of the occasion of revelation.[62] Gülen points out that even God Himself, who knows everything and every event better than anyone else, refers to the specific occasion of revelation to convey a general message to a mass audience. Gülen conveys these reports in various ways; sometimes he only mentions the report and makes no further comment (e.g., 18:28, 33:5 and 93:4), whereas sometimes he narrates these reports while warning his readers not to limit the meaning of the verses with these reports (e.g., 5:54[63] and 36:20.[64]) Gülen adds that if a scholar cannot widen the scope of a verse or interpret it in various ways; he should not be considered a real *faqīh* (not in the sense of jurist, but meaning a person who has a deep understanding of Islam).[65] His comment on verse 36:20 displays this approach clearly: no matter that the verse in question concerns unbelievers, hypocrites or Jews and Christians, whether its occasion of revelation indicates this or that event, environment or people, we should find a connection between the verse and our own conditions, personality or environment.[66] For Gülen this is the unique way to be continuously addressed by the Qur'an. Finally, he points out some verses that cannot be understood without reference to the occasion of revelation such as verse 87:9.[67] Having used linguistic and historical anecdotes Gülen concludes that the verse says, "Advise them because your advice will definitely benefit them." In this case the occasion of revelation is important in capturing the spirit of the Qur'an.

4.2. Qur'anic narratives and the notion of *isrāīliyyāt*

Qur'anic narratives constitute more than one third of the Qur'an and therefore, every Qur'anic student has to consider them. In the modern period

---

[61] Ibid.
[62] Tuncer 2006, p. 10.
[63] 5:54.
[64] 36:20 "Then there came running, from the farthest part of the city, a man, saying, 'O my People obey the messengers ....'"
[65] *Lā yakūnu ahadun faqīhan hattā yahmil al-āyah al-wāhidah ilā mahāmila muta'addidatin.*
[66] Gülen 2000b, pp. 331–32.
[67] 87:9 "Therefore give admonition in case the admonition profits (the hearer)."

there are two important issues concerning Qur'anic narratives; historical truthfulness and their interpretation in the light of *isrāīliyyāt* reports. Recently, some contemporary scholars have questioned the historic veracity of these narratives, and conclude that there is no obligation to think that these stories are historical facts. They are presented in the Qur'an as a fiction to provide strength to early Muslims at a distressing and hopeless time.[68] Others use various ways to rationalize their contents rather than denying their historical authenticity.[69] Expressing his dissatisfaction with both approaches, Gülen reveals that he has no doubt about the historical accuracy of Qur'anic narratives. He claims that in order to deny the historical truthfulness of these stories, some people choose an unwise understanding by equating them to metaphors or similes. In fact for Gülen, these stories are very vivid and have been taken directly from the lives of people now deceased. Similarly, Gülen argues that nobody has the right to deny their historical accuracy by examining them through the lens of symbolism.[70]

Nonetheless, he gives very important clues regarding the manner in which one should approach Qur'anic narratives. First of all, he strongly asks the reader to enter the heart of the dialogue and narration of these stories and apply them to their own lives. Thus, he states that if contemporary Muslims perceive the characters in these narratives as significant figures mentioned in Qur'anic narratives, in the same way as Prophets and saints who lived a long time ago, one never gets real benefit from these stories. According to Gülen, Muslims have to bring these accounts into their own daily lives, they have to internalize these figures and most importantly, they have to draw lessons from their stories within the confines of Qur'anic presentations and as far as Qur'anic narrative allows them to do so.[71] Gülen holds the view that the main purpose of these stories is to reveal to believers a small part of the universal rules that will persist until the Day of Judgment.[72] At this stage, according to Gülen, it is important to note that the reader should ask not only about the meaning of the narrative, but also about the effect of

---

[68] Şimşek 2008, pp. 368–69; Baljon 1961, p. 53.
[69] Rahbar 1956, pp. 325–32.
[70] Gülen 2000b, p. 327; Aydüz 2001, pp. 30–41.
[71] Gülen 1995a, pp. 188, 195; Gülen 2000b, p. 332.
[72] Gülen 2000b, p. 331.

that narrative in their life. Gülen's interpretation of the verse (18:94)[73] is very illustrative. This verse talks about how Gog and Magog spoiled the land. Consequently weak people asked Dhu al-Qarnayn to set a barrier between them and Gog and Magog. Gülen says that this barrier may be interpreted as the Great Wall of China or the Iron door in Caucasia. However, when we look at the issue in the light of other verses, it is difficult to identify it as a specific barrier only. It really needs additional serious study. Indeed, we need to look at the people behind the barrier rather than focusing on the barrier itself. As long as society stands firm with powerful and dynamic spiritual and ethical values, it will avoid Gog and Magog's sedition and disruption. Gülen also disputes the possible meaning of the verse and says that the main features of just rulers and the conditions for the continuity of states and similar questions should be considered in this particular narrative. Otherwise, we only achieve the narration of a story from the depths of the historical record. Indeed, the benefit of this story to the reader would be very limited.[74]

Similarly, after giving a brief account of the Prophet's meeting with jinn in the interpretation of the verse 72:1−2,[75] Gülen argues that the Prophet's experience of living in a complex and intricate physical and metaphysical world is beyond our understanding. Moreover, it is also beyond the realms of our responsibility to discuss the issue. What is important for us to concentrate on are the lessons that we can derive from the knowledge that the Prophet' message incorporates the group of jinn.[76] Concerning the people of Jonah in verse 10:98,[77] Gülen also displays his view about what is important in the Qur'anic narrative: "No matter where these people live, whether in Mosul, the village of Nineveh, or any other place, it does not change the result. The crux of the topic here is to re-evaluate God's warning and circum-

---

[73] 18:94 "They said: 'O Dhu al-Qarnayn! Lo! Gog and Magog are spoiling the land. So may we pay thee tribute on condition that thou set a barrier between us and them?'"

[74] Gülen 2000b, p. 240.

[75] 72:1−2.

[76] Gülen 2000b, p. 388.

[77] 10:98 "Why was there not a single township (among those we warned), which believed, so its faith should have profited it, except the people of Jonah? When they believed, we removed from them the penalty of ignomy in the life of the present, and permitted them to enjoy (their life) for a while."

stantial evidence in the verse and to continually guard against any possible danger on this path."[78]

From time to time he gives detailed analysis of the narrative to shed light on our current situation. To do so, he takes every element such as time, space, characters, and the social, political, and geographical conditions of the event into consideration.[79] This analysis allows him to make further comment on various contemporary issues. The Qur'anic verse 36:20 is worth mentioning in this regard, "Then there came running, from the farthest part of the city, a man, saying 'O my people obey the messengers.'" Basing his view on the exegesis of classical commentaries, Gülen elucidates the expression *aqsā al-madīnah* in his work. Briefly, he states that various exegetes interpret this expression in three ways; the remote part of the city, the upper class of the society and finally, influential people. Gülen, without implying his preference, concludes that the man mentioned in the verse came from a remote part of the city where rich and aristocratic people lived as if they distanced themselves from the local way of life and its belief.[80] He sometimes displays his preferences concerning rival interpretations of the narrative on the basis of a variety of textual and contextual evidence. In the interpretation of verses 11:70−71,[81] Gülen deals with the question of why Sarah (wife of the Prophet Abraham) was standing while her husband's guests were giving him good news. Having mentioned four possibilities, he inclines to the last one, and notes that when she heard she was going to give birth despite being an older woman, she began to menstruate. Following on from this comment Gülen never neglects saying that God knows best.

With regard to the *isrāīliyyāt* reports it is safe to assume that he takes a quite different approach from many modernist Qur'anic readers. Gülen thinks that *isrāīliyyāt* reports are neither completely true nor completely false. Therefore, we sometimes see *isrāīliyyāt* reports in his exegesis. However, there are other accounts of *isrāīliyyāt* which he criticizes severely. He does not remain silent when he comes across *isrāīliyyāt* reports concerning

---

[78] Gülen 2000a, p. 194.
[79] Gülen 2002, pp. 96−98.
[80] Gülen 2000b, pp. 329−30.
[81] 11:71−2 "And when he saw their hands reached not to it, he mistrusted them and conceived a fear of them. They said: 'Fear not! Lo! we are sent unto the folk of Lot. And his wife was standing (there), and she laughed: but We gave her glad tidings of Isaac, and after him, of Jacob.'"

Prophetic immunity from sin or any report that distorts a vital Islamic understanding. The criteria for the acceptance of these reports lie behind their conformity to Qur'anic narratives. For instance, in his explanation of Surah Naml (Ant), he says that modern thinkers should investigate the wisdom and significance of why this Surah begins with *hurūf muqatta'ah* (detached letters) and focus on the latest scientific developments in the study of ants. But if they forget the real purpose of God and start discussing whether it is a red or black ant or other details, the main aims behind the literal meanings of the verses disappear or die gradually.[82] Furthermore, in his exegesis he rigorously criticizes the people who use *isrāīliyyāt* as a tool to satisfy their own desires. While he is dealing with Korah in verse 28:76,[83] he says that some commentators attempt to find a kinship between Moses and Korah. Then he argues that the main reason for promoting this relationship is to show that despite Korah's closeness to Moses, he never benefited from such a great Prophet. In fact, there is no single explanation in the Qur'an and Prophetic tradition to justify their connection as relatives.[84]

As stated above, Gülen never provides the opportunity for any dogmatic misunderstanding in his exegetical approaches. His comment on verse 12:24[85] is very important in this context. Gülen argues that some commentators hold the view that the Prophet Joseph is free from every kind of human inclination, desires or lust as if he were not human, while others portray him as a person who suffers the pressure of these desires. Gülen, as an advocate of the middle way, says neither point of view is correct. According to Gülen, Joseph had desires but he was able to control them with his Prophetic determination under the guidance of God.[86] At the same time, he rejects all reports and interpretations that either deify or ascribe inferior status to the Prophet Joseph.

We rarely come across references to the Scriptures of the People of the Book and *isrāīliyyāt* in his explanation.[87] Gülen's approach reflects his sin-

---

[82] Gülen 1995a, p. 188.

[83] 28:76 "Now Korah was of Moses's folk, but he oppressed them ...."

[84] Gülen 2000b, p. 302.

[85] 12:24 "She verily desired him, and he would have desired her if it had not been that he saw the argument of his Lord ...."

[86] Gülen 2000a, pp. 199–200.

[87] There is very good example concerning the Prophet Solomon's employment of jinn in 34:12 (Gülen 2000b, pp. 324–25).

cerity in preferring the mode of a more sensitive classical exegetical tradition rather than being resistant to these types of reports for political or ideological reasons.[88] Furthermore, exegesis as an Islamic discipline is more flexible than any other basic Islamic science such as Islamic law, theology or Prophetic tradition. Instead of dwelling only on *asl* (origin and authenticity) in exegetical reports, experts from the past to the present focus on *fasl* (moral lessons). So Gülen sees no problem in following in their footsteps.

4.3. The notion of *naskh* (abrogation)

The denial of the phenomenon of abrogation in the Qur'an during the nineteenth and twentieth centuries is another important aspect of modern exegesis. When we look at Gülen's exegetical works, we see that he does not engage much with important verses related to the notion of *naskh*. It seems that he does not want to focus on such a technical issue in his general works. Nonetheless, in his other works he deals with the notion of abrogation from different angles. Instead of concentrating on the types of *naskh*, their number in the Qur'an, its relation to the Qur'an and *sunnah*, he prefers to look at the issue from a broader perspective. First of all, Gülen finds the theory of abrogation very meaningful. Thus discussion about whether the *naskh* really exists in the Qur'an is unimportant for Gülen. His only concern is to draw a big picture about the question of what *naskh* really is. In a similar way to Said Nursi,[89] Gülen gives primary importance to verse 13:39: "God erases whatever He wills, and establishes (whatever He wills). With Him is the source of ordinance." This verse illustrates how Gülen sees the notion of abrogation. For Gülen, abrogation is not a simple hermeneutical device of jurists, but it is an eternal law of God in the realm of human life. Abrogation is the name of every change in our life and universe. It is related to cultures, economies, social life, animate and inanimate creatures, and is also

---

[88] For instance, Abu Rayya considers Ka'b al-Ahbar a Zionist for the interpolation and insertion of these reports in the exegesis (Juynboll 1969, pp. 120–38).

[89] Gülen uses Nursi's argument here. According to Nursi, there are two significant concepts concerning changeable and unchangeable things. One is *imām-ı mubīn* which is related to the realm of the unknown or the unseen, *ghayb*. This is a notebook of divine destiny which hides the original forms of both past and future. In addition, it is a manifestation of God's attributes of *ilm* (knowledge) and *amr* (commandment). The other is *kitāb-ı mubīn* which is related to the realm of the seen, *shahādah*. This notebook is the manifestation of God's attributes *qudrah* (power) and *ījād* (invention) which is related to the formation of things in the world (Nursi 2006, p. 533).

related to their modification, adaptation, and ecological change.[90] Gülen continues as follows:

> According to Divine wisdom, God changes, annuls, abrogates what He wills in both His religious commandments (Holy Scriptures) and rules of nature. He sometimes changes societies, and systems, lets some nations perish and others exist. He manifests His names, *jalālī* (majesty, wrath and rage) and *jamālī* (beauty and blessing) in the universe. Through the manifestation of these names some people become happy, while others become sad. Similarly, He abrogates and changes some rules in His Divine law and brings forth another. Instead of the Prophet Adam's *suhuf* (divine text or pages) He declares the pages of the Prophet Noah. When the time comes He announces His new revelation to the Prophet Abraham. He takes something out of the old pages and inserts a new one, and then shapes it as a Holy Scripture to be presented to the Prophet Moses. Afterwards, he brings more dimension and depth to the book with Psalms and proclaims them to be from the mouth of the Prophet David. With the Gospel, He brings a spiritual dimension to humanity in addition to the Torah. Finally, through the words of the Prophet Jesus He gives the good tidings of Ahmad who enables the biggest change in human history.[91]

Although Gülen strongly believes that there is no change or abrogation in the fundamentals of faith, there are many changes in its secondary issues or details. To support this idea, Gülen compares the time of the Prophet Adam with childhood (*sabah*/early morning), and the era of the Prophet Muhammad, peace be upon him, with middle age (*asr*/afternoon). He holds the view that this is completely related to the maturity of humanity.[92] Obviously, he tries to say that people at the time of the Prophet Adam are different from the people of the Prophet Muhammad's time. Hence, change in some details is inevitable. Thus, Gülen considers the denial of *naskh* (abrogation) as the denial of the history of humanity on earth.

Nonetheless, rather than referring frequently to the notion of abrogation, Gülen is determined to see Qur'anic verses as very active and relevant. He goes even further and says that there are Qur'anic verses concerning the People of the Book that should be examined seriously by Muslims. Verse 3:188: "Think not that those who exult in what they have given, and love to be praised for what they have not done. Think not they are in safety from the doom. A painful doom is theirs," is a very good example of this. Gülen

---

[90] Gülen 2008a, pp. 104–112.
[91] Ibid.
[92] Gülen 2001, pp. 20–28.

states that there are many important lessons and advice for Muslims to derive from all the verses of the Qur'an, even though they address non-Muslims—unless such verses are abrogated. To support his approach, Gülen uses an important legal methodology, namely *shar'u man qablanā shar'un lanā* (the laws of previous religions are also law for us). Clearly, he tries to combine the ethical dimension of the verses with their legal enactment on the basis of the notion of abrogation.[93] Thus, instead of denying the content of the verses, he prefers to use every statement of the Qur'an.

Gülen is such a strong believer that he always finds enough mental resources to solve the various problems of modern men and women from Islamic sources. His trust in the capacity of Islamic sources brings us to another dimension of the notion of *naskh*, namely *ijtihād*.[94] In his classification of the basic Islamic sciences, *naskh* takes its place under the title of *mutammimāt* (complementary). He divides knowledge into two as *aqlī* and *naqlī*, and *naqlī* is also sub-divided into sections such as *muāmalāt* (transactions). Accordingly, *naskh* is found under this transaction and used in the understanding of Qur'anic law.[95] Gülen also uses this hermeneutical device in his rational and traditional explanations to pave way for a new *ijtihad*. However, in his usage, Gülen's point of view is quite different from both pre-modern scholars who reject *naskh* completely and contemporary scholars who accept it to prove that the Qur'an is simply a historical text and can only be understood in this specific historical context. Gülen is aware of the necessities of modern life and the many changes in society. Equally, he believes that Muslims can achieve advancement in modern life by depending primarily on their own tradition. Progress is not accomplished by freeing oneself from the accumulations of the past, but rather by building upon its foundations and developing its traditions by means of new solutions and discoveries. To sum up, his approach to the notion of *naskh* in his exegetical works is similar to the understanding of exegetes rather than that of jurists. Thus, he is interested in a more general rule of abrogation rather than a specific juristic approach.

---

[93] Gülen 1995a, pp. 181–82.
[94] For further discussion on *ijtihād* see İsmail Acar's chapter in this volume.
[95] Gülen 2006a, pp. 18–23.

4.4. The notion of *muhkam* and *mutashābih* (clear and allegorical verses)

Generally Qur'anic exegetes focus on three verses of the Qur'an when they discuss *muhkam* and *mutashābih*; (11:1) "a Scripture whose verses are perfected, *uhkimat āyātuhū*" indicates that all the verses of the Qur'an are *muhkam*; while (39:23) "God has sent down the fairest discourse as a Book, co-similar in its oft-repeated, *kitāban mutashābihan mathāniya*," shows that all the Qur'anic verses are *mutashābih*. Finally there is another type of verse (3:7) that states that some parts of it are *muhkam* and the others are *mutashābih*. The verse runs as follows:

> It is He who sent down upon thee the Book, wherein are verses clear that are the essence of the Book, and others ambiguous. As for those in whose hearts is swerving, they follow the ambiguous part, desiring dissension, and desiring its interpretation; and none knows its interpretation, save only God. And those firmly rooted in knowledge say, "We believe in it; all is from our Lord"; yet none remembers, but men possessed of minds.

Gülen deals with the notion of both *muhkam* and *mutashābih* from various perspectives. Primarily, he draws attention to the idea that one should not forget that this difficulty or ambiguity in *mutashābih* has nothing to do with God. Gülen, from the beginning to the end, emphasizes this and approaches the topic from the reader's viewpoint. Thus, only human beings are bound to *muhkam* and *mutashābih*. God, however, knows everything in all its detail. For those who want to understand the Qur'an, *muhkamāt* is very important, as Gülen maintains that these verses allow the reader to distinguish between right and wrong. He implies that there are *thābitāt* (eternally valid or firmly fixed things) in the Qur'an that need to be referred to continuously. So Gülen likens the *muhkamāt* to a searchlight that helps the reader understand *mutashābihāt*.[96] According to Gülen, *mutashābihāt* means the verses of the Qur'an that lack clarity. However, absolute ambiguity is not intended. He argues that there are various wisdoms behind the existence of *mutashabihat* in the Qur'an and therefore, it is wrong to see *mutashābihāt* as a static term.

Since the Qur'an is a living book, the interaction between it and the reader is very important. The more one immerses oneself in the Qur'an the

---

[96] Gülen 2005c, p. 2.

more one starts finding new insights in it.[97] So *mutashābihāt* indicates that there are abundant realities in the Qur'an, many of which are unknown to humankind. Through these verses the Qur'an forces believers to reflect upon and contemplate the Qur'an. Gülen strongly believes that these verses are open to inspire receptive people. He believes that the existence of such verses in the Qur'an is essential evidence for the universality of the Qur'an and Islam. Because there are both very knowledgeable and ordinary believers among the Muslims, the Qur'an addresses both intellectuals and the general population. Thus, the Qur'an is sometimes very precise and sometimes very deep in meaning and can be applied to a wide variety of issues. The understanding of *mutashābihāt* is also conditioned by time. In other words, when the exact time comes, the meaning will be understood by those who believe. This precise time, however, is related to the gradually occurring needs of people and events.[98]

Like many of his predecessors, Gülen divides *mutashābihāt* into four categories; *khafī* (hidden), *muskhil* (obscure), *mujmal* (concise) and *mutashābih* (unclear) and then narrows the scope of the absolute *mutashābihāt* in the Qur'an. Using the methodology of juristic language, Gülen suggests that *mutashābihāt* should be read in the light of *muhkamāt*. Even his indirect comment on the letter *waw* (whether it is a conjunctive particle – *waw al-ʿatf* – or a letter which shows the beginning of a new sentence – *waw al-'isti'nāf*-) about verse 3:7 supports this approach. In short, he adheres to the idea that many *mutashābihāt* will be clarified through the interpretation of knowledgeable scholars.[99]

Besides the existence of different levels of meanings, there is another important aspect of the existence of *mutashābihāt* in the Qur'an, namely the allegorical language of the Qur'an concerning some anthropomorphic verses. Because it is also related to theology, this is extremely important in Gülen's approach to the Qur'an. Firstly he says that to remove ambiguity (*majhūl*) by means of another ambiguity (*majhūl*) is not healthy. The literary skill of the Qur'an is very important in this regard. The Qur'an uses *tashbīh* (metaphor) and *tamthīl* (similes) to clarify some verses. Concerning God's attributes and names, miracles etc., Gülen says that the Qur'an always

---

[97] Ibid, p. 3.
[98] Sarıtoprak and Ünal 2005, pp. 447–67.
[99] Gülen 2005c, p. 4.

employs understandable concepts in its explanation of the unknowable. For instance, for those who do not believe in the virgin birth of Jesus, the Qur'an asks them to look at the way that Adam was created.[100] Despite the Qur'an's emphasis on *mutashābihāt*, many could not understand the delicacy of the issue and indulged in various discussions. Gülen describes the issue of the interpretation of *mutashabihat* as *mazallat al-aqdām* (slipping of the feet, lapse). Thus, the correct understanding of *mutahsābihāt* leads people to prove the existence of God without indulging in anthropomorphic explanations or denying the truth, *ithbāt bi-lā tashbīh wa tamthīl* and *tanzīh bi-lā ta'tīl wa inkār*.[101]

Finally, it is important to note that according to Gülen, the existence of *mutashābihāt* in the Qur'an is also an obstacle in facing the achievement of an exact translation of the Qur'an. Believing that the Qur'an cannot be translated, he is cautious even to use the term *maāl* (explanatory translation), because some verses contain *muhkam* and *mutashābih* together (there is an *ijtimā'* of *muhkam* and *mutashābih*) and therefore, the meanings cannot be easily identified by any translation.[102]

5. EXEGETICAL TRADITIONS

In this section, we will discuss Gülen's position in relation to various exegetical traditions in Islam. Although we are not going to go into detail, we will try to present Gülen's usage of mystical, theological, and legal verses in his exegesis.

5.1. Mystical interpretation of the Qur'an

Many Muslim thinkers express their dissatisfaction with the mystical interpretation of the Qur'an. One of the disadvantages of this attitude is the loss of the strong traditional connections between *fiqh akbar* (theology), *fiqh zāhir* (law) and *fiqh bātin* (Sufism). In contrast to many modern Qur'an readers, Gülen offers some mystical explanations in his commentary to reconnect the inner and outer dimension of modern men and women. When we look at Gülen's mystical interpretations, we see that in accordance with

---

[100] Gülen 2003, pp. 103–04.
[101] Gülen 2008a, pp. 179–83.
[102] Gülen 2000a, p. 140.

his previous approach, he follows a moderate line. Having mentioned the Prophetic report that indicates the different levels of meanings in the Qur'an, Gülen also argues that as with the branches and knots of trees, there are numerous deep meanings in the Qur'an.[103] Gülen believes that after explanation of the literal meaning, it is wrong to ignore the mystical interpretation of the Qur'an, but that this does not contradict the literal meaning. Since he wrote a four-volume mystical work[104] in which he thoroughly covers the Qur'anic text and mystical concepts, we will not re-visit that but will primarily focus on his less-known book about the mystical interpretation of the Qur'an. At this point, it is important to note that Gülen's mystical exegesis gives priority to quality rather than quantity in terms of the numbers of verses that he has dealt with.

Where his exegetical works are concerned, one of the most interesting issues that Gülen raises is the relationship between the reality of the Ka'bah and the reality of Ahmad (the Prophet Muhammad, peace be upon him). Having analyzed verses (2:144), (5:97), and 6:124) he also gives detailed information about the concept of *nur al-muhammadi* (the Light of the Prophet Muhammad) in the interpretation of verses (24:35) and (48:29). Briefly, there are different dimensions in the Prophethood of Muhammad, peace be upon him; one dimension is that of being a human, and the other is a spatial dimension. For Gülen, both the Prophet and Ka'bah were created together (as twins) in the "world of possibility" (*alam al-imkan*).[105] The reason for the Prophet's prayer and wish to direct his face to the Ka'bah lies in this metaphysical relationship. The Prophet wishes to re-unite with his twin (the beloved). On the other hand, the Ka'bah, the heart of the world and the space which connects the world with heaven is waiting to embrace his twin (the Prophet).[106] Gülen explains some mystical wisdom behind the birth of the Prophet in Mecca, near the Ka'bah and the Ka'bah's existence in the birthplace of the Prophet. Furthermore, he uses another mystical terminology, namely *maqām jam* (the place of meeting or the place that brings two into one). In short, the Prophet brings both the physical and spiritual

---

[103] Gülen 1992a, p. 4.
[104] See Gülen's *Kalbin Zümrüt Tepeleri I–IV*, Izmir-Istanbul: Nil Yayınları, 2005–2008. Also see Mehmet Y. Şeker's chapter in this volume for more detail.
[105] Gülen 2000a, p. 72.
[106] Ibid, pp. 148, 160.

realms together and represents some kind of middle way between two excesses. Gülen gives the Prophet David and Solomon as examples. According to Gülen, God allows David to deal with the physical world and provides everything for his service. Similarly, God also provides unseen creatures to assist Solomon. The reality of Ahmad, according to Gülen, represents the meeting place or space in these two dimensions, namely the unification of the physical and metaphysical realms.[107]

Gülen's approach to mystical interpretation allows him to use some technical terms such as *ma'iyyah* (togetherness with both God and the Prophet), *ubūdiyyah, ibādah* and *ubūdah* (level of worship), *qurb-bu'd* (closeness to God–remoteness), *ridā* (acceptance), *sakīnah* (tranquility) and the notion of *tawhīd* (the Unity of God) and many other Qur'anic terms. It is also interesting to note that following classical Muslim scholarship, Gülen uses some Arabic letters or dots to derive mystical interpretations from them. This kind of interpretation is rare. We can give an example from the beginning of the *basmala* which starts with the letter *b* (preposition) and the dot under this letter.[108] In addition to his own interpretations, Gülen also quotes from Muslim mystics such as Imām Ghazzali, Mawlānā Jalāl al-Dīn al-Rūmī, Ibn 'Arabī, Imām Rabbānī, Ibrāhīm Haqqī, Mawlānā Khālid and Said Nursi. However, Gülen never considers his mystical exegesis as the final interpretation of the verse. Furthermore, he is so careful that he frequently uses some precautionary expressions in his mystical interpretations.

5.2. Theological exegesis

One of the important features of modern exegesis is to place Qur'anic commentary ahead of all other disciplines and expect it to fulfill the function of every other Islamic discipline. Thus, Gülen's approach in this regard is worth investigating. It is safe to assume that Gülen has great respect for the traditional division of Islamic disciplines. It is understood that he does not generally use exegesis to discuss theological issues. Instead, he repeatedly redirects his reader to theological literature. We also have a volume written by Gülen which is specifically compiled to deal with theological issues.[109] None-

---

[107] Gülen 2000b, pp. 325–26, 354.
[108] Gülen 1997a, pp. 78–79.
[109] See Gülen 1996a, 1996b, and Zeki Sarıtoprak's chapter on Gülen's theology of social responsibility in this volume.

theless, from time to time Gülen tackles some theological questions in his exegetical works without going into details. Many of his theological explanations are provided in his work as additional information. Despite the originality of his own discourse, he seems to follow the Sunni framework in his analysis.

Gülen's main focus on theological issues in his exegesis is mostly related to the absence of sin in the natures of the Prophets. The Prophet Jonah's departure from his town without waiting for God's response,[110] and the Prophet Solomon's smiling posture in verse 27:19[111] are important examples. Gülen makes a great effort to analyze sensitively some dogmatic verses of the Qur'an. For instance verses of 4:142[112] and 3:54[113] which talk about God's *khud'a/makr* (cheating!) can be mentioned. Gülen criticizes some translations and focuses on the implications of these translations. In brief, he says that no one has the right to imply that God is trying to cheat people in the same way that people cheat each other. God's aim in these verses is to convey the meaning that whoever cheats someone, will have his cheating come back to him; he will fall into his own trap or God will definitely bring his plot back to him.[114] Gülen's discussion of the teaching does not follow a systematic theological pattern in his exegetical works. Nevertheless, he sometimes gives detailed information about some important issues such as the relationship between the Will of God and the will of human beings. In

---

110 21:87 "And (mention) Dhu'n-Nun (Jonah), when he went off in anger and deemed that We had no power over him, but he cried out in the darkness, saying: 'There is no Allah save Thee. Be Thou Glorified! Lo! I have been a wrong-doer.'" Gülen approaches this verse from a theological perspective and says that the ordinary believers' actions can be considered mistake on the part of *muqarrab* (the closest people to God). Because Jonah left his hometown before he received a revelation to do so, his departure is considered a lapse rather than sin (Gülen 2000b, pp. 266–69).

111 The translation of the verse 27:19 is as follows: "So he (Solomon) smiled, wondering at her (and) word, and said: 'My Lord! Grant me that I should be grateful for Thy favor which Thou hast bestowed on me and on my parents, and that I should do good such as Thou art pleased with, and make me enter, by Thy mercy, into Thy servants, the good ones.'" According to Gülen, the Qur'an uses the term *dahk* for Solomon's smile and this smile is different from excessive or louder smile of ordinary people (Gülen 2000b, p. 295).

112 4:142 "The hypocrites they think they are surpassing Allah, but he will surpass them: when they stand up to prayer, they stand without earnestness, to be seen of men, but little do they hold Allah in remembrance."

113 3:54 "(And Unbelievers) plotted and planned, and Allah too planned, and the best of planners is Allah."

114 Gülen 2000a, p. 83.

the interpretation of verse (2:10)[115] Gülen says that some exegetes deal with this verse from the perspective of the rule *al-jazā min jins al-amal* (the punishment of the person in accordance with his actions). According to Gülen, this explanation is not satisfactory. Gülen elucidates that some people have very bad intentions, and if they have any opportunity to put their bad intentions into practice, they immediately do so. This verse shows the vicious circle between their intentions and actions.[116] Then, he tries to provide a definition for the notion that humanity has a will based on the understanding of the Mu'tazilites and Jabriyyahs.[117]

Another important issue on which Gülen concentrates in his exegesis is the act of repentance just before death. Gülen points out the quality of the repentance of Pharaoh mentioned in verse 10:90.[118] He explains this verse in the light of another verse 40:85.[119] Having used some intertextual evidence such as the way of Pharaoh's repentance, "I believe that there is no god except Him Whom the Children of Israel believe in," Gülen concludes that people like Pharaoh are strong materialists and it is very difficult for them to accept faith. By not mentioning Moses' name, he conceals the truth of his messengership through whom God revealed his message at that time. Thus, Pharaoh commits a sin while he is uttering the words "I believe."[120] Apart from these issues, Gülen also debates some theological problems such as whether jinn know the unseen future or not,[121] the identification of the holy spirit in 2:87,[122] and the deep theological meaning of the words *rahmān* (in relation to *wāhidiyyah*) and *rahīm* (in relation to *ahadiyyah*).[123] Clearly, Gülen maintains an understanding of classical theology, but also, in the meantime, he addresses modern readers through bringing in some new

---

[115] 2:10 "In their hearts is a disease; and God has increased their disease …"

[116] Gülen 1997a, pp. 184–85.

[117] Gülen 2000a, p. 37.

[118] 10:90 "We took the Children of Israel across the sea: Pharaoh and his hosts followed them in insolence and spite. At length, when overwhelmed with the flood, he said: 'I believe that there is no god except Him Whom the Children of Israel believe in: I am of those who submit (to Allah).'"

[119] 40.85. But their faith when they actually saw Our mighty punishment could not avail them: (that is) God's way (of dealing with humankind, a way) which has always been in effect for His servants. And so the unbelievers have lost altogether.

[120] Gülen 2000a, pp. 191–92.

[121] Gülen 2000b, p. 327.

[122] Gülen 2000a, pp. 62–63.

[123] Gülen 1997a, pp. 90–93. Also pp. 20, 192–93.

issues and different explanations. It is also important to note that the quantity of theological discussion in his exegetical works is very limited.

5.3. Legal exegesis

Although basic Islamic disciplines have very strong connections between each other and complement each other, there are also differences among them as well. The science of jurisprudence has superior status over many other Islamic disciplines. Gülen, however, does not use this discipline in his exegesis to pave the way for his legal opinions. Although the existence of his many legal judgments assigned him the status of a *mujtahid*, he preferred to preserve a distinction between exegesis and jurisprudence. Nevertheless, it does not mean that he has nothing to say about legal issues in his exegesis. It has been observed that he sometimes deals with legal issues but not extensively. His legal exegesis implies that he approaches the issues from the exegetical point of view rather than juristic evaluation. For instance, he has a specific chapter (legal judgments) in his book *Fatiha Üzerine Mülahazalar* where he discusses the inner meaning and function of *basmala* from the perspective of various schools of thought. Similarly, we find his legal arguments in the interpretation of the word *shatr* (towards) in the verse (2:144). With regard to that verse, he discusses the direction towards Ka'bah in accordance with traditional commentaries.[124] It is also important to note that Gülen strikes a good balance between law and ethics (morality). His Qur'anic judgment focuses on this balance. In other words, law does not solve every problem unless it is being supported by strong ethical values. Thus he extends the meaning of the verses beyond their legal limitations. For instance, concerning interpretation of verse 2:115,[125] Gülen argues that this verse suggests that believers not only search for the direction of the Ka'bah before they pray but also insists on their not forgetting God at any time in their daily lives.[126]

6. MODERN ISSUES

Under this heading it is possible to discuss various issues in the context of Gülen's exegesis such as his frequent emphasis on social and ethical issues,

---

[124] Gülen 2000a, p. 75.

[125] 2:115 "To Allah belong the East and the West: whithersoever ye turn, there is the presence of Allah. For Allah is All-Embracing, All-Knowing."

[126] Gülen 2000b, p. 284.

psychological analysis in his commentaries, and finally various remarks and deductions that conclude his exegesis. However, there is not enough space in this chapter to show the various features of Gülen's exegetical analysis. Thus we are going to focus on one issue only, namely Gülen's scientific exegesis.

6.1. Scientific exegesis

An important aspect of Gülen's exegesis is his approach to scientific interpretation. While discussing his method, we will also refer briefly to the notion of the miracle that takes place in his exegesis. It has been observed that in comparison to some of his contemporaries, Gülen displays a moderate attitude towards scientific explanation. According to Gülen, the Qur'an is not a book of science[127] and as a result, he does not see the discussion of scientific details as the primary part of exegesis; instead, he considers it a secondary hermeneutical device that supports the essential meaning of the verses. He states precisely that the Qur'an neither rejects scientific interpretation completely, nor gives it sacred status.[128] First and foremost the Qur'an presents itself as a book of guidance, a universal message, and a book of life. So, the meaning of life and the relationship between the Creator and His creatures are more significant than scientific explanation. Therefore, Gülen believes that the Qur'an focuses on the things that have priority in the presence of God. Nevertheless, Gülen does not dismiss scientific interpretations in his exegesis. Gülen holds the view that the Qur'an stems from God's attribute of *kalam* (speech) while the universe and everything in it is derived directly from His attributes of *qudrah* (power) and *iradah* (will), indicating that God creates and forms everything in a perfect manner. Then he concludes that if the word and work of God are the reflections of the above-mentioned attributes, there should be a necessary harmony between them. He further argues that it is an obvious error to perceive a conflict between science and the Qur'an. In Gülen's perspective, it is similar to a man having two eyes that work together and never contradict each other.[129] Thus one should not disregard either of them. Interestingly, he makes a distinction between *ilm* (real science or knowledge) and *bilim* (expressed in Turkish as meaning a more

---

[127] Gülen 1992a, pp. 5–6.
[128] Gülen 1998a, p. 40.
[129] Ibid, p. 34; Gülen 1997a, p. 27; 1992a, pp. 5–6.

materialistic knowledge). He argues that the former is the common property of Muslims that leads to Absolute Truth (God), while the latter is the
product of a sheer positivistic understanding of science. [130]

Thus, the exegete should be very careful in using science in his exegesis. Because whatever advanced level may be achieved by science, no one
can fully comprehend both the mystery of the universe and the Qur'an.
Although Gülen has complete trust in the scientific truthfulness of the
Qur'an, he is still very careful not to read the Qur'an completely in the
light of scientific developments. He argues that if we do not want to fall
into error, we should believe only in facts that cannot be rejected. Therefore, we have to study science according to its own rules, but if we believe
in its discoveries we should not think that we have exhausted the Power
of God. There might be many things that we do not accept today but will
be accepted in the future. The exegete should not hurry to bring unprov-
en scientific developments together with the eternal words of God. Thus
he insists on not narrowing the significance of Qur'anic verses. There will
always be unknown things in the scientific realm, *al-mawjūd (or al-
ma'lum) al-majhūl*/unknown known.[131] He also criticizes some Muslim
commentators who try to associate every new scientific discovery with
verses from the Qur'an. According to Gülen, such an approach would
imply that Muslims have an inferiority complex about science, which
would also allow them to put the Qur'an on a secondary level.[132]

Furthermore, when the exegete has difficulty in reconciling a fundamental incompatibility between the Qur'an and what is thought to be a
scientific finding, he should not attempt to distort the truth of the Qur'an,
but has to reconsider the scientific explanation. In other words, an established scientific discovery cannot be in contradiction with the Qur'an; if it
is thought that there is, then the scientific finding in question might need
further research. Gülen sheds light on the fact that some passages related
to time clearly prove the fallacy of out-dated scientific discoveries. Such
examples reveal Gülen's confidence in the information contained in the

---

[130] Gülen 1998a, p. 34.
[131] Gülen 2000b, p. 346. In his scientific explanation, Gülen always uses the word *fihi nazar*
which means that this is not an absolute interpretation, there might be others (Gülen 1992b,
pp. 2–5).
[132] Gülen 2001, pp. 128–29; 1992b, pp. 2–5.

Qur'an.[133] He also strongly believes that a part of the Qur'an will be explored in every scientifically competent age.[134] He supports this explanation with the verse 41:53: "Soon will We show them Our signs in the (furthest) regions (of the earth), and in their own souls, until it becomes manifest to them that this is the truth. Is it not enough that thy Lord doth witness all things?" According to Gülen, the expression of *sa-nurī* (We will show) in the form of the future tense demonstrates clearly that the Qur'an speaks to the first addressees of the Prophet by saying, "you do not know many of Our verses and signs, We will show them in the future." Regarding the phrase "to whom We will show them," Gülen focuses on the Arabic expression *him* which means "them" in this verse. To put it another way, the Qur'an says "not you" but "they" who will come in the future will know. Finally, he comments on the expression of *yatabayyana* (it becomes manifest to them) and states that the Qur'an will explain everything as time passes, and each explanation and discovery will be fulfilled through previously explored facts. Humanity's only task is to make a serious effort to search the Qur'an for answers. In this way, the Qur'anic truth will gradually emerge.[135] Thus, Gülen states that the Qur'an addresses not only current time but also the time up until the Day of Judgment.

At this juncture, it is important to find an answer to the question concerning the eligibility of scientific exegesis. According to Gülen, in order to comment on Qur'anic verses from a scientific point of view, one should primarily have a very strong faith in the Qur'an. Moreover, exegetes need to explore the Qur'anic world without becoming weary of the search. One has to keep using a very well-established methodology in interpreting the Qur'an. Finally, Gülen reminds the reader that advanced knowledge of Arabic, and expertise in social, scientific and Islamic sciences are imperative for a proper interpretation. As he repeats several times, these requirements indicate that scientific exegesis of the Qur'an is beyond the limited understand-

---

133 Gülen 1992a, pp. 5–6. In another place, Gülen likens scientific development to people's clothes. When these scientific discoveries become old enough, people throw them away like old dresses (Gülen 1998a, p. 49).

134 Gülen 1992a, pp. 5–6.

135 Gülen 2000b, p. 346. Gülen points out that the Qur'anic expressions *tafakkur, tadhakkur,* and *tadabbur* which means "contemplation" encourage believers to seek scientific knowledge from the Qur'an (Gülen 1998a, pp. 43–45).

ing of individuals in the modern period. Consequently, Gülen calls for a collective effort to accomplish a scientific exegesis.[136]

When we look at Gülen's own scientific interpretation, it is obvious that he uses various hermeneutical and scientific devices. Although his scientific interpretation of verses is limited in quantity, they are rich in quality. For example, he gives plenty of details about the creation of everything in pairs[137] and the power of the atom in Surah Saba' (34:3).[138] Gülen draws attention to the linguistic analysis of the word *kull* (every) in verse (51:49). He explains that if the word kull becomes a noun phrase attached to the indefinite noun *shay* (thing), it signifies generality. On the basis of this elucidation, Gülen concludes that everything in the universe is created in a pair. Atoms are not exceptions. Nonetheless, he assists us to understand that people who witness the revelation of the Qur'an did not know atoms, electrons, protons or neutrons. Today, we know that every creature exists as part of a pair.[139] Gülen is always cautious in his grammatical analysis of the Qur'an in the light of modern science. He reiterates that we can never exhaust the treasures of the Qur'an as measured by today's level of scientific developments. In fact, we do not know what atomic physics will show us in the future. Furthermore, Gülen also comments on the above-mentioned second verse and says that the expression *mithqāla dharrah* (atomic weight) refers to the theory of the existence of atomic weight in every element, which has only been discovered very recently.[140] In addition, he focuses on Lorenzi's electron theory, the explosion of neutrons, and the formation of energy after a reaction etc. and finds different scientific hints in various verses of the Qur'an.[141]

There are other verses where Gülen's approach is made from a scientific point of view; these include the expansion of space,[142] the circular shape

---

[136] Gülen 1998a, p. 33.
[137] 51:49 "And all things We have created by pairs, that haply ye may reflect."
[138] 34:3 "Those who disbelieve say: 'The Hour will never come unto us.' Say: 'Nay, by my Lord, but it is coming unto you surely. (He is) the Knower of the Unseen. Not an atom's weight, or less than that or greater, escapeth Him in the heavens or in the earth, but it is in a clear Record.'"
[139] Gülen 1997, p. 32.
[140] Ibid, pp. 33–34.
[141] Ibid, pp. 34–35.
[142] 51:47.

of the earth,[143] its compressed nature or the earth's polar extremes,[144] the heavens and the earth being at first one piece and their partition, the creation of every living thing from water,[145] the formation of milk in a cow's body,[146] the rotation of the sun in its specific orbit,[147] the separation of the two seas, and so on and so forth.[148] Some of Gülen's scientific interpretations go beyond the limitations of the exegesis. His information about the creation of human beings and the formation of the fetus and its various stages in the womb[149] are good examples of his comprehensive interpretation. Similarly, he gives a lengthy explanation about the phenomenon of winds to fertilize clouds and bring rain.[150] But Gülen never disregards the real reason behind all these incidents in his analysis. His strong statement concerning rain is worth mentioning here: "Whether rain is caused by positive and negative drops, clouds or any other thing; the main point is that the real formation is carried out by God. He is the One who reconciles winds and clouds, negative and positive."[151] Thus Gülen intentionally brings God to the attention of the reader on every occasion. After summarizing both classical and modern approaches to the verses, he focuses on the scientific interpretation.

On the other hand, he frequently warns the reader about some deficient scientific interpretations. At this point, it is worth mentioning the association of the *dābbah* (beast) with the AIDS virus in the explanation of verse 27:82.[152] According to Gülen, the verse, in its content, talks about the appearance of the beast when the signs of the Day of Judgment are apparent. He analyzes several words in this verse together with many Prophetic traditions and then concludes that to confirm that the verse is referring to the AIDS virus is to narrow its scope. According to Gülen, these kinds of

---

[143] 70:30.

[144] 39:5.

[145] 21:30.

[146] 16:66.

[147] 36:38.

[148] 55:19–20.

[149] 22:5; 22:12–14.

[150] 15:22; 24:43.

[151] Gülen 1997, p. 39.

[152] 27:82 "And when the Word is fulfilled against them (the unjust), we shall produce from the earth a beast to (face) them: He will speak to them, for that mankind did not believe with assurance in Our signs."

interpretations are not objective and are generally contrary to the meaning of the verse.[153]

Gülen sincerely believes that the truth is not something that the human mind produces. Truth is independent of human production, and is created by God. As the words of God manifest the works of God in the universe, the Qur'an is in complete harmony with nature. They do not contradict each other. Having said that, Gülen then confirms the reliability of the miracles mentioned in the Qur'an. Indeed, he offers various logical explanations to strengthen the validity of the miracles. His strongest evidence for the miracles is the Qur'an itself. Thus, he criticizes many scholars who do not accept the miracles mentioned in the Qur'an and Prophetic tradition. Contrary to those exegetes, Gülen not only accept these miracles but also provides some scientific explanations. The narrative in verse 2:73[154] about the identification of the killer is a proper example of Gülen's science-based explanation of the miracles. Gülen reveals various dimensions of the verse as follows. Firstly, he acknowledges it as a miracle. Gülen also believes that this verse encourages humanity to go further in scientific exploration. He then gives some information about how some brain cells stay alive after death. This verse should be read in the light of modern genetics, biology and autopsy practices. For example, he comments that this verse may shed light on the identification of the unknown killer in the future.[155] Although he is careful about not falling into the trap of rationalization of the miracles, he encourages modern thinkers to pay attention to the miracles attributed to the Prophets in the Qur'an, and to be inspired by them to conduct further scientific research.[156]

7. CONCLUSION

What is Gülen's place among Qur'anic exegetes? Some might see him as a stereotypical traditionalist who embellishes his exegesis with some modern discourse. For others, who approach him more sympathetically, he is a progressive Muslim intellectual who has sufficient religious and scientific background to offer changes to the interpretation of various Islamic disciplines.

---

[153] Gülen 1998a, p. 48; Gülen 1996b, pp. 133–36.

[154] 2:73 "So We said: 'Strike the (body) with a piece of the (heifer).' Thus God bringeth the dead to life and showeth you His Signs: perchance ye may understand."

[155] Gülen 2000a, p. 59.

[156] Gülen 1998a, p. 35; 2000a, p. 50.

In the light of our analysis, it is safe to assume that Gülen is actually a representative of the Ottoman exegetical school; he is well-acquainted with classical commentaries and established tradition and while at the same time he is also familiar with modern science. Because of this strong connection, it is inappropriate to view his exegetical efforts merely from the perspective of intellectualism.

Concerning the methodology of the exegesis, Gülen is representative of *via media*. He uses reports on "the occasions of revelations" while sometimes criticizing these reports. His approach to the notion of *isrāīliyyāt* follows a similar pattern. When looking at his analysis of the notion of abrogation and *muhkam* and *mutashābih*, we notice his broader understanding of the issues. To sum up, we can situate Gülen somewhere between traditionalist and modernist scholars in his evaluation of these hermeneutical devices. Gülen stays on the middle ground while interpreting the nature of the Qur'an, the relationship between scientific developments and Qur'anic verses, etc. He also argues against the wholesale adoption of a scientific, literary, or classical approach. Instead, he suggests that Muslim scholars and interpreters of the Qur'an should use an approach that is rooted in Islamic tradition and experience, without neglecting modern developments. With regard to the mystical, theological, and legal interpretation of the Qur'an, we see his style as being moderate and following traditional literature, while giving credit to modern interpretations and scientific explorations.

Gülen's quotations of contemporary thinkers, philosophers, and theologians from West and East are worth exploring in a separate work. It is also important to note that Gülen brings the idea of interfaith dialogue to his exegetical endeavor though we have not discussed it here since it is beyond the scope of this chapter. If his exegesis is considered in the light of interfaith dialogue, it would be an original contribution to the literature of modern Muslim exegesis. Finally, Gülen's analyses have social, psychological, cultural and philosophical dimensions that differentiate his Qur'anic exegesis from that of his many classical counterparts.

CHAPTER TWO

Fethullah Gülen's Thought on *Hadith*

Halim Çalış

1. INTRODUCTION

The goal of this chapter is to explore Fethullah Gülen's thought regarding the *hadith*, a discipline that explores the Prophetic traditions. It is confined to summarizing Fethullah Gülen's ideas on the subject—an effort without a precedent according to my research—through examples taken from his works without presenting detailed discussions on a specific matter or attempting to cover everything under the title of *hadith*.

Studying a scholar as versatile as Fethullah Gülen requires exploring the diversity of his thinking; this is necessary in order to fully understand his position with respect to *hadith*. This study, therefore, looks into his attitude towards *hadith* in three subsections that will reveal (a) how he uses and interprets *hadith* in his works as a "commentator" (b) what contribution he makes as a "teacher," and (c) what point of view he holds in the face of contemporary debates over *hadith*. But first of all, it would be helpful to provide some brief information on *hadith*.

2. *HADITH*: A SUMMARY OF THE CLASSICAL VIEW AND CONTEMPORARY APPROACHES

Hadith, literally meaning "something new" or "talk," is a term used for the tradition attributed to the Prophet Muhammad, peace be upon him, and includes what he said, did, or tacitly approved.[157] Reports regarding the physical and moral characteristics of the Prophet are also considered as *hadith*. The science whose subject is the *hadith* of the Prophet is also called

---

[157] In some cases, sayings of the Prophet's Companions are also called *hadith*.

hadith. Sunnah, on the other hand, refers to the Prophet's customs, practices and religious rules drawn from his actions.

A *hadith* has two main parts: *sanad* (the chain of transmitters) and *matn* (the text narrated). The number of transmitters varies from only a few transmitter names to some very long chains. In the *sanad* section, some particular Arabic verbs and prepositions are used such as *haddathanā* (he narrated it to us), *akhbaranā* (he informed us), or *'an* (from, on account of). *Matn* also may differ in their length. Most of the *matn* only consist of the Prophet's statements but there are many *hadith* in which the Companions talk about the Prophet's actions and customs. Considerable amounts of this type begin with the Arabic verb *kāna* that is translated as "the Prophet used to (do ...)."

Scholars have categorized *hadith* into several groups according to different conditions like the number of transmitters or their levels of authenticity. As a result, many types of *hadith* have been defined in reference to the "number of transmitters," "the nature of *sanad*," the "special feature of *matn* or *sanad*," "acceptable traditions," and "rejected traditions."[158]

The preservation and compilation of *hadith* are two critical subjects in the history of *hadith* tradition. During the lifetime of the Prophet, preservation meant memorization. Besides memorization, debate exists over whether *hadith* were recorded in writing in this period and there are conflicting narratives in Islamic sources. Some narratives state that the Prophet forbade the Companions to write statements beyond the Qur'an, while others convey his permission to write. The sources even mention some scripts (*sahīfah*) in which some Companions such as 'Abd Allāh b. Amr collected some *hadith* of the Prophet. Scholars generally explain this contradiction as follows. When the Companions did not have enough experience to distinguish between Qur'anic verses and *hadith*, the Prophet forbade them to write his *hadith*, fearing that some non-Qur'anic utterances might get mixed into the Qur'anic revelation. But as the years passed and he became confident that the two would be delineated, he permitted some well-versed Companions to write his words. But, while some Companions may have written *hadith*, we must acknowledge that *hadith* was for the most part transmitted orally until it was committed to paper.

---

[158] For further information, see Robson 2008.

According to recent research, there were around four hundred traditionists (*muhaddith*) who wrote *hadith* between the second half of the first century of Islam (700) and the first half the second century (800).[159] One factor that accelerated this activity might be the official order of Caliph ʿUmar b. ʿAbd al-ʿAzīz (d. 101/720)[160] regarding compilation of *hadith*. Ibn Shihāb al-Zuhrī (d. 124/742), who was known as a great scholar and who collected everything available to him about the *sunnah*, was among those scholars who carried out the order. Thus, during the second and the third centuries (800–900) intense efforts were made to collect and record *hadith*. *Hadith* works produced in this time were mostly structured on either the subjects of *hadith* (*musannaf*) or the names of the first transmitters, namely the Companions (*musnad*). However, during this process there were political and sectarian disputes that resulted in many fabricated *hadith* (*mawdūʿ*) as these struggling groups sought to justify their political or theological position. These *hadith* came into circulation, so scholars developed a science of criticism for *hadith* (*al-jarh wa al-taʿdīl*). This criticism was entirely about the *sanad*, that is the reliability of the transmitters (in terms of their piety, accurate memory, and lack of contradiction with well-known reliable narrators). The uninterrupted connection between them verified the authenticity of the *hadith* under discussion.

Based on their fulfillment of these conditions, *hadith* were divided into four groups: sound (*sahīh*), good or lesser than *sahīh* (*hasan*), weak (*daʿīf*), and invalid (*saqīm*).[161] Finally, critical scholars attempted to form collections that contained the most reliable *hadith* as were possible. Among them, two collections, *Sahīh al-Bukhari* and *Sahīh al-Muslim*, gained the reputation as the most reliable books of *hadith*. They contained only sound *hadith*s, consequently classical scholars generally did not question the authenticity of the traditions included by Bukhari (d. 256/870) and Muslim (d. 261/875). Besides these two, the *Sunan*s of Abu Dāwūd (d. 275/888), al-Tirmidhī (d. 279/892), al-Nasāī (d. 214/303), and Ibn Mājah (d. 273/887) constitute the most reliable six books (*al-kutub al-sitta*).

Classical Sunni understanding is distinguished by the following two ideas regarding its approach to *hadith*: First, the *hadith* the classical scholars

---

[159] Kandemir 1988, XV.32.
[160] Dates are After Hijrah (Islamic calendar) / Common Era.
[161] Robson 2008.

verified as being sound are absolutely reliable and authentic, so there is no need to criticize or re-evaluate them. In addition, all the Companions are accepted as trustworthy. Second, it is obligatory to act upon sound *hadith*. *Hadith*, in this sense, has been considered the second authority in Islam after the Qur'an. Qur'anic verses enjoining Muslims to obey the Prophet have been taken as accounts that prove the religious authority of *hadith*. Classical Sunni scholars emphasize two important functions of a *hadith* (a) it interprets the Qur'an by explaining unclear points[162] or adding information[163] and (b) it sets forth law that is not present in the Qur'an.[164] As a matter of fact, many Muslim scholars consider both the Qur'an and *hadith* as divine revelations except that the wording of *hadith* belongs to the Prophet (*al-wahy ghayr al-matluw*: the unrecited revelation).

From the beginning of the nineteenth century, Western scholarship presented a different approach from Muslim scholars concerning *hadith* by regarding most *hadith* as fictitious. Two Western scholars, Ignaz Goldziher and Joseph Schacht, became the first flag-bearers of a great skepticism about *hadith*. Goldziher concluded that the *hadith* is not a historically reliable source concerning the time of the Prophet and the Companions. He argued, rather, that *hadith* reflects the time of later generations which means that they were generated during the later period.[165] Schacht, who studied the origin of Islamic jurisprudence, argued that legal traditions appeared long after the Prophet and every one of them must be taken as inauthentic until the contrary is proved.[166] Montgomery Watt, on the other hand, offered an alternative view, that the *sīrah* genre (compilations about the life of the Prophet) has "a basic core of material which is sound."[167] So, Islamic tradition can be taken as historically reliable, for Watt, at least in its essence. There is another group of scholars such as Josef van Ess, Gregor Schoeler and Harald Motzki who

---

[162] *Hadith* collections have sections as regards the interpretation of the Qur'an (*tafsīr*).

[163] For example, *hadith* provides much more elaborate information about the end of the world, the hereafter, hell and paradise etc., than the Qur'an.

[164] For instance, the unlawfulness for someone to marry his wife's aunts is established by *hadith* in Islamic jurisprudence.

[165] Stern 1967–71, II.19.

[166] Schacht 1967, p.149. Some scholars, coming after Schacht, rejected his ideas while others followed him. See: Motzki 2004, p. xxiv. Kandemir summarizes and refutes the arguments of some Western scholars who shared Goldziher and Schacht's skepticism towards *hadith* such as Leone Caetani, Henri Lammens, David Samuel Margoliouth, Reynold Alleyne Nicholson, Alfred Guillaume and Philip Khuri Hitti. See Kandemir 1988.

[167] Watt 1988, p. 1.

position themselves between those who reject Muslim tradition completely and those who accept it unquestionably.[168] Their strategy is to avoid "general statements about the historical reliability of the *hadith*" and to postpone "judgments about individual *hadith*" until they are examined.[169]

Some contemporary Muslim scholars also criticize *hadith* and raise doubts concerning their authenticity. Movements of *sola scriptura* in the Islamic world, which became popular during the latest centuries, are partly the result of scholarly distrust of *hadith*.

3. FETHULLAH GÜLEN AND *HADITH*

Although his biography includes no *hadith* study in his early education,[170] it is not difficult to guess that young Fethullah, who was fond of listening to sermons and religious talks (*sohbet*), became familiar with many traditions of the Prophet at a very early age. His thirst to know about the lives of prominent Muslim figures, especially the first generation, the Companions of the Prophet Muhammad, peace be upon him, seems to have been passed on to him from his father who studied the biographies of the Companions to such an extent that he frayed the pages of the books he was using.[171] When he was able to read, Gülen studied his father's books, which were written in Ottoman script, again and again to the extent that he almost memorized them.[172] Having been impressed by what he learned about the Companions, he became an "admirer of the companions."[173] When he started preaching at fourteen, he would prepare sermons based on Arabic sources such as *Durrat al-wā'izīn*, which included commentaries on many Qur'anic verses and Prophetic traditions.[174]

---

[168] Motzki 2004, pp. xxviii–xxix.

[169] Ibid, pp. xxviii.

[170] He started his education by memorizing the Qur'an and then took lessons on the grammar of the Arabic language, as was the tradition in classical *madrasah* education. See Erdoğan 2006, pp. 28, 36. Also accessible at http://tr.fgulen.com/content/view/3502/128/.

[171] Ibid, p. 27.

[172] Ibid, p. 36.

[173] http://tr.fgulen.com/content/view/3502/128/. Knowledge of persons (*'ilm al-rijāl*) is considered a very important part of *hadith*. It is interesting that Gülen began to pay attention to this dimension of *hadith* during the very early years of his education.

[174] See http://tr.fgulen.com/content/view/3502/128/. *Durrat al-wa'izin*, also known as *Durrat al-nasihīn*, was a very popular book for preachers. It was written by Hopalı Osman Efendi (d. 1825), an Ottoman scholar. See Uludağ 1988, X. p. 32.

After completing his short informal religious education, Gülen left his hometown, Erzurum, and went to Edirne. While he was working as an officially appointed imam in Edirne, he continued to educate himself by reading about various Islamic disciplines including the *hadith*.[175] During this period, for example, he read the entire *Saḥīḥ al-Bukhari* for the first time. For a young person of eighteen or nineteen, this was so unexpected at that time that his teacher in Erzurum did not want to believe that Gülen had read the text of *Bukhari*.[176] In essence, his reading of this voluminous *hadith* collection was a challenging attempt by an eager young scholar who was not content with the "unsatisfying" lessons taught in classical educational institutions and who wanted to explore classical Islamic sources on his own. From this point on, he continued to study *hadith*. "I spent my whole life," he says, "studying the *sunnah*."[177]

Readers of Gülen's works readily note that his interest in the science of *hadith* is more intense than his concern for any Islamic discipline. We should note that most of his published books, through which we can try to understand his ideas, are actually his sermons and lectures.[178] Before his activities in education and interfaith dialogue, Gülen became a public figure in Turkey first through his influential sermons. He, as noted above, delivered his first sermon at fourteen. From 1959, when he was officially appointed as an imam, up to 1991, he spoke in public frequently in most Turkish cities and even abroad.[179] His lectures and conferences, which took place not only in mosques but also coffee houses and community centers, were on various ethical and religious matters and also on moral standards and social issues. His sermons, which were filled with vast knowledge and emotion, made a great impact on the public, and from early days on they were recorded. Thousands of his speeches, in the form of audiocassettes, videocassettes, CDs and DVDs, are currently in circulation today. One of the innovative aspects of his preaching is that he was able to explain many subjects in lecture series,

---

[175] Erdoğan 2006, pp. 85–86.

[176] Ibid, p. 45.

[177] Ünal 2003, p. 307.

[178] Gülen's books can be divided into three categories: the ones composed of his public lectures, the ones compiled from private conversations delivered to visitors and students, and the ones made up of articles published in various periodicals. In addition, several interviews with him have been published.

[179] http://en.fgulen.com/about-fethullah-Gülen/life-chronology/1055-1941-1993.html.

and some of these were published and became bestsellers in Turkey and were translated into many languages. Among them, *Sonsuz Nur* (vols I–III), dedicated to a narration of the life of the Prophet, can be considered the only book directly related to the science of *hadith*. However, Gülen presents his ideas about *hadith* in his other works as well.[180]

Contemporary scholars of various Islamic disciplines such as Suat Yıldırım and İbrahim Canan and intellectuals such as Ali Bulaç and Ali Ünal acknowledge Gülen's deep knowledge and expertise on the science of *hadith*. Ünal states that Gülen has competence (*yad al-tūlā*) in *hadith*, *sīrah* and especially the philosophy of *sīrah*.[181] According to Bulaç, Gülen is "one of the most distinguished representatives of the intellectual '*ulama* type" who have knowledge of both Islamic and modern sciences.[182] Bulaç points out that among the key features of his intellectual-'*ālim* persona, apart from his profound understanding of Islamic sciences and Islamic methodology, is his deep knowledge of biography (*'ilm al-rijāl*) in *hadith*. Yıldırım maintains that *Sonsuz Nur*, one of Gülen's main works, is enough to show his thorough knowledge of the philosophy of *sīrah* (*fiqh al-sīrah*).[183] Canan, a professor of *hadith* from Turkey, attempts to explain all of Gülen's positions in view of *hadith* in his work.[184]

3.1. Gülen as a commentator on *hadith*

One who skims through Gülen's books will clearly see that his discourse is heavily based on Qur'anic information and *hadith*. Since he is a preacher, it is not unusual that his main sources are the Qur'an and the *sunnah*. Therefore, when he speaks about a religious or non-religious subject, he juxtaposes many Qur'anic verses and *hadith* and occasionally provides a multi-dimensional interpretation of *hadith* through which he engages in linguistic analysis and discusses the authenticity of the traditions and the reliability of the transmitters and so forth. Sometimes, listeners ask him directly for his comments on particular *hadith*. In addition, Gülen reserves a very long section for the interpretation of some individual *hadith* in his work *Sonsuz Nur*.

---

[180] Although these are scholarly books, readers should not always expect an academic style in Gülen's writings as they were transcribed from his speeches.

[181] Ünal 2003, p. 307.

[182] Bulaç 2006, pp. 100–101.

[183] Yıldırım 2003, pp. 17–18.

[184] Canan 2007.

We should first mention that one of the most notable characteristics of Gülen's discourse is that he reinforces and enriches narration with many anecdotes from the history of Islam and biographies of Muslim figures concerning the subjects he discusses.[185] Gülen picks examples mostly from the life of the Prophet and his Companions because he considers them the most relevant models for all Muslims.[186] This being the case, according to Gülen, *al-ʿasr al-saʾādah* (the Age of Happiness), that is the age of the first Muslim generation, provides a crucial source for solving all of the problems that Muslims will encounter to the end of the world.

When interpreting a *hadith*, Gülen always deals with it in the light of the Qurʾan and its exegesis. According to him, those *hadith* transmitted by one or only a few persons (*āhād*)[187] must be understood through knowledge derived from the relevant Qurʾanic verses. He also benefits from other traditions in order to solve ambiguities in the *hadith* involved. The following comment is a helpful example to show how Gülen unravels the mystery around a *hadith* by engaging in discussion of verses of the Qurʾan, other *hadith* and linguistic explanations. He is asked about his interpretation of the tradition stating that "God created Eve from a rib."[188] First, he underscores two Qurʾanic verses that mention Eve's creation: "O humankind! In due reverence for your Lord, keep from disobedience to Him Who created you from a single human self, and from it created its mate, and from the pair of them scattered abroad a multitude of men and women"[189] (4:1) and "He has created you from a single human self, and then He has made from it its mate ..." (39:6). The word *nafs* (translated as "human self") in the verses, which is a feminine noun in Arabic, points out the essence or the nature of Adam, not his physical body. The verses never mention Adam's

---

[185] Gülen 2007a, p. 84.

[186] Gülen 2002, p. 21–26; Ergene 2005, p. 120; Gülen 2004b, p. 97.

[187] *Ahād* is the technical term used for narrations that do not fulfill the conditions of a *mutawātir*, i.e., the narration is transmitted by such a large number of people that it is impossible to think that they all lied.

[188] The full version of the tradition is as follows: Abu Hurayrah narrates "The Messenger of Allah said, 'Treat women nicely, for a woman is created from a rib, and the most curved portion of the rib is its upper portion, so, if you should try to straighten it, it will break, but if you leave it as it is, it will remain crooked. So treat women nicely'" (Bukhari, *Sahīh al-Bukhari*, Anbiyā, 1 and Nikāh, 80; Muslim, *Sahīh al-Muslim*, Radā, 61).

[189] The translations of the Qurʾanic verses are from Ünal's *The Qurʾan with Annotated Interpretation in Modern English*, NJ: The Light Inc., 2006.

name but clearly state that God created Eve from that "self" (*nafs*) using the feminine enclitic pronoun (*hā*) that refers to *nafs*. Thus, the verses do not express that God created Eve "from Adam himself" or "Adam's body." On the other hand, there are statements in the *hadith* under discussion that emphasize women's fragile and emotional nature. What follows is that the Prophet implies this in the nature of women by employing the metaphor of the "rib." Using this similitude, the Prophet provides a visual picture of women's natures. So, Gülen prefers to give the *hadith* an allegorical meaning that highlights the physiological nature of women rather than the physical material that Eve was created from. He also conjures up another *hadith* to reinforce his interpretation.

Speaking about a camel that had run away, the Prophet says, the "camel was created from Satan." It is clear, in Gülen's view that the Prophet points out satanic behavior rather than Satan himself. Likewise, Gülen states, people use this kind of metaphor in their daily conversations. For example, they call an insensitive person "wooden" (in Turkish) or when speaking about a wicked man, they say "he is Satan." Finally, Gülen refers to the relevant biblical verse which states that Eve was created from Adam's rib and ends by saying that God might have really created Eve from one of Adam's parts, for this is not impossible for God. As a matter of fact, Adam's creation without any ancestor was a miracle in itself.[190]

Gülen asserts that like the Qur'an, the Prophet's statements also have ambiguous or parabolic expressions (*mutashabihat*) whose meanings are not clear or not completely agreed upon and definitely need to be interpreted.[191] For the *mutashabihat* of the *hadith*, he tends to allegorical interpretation. For example, he interprets anthropomorphic expressions of the *hadith* that refer to God as His divine attributes, just like classical *sunni kalam* (systematic Islamic theology) scholars do.[192] Furthermore, he applies the same methodology for *hadith* that has been used by Sufis who support the idea of the Unity of Existence (*wahdah al-wujūd*) as proof for their ideas. Gülen actually makes a great contribution to Sufism with his books, especially with

---

[190] Gülen 1998c, pp.154–62.

[191] Ibid, p. 123.

[192] For example, Gülen discusses the following *hadith*: "Allah put His hand on my chest ... I felt the coolness of His hand on my chest." He explains this *hadith* by the Prophet's attainment of God's mercy and his comprehension of spiritual realities and secrets of the heavens, etc. (See ibid, p. 124).

the one entitled *Kalbin Zümrüt Tepeleri* (published in English as *Emerald Hills of the Heart*) in which he introduces and discusses Sufi terminology with sophistication, while ultimately not approving of the idea of the Unity of Existence. In this regard, it would be helpful to cite here his explanation of one of the most quoted *hadith* by the followers of the Unity of Existence. The *hadith* asserts that when a person keeps coming nearer to God through obligatory worship and supererogatory deeds, he reaches a certain point so that God becomes his hearing with which he hears, his seeing with which he sees, his hand with which he grasps, and his foot with which he walks.[193] The meaning that Gülen offers for this *hadith* is utterly figurative:

> It means that God shows him what he looks at correctly … when he [the person] hears a good call inviting to the truth he felt eagerness in his spirit in the name of God and his spiritual progress starts … when he speaks, God makes him speak truthfully …[194]

One may ask what makes Gülen correct in his ruling out literal meanings for some *hadith* in his comments. In other words, what are the criteria in taking a statement of the Prophet as a metaphor? First of all, *hadith*, as with the Qur'an and the other sacred texts, are open to interpretation. That is why different legal and theological Islamic schools sometimes use the same Qur'anic verse or a tradition to argue opposite opinions.[195] So a pre-accepted viewpoint determines the destination of the interpretation. It is apparent that the viewpoint Gülen adopts is that of mainstream Islam because, as we will discuss later, he observes the principles of mainstream Islam while commenting on *hadith* and he defends the arguments made by classical *sunni* scholars. However, Gülen's Sunnism can also be characterized as (a) being intent on solving the problems that emerge in modern times by using the flexibility that already exists in the essence of religion and (b) being respectful of Sufism. In brief, if a *hadith* contradicts the *sunni* perspective in its literal meaning, Gülen prefers the allegorical interpretation.

For example, in a long *hadith* narrative, we read that Prophet Abraham had to commit "*kadhib*" three times in his life. Gülen takes the word

---

[193] Bukhari, Riqāq, p. 38.

[194] Ibid, p. 200.

[195] For examples of the linguistic discussions that have resulted in different legal and theological opinions between Islamic sects see 'Abd al-Wahhāb 'Abd al-Salām Tawīlah. 1993. *Athar al-lughah fī ikhtilāf al-mujtahidīn*, Cairo: Dār al-Salām.

"*kadhib*," which literally means "lie," as "allusion" (*ta'rīd*) complying with the *sunni* principle that all the Prophets are impeccable (*ma'sūm*). Hence, he explains that the Prophet used *kadhib* rather humorously in this context, and he gives further examples on the Prophet's other witty sayings and this specific *hadith* fits into that category.[196] Another example is his comment on the *hadith* that announces that "Allah created Adam in His complete shape and form."[197] There is another version of this tradition which Gülen employs in his comment: "God created man in the form of the All-Merciful (*al-Rahmān*)."[198] He makes a great effort to interpret both these *hadith* in an allegorical way in order to avoid anthropomorphic implications that would contradict the principles of mainstream Islam.[199]

Gülen's loyalty to *sunni* doctrine does not prevent him from addressing contemporary problems and producing modern interpretations that may not be found in classical works. In the following passage, he explains the object of modern interpretations:

> Among things that we most need is to present new interpretations, as time changes, of the Book [the Qur'an] and the *sunnah* without distorting their essence in terms of exploring their dimensions that remained undiscovered up to the present day ... What is important is to process this material (the Qur'an and the *sunnah*) and to discover their jewels that may vary in different ages and periods considering variation ... Indeed, alongside loyalty to the essence and the basic fundamentals (of the Qur'an and the *sunnah*), comprehension of present time is also very important. For me, this is the meaning of the revival (of Islam), *tajdīd*.[200]

In this regard, Gülen is able to derive original answers to the questions raised in modern times using *hadith* material. Before discussing the examples, we should note his opinion that those who try to understand and interpret *hadith* should not take modern sciences as the only criterion. Since human reason and the sciences are limited and dependent on the capacities of humans, some information given in the Qur'an and *hadith* may be beyond human perception. Gülen, for example, criticizes some modernist commen-

---

[196] Gülen 2008b, pp.504–511.

[197] Bukhari, Isti'dhān, 1; Muslim, al-birru wa al-sila wa al-ādāb, p. 115.

[198] al-Dāraqutnī 1981, p. 37; al-Shaybānī 1979, p.229.

[199] Gülen 2007b, pp. 158–66. Interestingly, biblical commentators have understood the following biblical verse metaphorically. It is parallel to the *hadith* under discussion: "So God created man in his own image, in the image of God he created him; male and female he created them," (Gen 1: 27). See Çalış 2007, pp. 16–20.

[200] Gülen 2006b, pp. 71–73.

tators who reject, possibly under the influence of positivism, some traditions of reliable *hadith* compilations that narrate that the Prophet was exposed to a spell.[201] So, human reason and scientific facts are welcome as long as they assist but do not determine the process of interpretation.

An example is now provided to show how the commentator uses an irrelevant *hadith* to solve a problem that can be encountered only in the modern age. In answer to a question about how a Muslim should perform his or her daily prayers in the polar zone where days and nights last six months, Gülen recalls an eschatological *hadith* in which the Prophet talks about the time of the Antichrist (*Dajjāl*). When the Prophet says, "The Antichrist will stay on this earth for forty days. The length of the first day will equal one year, the second day will be like a month, the third day will be like a week, and the remaining days will be normal," the Companions ask the Prophet the following, "Do the prayers for one day suffice for that day that will equal to one year?" The Prophet replies, "No, you estimate and calculate!"[202] In his answer, Gülen concludes that those who have to pray in the polar zone should calculate the times of the daily prayers by considering the timetable of the nearest "normal" territory.[203] In another comment, he says that the Black Stone (*al-hajar al-aswad*) may be a meteor. He bases his viewpoint on some traditions that acknowledge its heavenly origin.[204] Furthermore, he approves the religious permissibility of fiction-writing, which has been debated by Muslims in modern times. He calls attention to the style of the Qur'an and Prophetic discourse that provides messages through many narratives.[205]

Gülen frequently explores the formal characteristics of *hadith*, elaborating the discussion with technical details. In this sense, he sometimes specifies the level of authenticity of the narration. If the *hadith* is weak, he generally informs the readers about its weakness.[206] He considers the use of weak *hadith* on moral subjects, apart from legal issues, acceptable.[207] It seems that he follows the principle adopted by Said Nursi that "weakness in authentic-

---

[201] Gülen 2006c, p. 53.

[202] Muslim, *fitan*, p. 110.

[203] Gülen 1998b, pp. 129–30.

[204] Gülen 2001, p. 121.

[205] Gülen 1995b, pp. 330–32.

[206] For example, see Gülen 1998b, pp. 29, 162; 1998d, p. 127; 2004a, p. 58.

[207] Canan 2007, pp. 117–33.

ity of a narrative does not necessarily entail falsity of its meaning."[208] However, two points need to be made clear here: first, Gülen is careful to distinguish the *hadith* that are categorized as "encouraging-discouraging" (*targhīb-tarhīb*) from the legal ones.[209] Second, if a weak *hadith* conflicts with the *sunni* point of view on a certain issue, he rejects it.[210]

Gülen sometimes refers to linguistic and rhetorical analysis of *hadith*. In his view, it is necessary to be aware of the language of traditions in order to avoid false interpretation. An interpretation, according to him, should not go beyond the limits of the language of *hadith*[211] by conflicting with the rules of Arabic. Likewise, a commentator should know when he or she would prefer to assign an allegorical meaning to the text rather than a literal meaning. The following passage is an interesting example because it shows the difference between literal and allegorical meanings:

> Some people have interpreted Qur'anic verses and *hadith* in a hurry without considering the consequences. Most of you must have heard that they suggested the following comment about the *hadith* in which the Prophet said, "Run away from leprosy as if it is a lion!" They said, "Do you know why the Prophet employed the simile of the lion? Because the germ of leprosy looks exactly like a lion!" They commented on the *hadith* thus in order to be seen as scientific and to show how the Prophet miraculously foretold the future. This was so thoughtlessly commented on that its promulgator did not worry about the possible damage to religion that would occur when people would see the germ under the microscope and would understand that it had nothing to do with a lion.[212]

Another reason for Gülen's attention to linguistic and rhetorical discussions while explaining traditions is his dedication to proving the greatness

---

[208] Nursi 2001, p. 360; Ünal, İsmail, 2001, pp. 86–87.

[209] For example, see Gülen 2006c, pp. 231–32. Here, Gülen explains the *hadith* stating that "who spreads salutation, feeds people, and who visits relatives will enter paradise." Thinking that the main purpose of this statement was to encourage people to do these good things, Gülen concludes that this *hadith* is about "some" qualities that help people enter paradise. So, one cannot say that those who fulfill these three will surely enter paradise or those who do not do these will definitely go to hell.

[210] For example, see Gülen 1995b, p. 43. Gülen rejects the narrations that assume that the Prophet was about to commit suicide when the revelation was interrupted at the beginning of his Prophethood. In addition, see Gülen 1995a, p. 181. Gülen rejects reports that ascribe a stutter to the Prophet Moses because he believes that all the Prophets are perfect both physically and spiritually. Only in this way can they be perfect models for their followers. Any deficiency in them may cause hesitation in people and may cause misperception of God's message.

[211] Gülen 1998c, p. 56.

[212] Ibid, p. 55.

of Prophetic eloquence to the extent that he counts it as one of the Prophet's miracles. Gülen, who approaches the traditions with a great confidence and wholeheartedness, repeatedly calls the Prophet "the Sultan of speech"[213] and frequently asserts his having *jawāmiʿ al-kalim* (i.e. the ability to narrate many meanings through the most concise expressions), a term proclaimed by the Prophet himself: "I have been sent with *jawāmiʿ al-kalim*."[214] As a result, in a section of his book *Sonsuz Nur*, Gülen illustrates how the Prophet was able to convey many truths through very short expressions. Gülen also often provides extra information about the events and persons that take place in a given *hadith*.[215] In addition, he mentions the occasions these traditions were laid down so that the readers can know the reasons behind the statements of the Prophet.[216] With all of these, he seems to draw a general picture of the context in which the *sunnah* took its shape. Indeed, to know the historical background and the cultural context is crucial to fully grasping the meaning of any historical text. The following passage is uttered about the Qur'an, but it may be considered totally valid for our discussion as knowing the context of the *sunnah* can provide us with better understanding:

> To study the historical background of the stories [told in the Qur'an] taking the philosophy of history into consideration, to be acquainted with the nations (mentioned in the Qur'an) and their characteristics... and to analyze the narratives of the Qur'an through examining all the periods up to the Prophet Muhammad, peace be upon him, will open up new horizons for people. On the contrary, any attempt to understand the Qur'an without considering these (above-mentioned factors) would be peculiar, like trying to analyze Shakespeare's eloquence in his works without having any idea about the Elizabethan era and its lifestyle. Other than that, [the person] who tells the stories of the Qur'an is Allah, who sees the past and the future as one point at the same time and turns them over and over in His hand of disposal. Needless to say, His narration is beyond every comparison and is extraordinary and magnificent.[217]

To summarize, this section has shown that Gülen comments on *hadith* in the light of information deduced from the Qur'an and other *hadith*. The position of mainstream Islam determines his priorities in interpretation espe-

---

213 See Gülen 2008b, p. 288.
214 Bukhari, taʿbīr, 11; Muslim, masājid, 5.
215 For example, see Gülen 1998b, pp. 63–64; 1998d, p. 16–22, 168–77; 2008b, p. 59, 119.
216 For example, see Gülen 1998c, p. 159; http://www.herkul.org/kiriktesti/index.php?article_
    id=5633
217 Gülen 1995a, p. 195.

cially in theological subjects such as the incorporeality of God. He occasionally talks about the technical details of a *hadith* but not as an academic exercise. He also attaches great importance to the eloquence of Prophetic statements.

3.2. Gülen as a teacher of *hadith*

What was said in the previous section reflects Gülen's ideas which were presented in public and therefore intended for people who are not expert in the science of *hadith*. However, he has also been providing scholarly instruction for divinity school graduates. He started his lessons and lectures specifically in the field of *hadith* in a mosque in the 1970s.[218] The first attendees were students from religious high schools (İmam-Hatip Lisesi) and Islamic seminaries (Yüksek İslam Enstitüsü). The lessons that were interrupted by the military coup in 1980 started again in 1985[219] and have continued up to the present day with graduate students whose numbers have varied over time. According to the testimonies of students who attended these lessons, they studied books written on various major Islamic disciplines such as *tafsīr*, *fiqh*, *tasawwuf*, and *hadith* under the tutelage of Gülen.[220] Among these books, the ones related to *hadith* consist of the major *hadith* compilations, their voluminous commentaries, and some other works on the methodology of *hadith*.[221] The method of the lessons is as follows: students prepare for the text in advance. When they read the text in the presence of Gülen, they ask questions about the format or the content of the text and Gülen answers and explains. In addition to reading the text, they peruse the transmitters of the *hadith* (*rijāl*)[222] under discussion through the computer program projected on the board. They use several software programs made for Islamic disciplines including *hadith* and get information from them instantly in the lesson. Study of the *rijāl*, in fact, began with information cards prepared by Gülen himself many years ago and it evolved through the overhead projector first and the modern video projector subsequently.

---

[218] Erdoğan 2006, p. 134.

[219] Kurucan 1995, p. xxiii.

[220] Canan 2007, pp. 78–83.

[221] Canan provides a list of books perused by Gülen with his students. See Canan 2007, pp. 80–83.

[222] The word *rijāl* literally means "men" though there are many women transmitters and experts on *hadith*.

The science of the transmitters (*rijāl*) is of great importance for Gülen. He believes that the healthiest evaluation of *hadith* is possible only through knowing its *rijāl*. Therefore, he teaches students theological and jurisprudential opinions of the *rijāl*, their position in the eyes of critics in terms of reliability, the structures of connections between them (such as "who receives a *hadith* from whom" or "who is teacher of whom" etc.), and other biographical information. Thus students are able to see activities of transmission that occurred in a certain time and place as a whole. In addition, Gülen does not neglect to relate hagiographical stories about the *rijāl* that may stimulate the students to be like them. In this sense, he acts not only as a scholar who teaches the biographies of Muslim figures, but also as a spiritual guide who attaches importance to practicing their moral qualities. What is more, we can say that the practical side of knowledge, as in our example, is Gülen's main concern because he believes that the purpose of learning must be appropriating for oneself what is learned.

Recent research on the chain of transmitters (*isnād*) has shown the importance of this field. Some contemporary scholars utilize the *isnād* analysis as a method through which they can evaluate the historical reliability of the *hadith*. They believe that they are able to make sound judgments about the authenticity of *hadith* using the *isnād* tradition.[223] Sharing the same point of view, Gülen thinks that our evaluation of a *hadith* can be sounder than in the past because of the comprehensive approach to variant versions of *hadith* and its transmitters:

> Hence, one should benefit from every opportunity provided by high technology; if the subject is *hadith*, for example, he or she should reexamine books of the *rijāl* and check the text according to the textual criteria… If it is done in this way, this will never harm the great reputation of either Bukhari or Muslim. However, judgments of today made with the aid of computers would be, I believe, sounder than the judgments of the past.

In short, for Gülen, it is imperative to pay attention to three interdependent studies when studying *hadith*: text analysis, *isnād* analysis and perusal of variant commentaries.

---

223 For example, see Motzki 2001, pp. 1–34. This article, in which Motzki deals with debates on the collections of the Qur'an, is a beautiful example that shows how a scholar achieves sound judgment on a historical event using data that the *'ilm al-rijāl* provides. In brief, through source criticism, textual analysis, and more importantly *isnād* analysis, Motzki is able to develop a more satisfying explanation than those who reject using *hadith*.

4. GÜLEN AND THE DEFENSE OF THE CLASSICAL VIEWPOINT

As we discussed earlier, questions have been raised about the traditional Muslim understanding of *hadith* for the last two centuries. Criticism focuses on how we can realize the authenticity of *hadith*. Skepticism around their authenticity results in a rejection of *hadith* as a source for both theological and jurisprudential matters. Gülen also gave his attention to this subject reserving a series of lectures to the defense of the classical view which later became the third volume of *Sonsuz Nur*, his work dedicated to the life of the Prophet.[224] In this volume, he discusses the description of the *sunnah*, its categories and functions. He also explains how *hadith* were preserved and the factors that played a role in their preservation. Lastly, he talks about the two most important generations of the chain of transmitters, namely the Companions of the Prophet (*ashāb*) and their followers (*tābi'ūn*). In this section, we will summarize Gülen's ideas related to the subject.

In the *Sonsuz Nur* (vol. 3), Gülen usually prefers to use the term *sunnah* because it seems to be broader in scope than *hadith*. However, what appears from the descriptions he provides is that these two terms are interchangeable:

> *Sunnah* literally means "a conduct and a good or evil path to be followed." This is the meaning used in the following *hadith*: "Those who establish a good path in Islam receive the reward of those who follow it, without any decrease in their reward. Those who establish an evil path in Islam are burdened with the sins of those who follow it, without any decrease in their burden."[225]

This term also has different terminological connotations according to each group of traditionalists, methodologists, and jurists. Traditionalists view it as including everything connected to the religious commandments reported from the Messenger and categorized, according to the Hanafī legal school (followers of Abu Hanifa), as obligations, necessities and practices particular to or encouraged by the Prophet himself as recommended and desirable. Methodologists consider it to be every word, deed, and approval of the Messenger as related by his Companions. Jurists, who approach it as the opposite of innovation in religion (*bid'ah*), consider it a synonym for

---

[224] The subtitle of this volume is "Establishing the Sunna and Its Role in Legislation" (Sünnetin Tesbiti ve Teşri'deki Yeri).

[225] Muslim, zakāh, 69; Ibn Mājah, muqaddima, 203.

hadith. They use it for the Prophet's words, deeds, and approvals, all of which provide a basis for legislation and categorizing people's actions. Derived from the word *haddatha* (to inform), *hadith* literally means tidings or information. Over time, it has assumed the meaning of every word, deed, and approval ascribed to the Messenger.[226]

According to Gülen, the *sunnah* (in terms of the Prophet's customs that are related to religiosity rather than his personal customs such as his style of clothing) has two major functions. First, as the second source of Islamic legislation after the Qur'an, it determines some religiously unlawful/prohibited (*harām*) and lawful/allowed (*halāl*) acts that are not mentioned in the Qur'an. For example, the unlawfulness of eating the meat of domestic donkeys and wild animals and that of marrying the female cousins of one's wife are laid down by the *sunnah* at the same time.[227] Second, it interprets the Qur'an.[228] Such interpretation comes true through the following methods:

i.   The *sunnah* clarifies some ambiguities in the Qur'an. For example, when the verse "Those who believed and did not mix their belief with wrongdoing: for them is security and they are those who are truly guided" (6:82) was revealed, the Companions, well aware what wrongdoing meant, asked the Messenger fearfully: "Is there one among us who has never done wrong?" The Messenger explained: "It's not as you think. It's as Luqman said to his son: 'Don't associate any partners with God; surely, associating partners with God is a grave wrongdoing'" (31:13).[229]

ii. The *sunnah* expands upon what is mentioned only briefly in the Qur'an. For example, there is no detail about daily prayers in the Qur'an. These details, such as their times, sorts, forms, etc. are given by the *sunnah*.[230]

iii. The *sunnah* specifies what is generally stated. For example, while the Qur'an lays down general principles of inheritance, the *sunnah* asserts that the Prophets do not leave anything to be inherited and

---

[226] Gülen 2000d, p.13; English translation is from: http://www.infinitelight.org/content/view/742/4/.

[227] Ibid, p. 3.

[228] Ibid, p. 25.

[229] Ibid, p. 26–27; trans. from http://www.infinitelight.org/content/view/746/4/; Bukhari, *ibid.*, tafsīr, 31.

[230] Ibid, pp. 28–29.

what they leave is for charity. In addition, a killer of her/his testa-
tor cannot take any share of the inheritance. These exceptions are
known only by means of the *sunnah*.[231] Thus, the *sunnah* specifies
the general rules of inheritance established by the Qur'an.

iv. The *sunnah* limits what is left unconditional by the Qur'an. For
example, the Qur'an decrees: "O you who believe! Consume not
your goods among yourselves in vanity (through theft, usury, brib-
ery, hoarding, and so on), except it be trade by mutual agreement"
(4:29). Islam encourages trade as a livelihood, as long as it is carried out according to Islamic law. One condition, as stated in the
verse, is mutual agreement. However, the Messenger decreed: "Do
not sell fruits until their amount is definite in the tree (so that the
amount to be given as alms can be determined)" and: "Do not go
to meet peasants outside the market to buy their goods (Let them
earn the market prices of their goods)."[232]

"As with the Qur'an," Gülen states, the "majority of the *sunnah* was
preserved through memorization and writing so that it could be passed
down to us."[233] In this sense, he includes the *sunnah* in the meaning of the
following Qur'anic verse: "Truly, it is We who have revealed the *dhikr* [lit-
erally means remembrance. In this verse, it is understood as the Qur'an] and
We will be its guardian" (15:9). In fact, the Qur'an and the *sunnah*, in Gül-
en's opinion, are coming from the same source, namely divine revelation. He
agrees with those who refer to the *hadith* as the "unrecited revelation" (*al-
wahy ghayr al-matluw*),[234] meaning that the traditions of the Prophet, like
the Qur'an, "the recited revelation" (*al-wahy al-matluw*), are also revelation.
The only difference is that the wording of the *hadith* belongs to the Prophet; so its recitation is not considered worship.

Gülen lists several motives playing a role in the historical preservation
of the *sunnah*.[235] First, the Qur'an urges Muslims to follow the Prophet and
embrace all that he teaches. He cites the following two verses of the Qur'an
on this subject: "… whatever the Messenger gives you, accept it willingly,

---

[231] Ibid, p.30–31.
[232] Ibid, p. 31–32; trans. from http://www.infinitelight.org/content/view/746/4/.
[233] Ibid, p. 35.
[234] Ibid, p. 36; Gülen 1998c, p. 135.
[235] Gülen 2000d, pp. 36–50.

and whatever he forbids you, refrain from it" (59:7). "Assuredly you have in God's Messenger an excellent example to follow, for whoever looks forward to God and the Last Day, and remembers and mentions God much" (33:21). Second, the Prophet himself exhorts Muslims to practice his *sunnah*. Again, Gülen presents many examples from the *sīrah* tradition. Third, the Companions were desirous of learning and teaching the *sunnah*. Fourth, the Companions witnessed many unforgettable scenes in the life of the Prophet, so they easily kept them in their memories and conveyed them to the others. Fifth, the Companions were extremely serious and careful in transmitting what they knew about the *hadith*. Sixth, the messages of the Qur'an and the Prophet created such a fertile environment that the first interlocutors were transformed from being a primitive community to the founders of a new civilization in a short period of time. Gülen often emphasizes the brilliant intelligence and marvelous powers of memory of the first bearers of the Qur'anic and Prophetic messages. The existence of these abilities, which were planted and sprouted in their nature in a propitious atmosphere, was due to the Prophethood of Muhammad, peace be upon him.

Gülen disapproves of those who assert that most of the traditions known as sound were fabricated during later periods. He states that the Companions and the generation that followed them (*tābi'ūn*) preserved *hadith* with great deliberation, thanks to the Prophet's occasional warnings about erroneous citing from his words.[236] He also recalls many examples from these two generations about their cautiousness and efforts to narrate *hadith*. At the same time, he accepts the fact that many fabricated *hadith* were incorporated into the corpus because of sectarian, political, or economic purposes despite all the efforts of traditionalists. But these fake traditions were identified by experts and compiled in books so that people should distinguish them from reliable *hadith*.[237] These books in which unreliable traditions were recorded would be a genre in Islamic literature with the name *mawdū'āt*. As a result, according to Gülen, after knowing of all these painstaking studies, raising doubts about the authenticity of those *hadith* identified as sound is misguided.[238] To this end, he explains with great care some *hadith* later labeled fictitious, although they occur in the sound *hadith* col-

---

[236] Ibid, pp. 62–63.
[237] Ibid, pp. 79–85; Gülen 2007a, p. 242.
[238] Gülen 2000d, pp. 79–85; Gülen 2007a, p. 242.

lections such as those of Bukhari and Muslim, because they seem to be unreasonable at first glance. In this way, he attempts to show that a superficial approach to these *hadith* under question could be misleading.[239]

Another important point Gülen touches on is the debate over whether traditions were written down during the lifetime of the Prophet. He records both groups of narratives that ostensibly contradict each other, and mentions both the Prophet's prohibition and permission for the Companions to write down his statements.[240] After considering all the narratives involved, subsequently he draws the conclusion that many traditions were written by some Companions such as Jābir b. 'Abd Allah and Ibn 'Abbās. In addition, the content of some scripts (*sahīfah*) such as that of Hammām b. Munabbih, who recorded many *hadith* from Abu Hurayrah, survived in *hadith* collections up to the present day.[241] Gülen agrees with Ahmad Muhammad Shākir, a contemporary *hadith* scholar, who maintains that Prophetic proclamations forbidding the Companions to write down *hadith* were either abrogated afterwards or were made because of the fear that *hadith* might get incorporated into Qur'anic verses.[242]

Since he is aware of criticism raised by Western scholars against some Companions called *mukthirūn* (who narrated more than one thousand *hadith*) such as Abu Hurayrah, 'Abd Allah b. 'Abbās, 'Āisha, and 'Abd Allah b. 'Umar, Gülen devotes a long chapter to the Companions in general, and to the *mukthirūn* in particular.[243] The Companions occupy a special place in Gülen's understanding to the extent that he almost equates them with religion itself because Islam was passed on by them to the next generations.[244] Therefore, to stand up for them denotes a defense of religion. They are not only the most important medium to safely convey religion to future generations of Muslims but also provide an example of a model community for Muslims for all times. An undistinguished person among the Companions is considered more virtuous than any other Muslim who is not a Companion, even the most notable ones such as 'Umar b. 'Abd al-'Azīz.[245] In this sense,

---

[239] Gülen 2000d, pp. 90–106.
[240] Ibid, pp. 124–31.
[241] Ibid, p.131.
[242] Ibid, p. 132.
[243] Ibid, pp. 139–81.
[244] Ibid, pp. 158.
[245] Ibid, p. 142; Gülen 1998c, p. 248.

the lifestyle of the Companions is the criterion for Gülen, who embraces as his life's purpose resemblance to them. He admires the Companions so much that he believes that the more closely a person models oneself on them, in terms of their lifestyle, the more closely it shows one's level of piety.[246] Furthermore, he states that the Companions were one of the miracles given to the Prophet.[247] This means that God reinforced the Prophet's messages with these "chosen" people just as He did with miracles. As a result, Gülen takes pains to explain everything through examples taken from the lives of the Companions. As for their position in the *hadith*, Gülen agrees with the opinion of the classical *'ulamā* (scholars) that all the Companions are reliable transmitters (*'udūl* [sin.] *'ādil*) which means that critics do not submit them to criticism.

5. FURTHER REMARKS REGARDING CONTEMPORARY ISSUES

Besides the above-mentioned points made in defense of the classical *sunni* point of view, Gülen presents some other noteworthy thoughts by which he aims to emphasize the effectiveness of the *sunnah* for today and to invalidate criticism about its acceptability and practicability. In short, he underscores the historicity of some parts of the *sunnah*, considers some of its practices in light of principles deduced from the totality of the corpus, and evaluates the practices according to their role and importance in religious life. We will be brief in order not to extend the limits of this study but I believe that the distinction between Gülen's thoughts and the classical standpoint needs to be further studied.

Gülen classifies the *sunnah* into two parts: (a) personal customs of the Prophet such as his style of clothing, and (b) his customs relating to religiosity. The latter is universal and concerns every Muslim while the former is contextual. Nevertheless, he clearly declares that a Muslim who practices the personal customs of the Prophet will be rewarded in the hereafter.[248] Therefore, when accentuating the historicity of some practices of the *sunnah*, Gülen does not seek to hurt the feelings of Muslims who sincerely imitate the Prophet's personal habits. For example, in his analysis of a well-known custom of the Prophet, the use of *miswāk* (a stick of wood used as a tooth-

---

[246] Gülen 2007a, p. 84.
[247] İsmail Ünal 2001, p. 211.
[248] Gülen 2000d, p. 1.

brush), he makes two points: first, the purpose of this *sunnah* is to provide advice on cleaning your teeth and a modern toothbrush and toothpaste can substitute for the *miswāk*. Second, the *miswāk* should not be ruled out in cleaning your teeth because it may have some beneficial features.[249] From this example one can see that Gülen avoids two extremes concerning the practices of the Prophet. He presents the same moderate approach about beard shaving, stating that having a beard is indisputably a *sunnah*, but shaving it is not prohibited by religion (*haram*). So, those who shave their beards for special reasons should never be condemned.[250]

Gülen accepts the fact that everything may not be found in the Qur'an and the *sunnah*. In such cases, he focuses on the general principles of the *sunnah*. For example, in response to a question about multinational corporations that are a reality in today's world, he states that Muslims should apply mercantile methods compatible with the "spirit" of the Qur'an and the *sunnah* even though they cannot find every detail for managing modern businesses in these sources.[251] In this sense, for him, all innovations in religion (*bid'ah*) are not erroneous. For example, he considers recitation of poems celebrating the birth of the Prophet (*mawlid*) as a "good innovation" (*bid'ah hasana*) that should not be rejected because it is in praise of God and the Prophet, and is celebrated by the Qur'an and the *sunnah*.[252]

Gülen complains about those who reduce the *sunnah* to fruitless discussions that occur between different Islamic schools. For example, he relates in sorrow, that he has been offended by being caught up in unfortunate discussions such as whether to perform a supererogatory prayer after an obligatory prayer is more meritorious than a litany of praise to God. Muslims who hurt each other for such unessential details, violate the more important principles established by the *sunnah*. According to him, other subjects of the *sunnah* such as kindness, mercy, true religion etc. deserve more attention.[253] At this point, why Gülen momentously calls attention to an interpretation of Islam that is influenced by and in harmony with Sufism, brings into question the necessity of putting everything in order according to their

[249] Gülen 2008b, pp. 185–87.
[250] Gülen 1995b, pp. 298–99.
[251] Gülen 2007c, p. 61.
[252] Gülen 2008c, p. 158.
[253] Can 1996, pp. 35–36.

importance. Accordingly, Gülen favors presenting Islam well by embracing tradition, saying, "Make things for people easy and do not make them difficult! Give people good tidings and do not frighten them!"[254] As a result, introducing Islam with an emphasis on its core teaching, which is ease and gentleness, is Gülen's priority. For example, one who prefers the clothing style of his community and does not imitate the Prophet in this matter in order to give Islamic messages to others more effectively so as not to be alienated from the society they live in, deserves nothing but admiration.[255]

Likewise, in these days, when Islam has been subjected to condemnation because of polygamy for example, Muslims must be self-critical. Gülen explains the Prophet's marriages in a historical and cultural context.[256] As for today, to deliver Islam from these attacks that overshadow its many beauties is more important than practicing a *sunnah* connected with a certain "context" which does not relate to the universal values of the *sunnah*.[257]

Our last example has much more serious implications than the previous ones. Gülen brings a totally new approach to the Islamic principle epitomized by the formula "enjoining good and forbidding evil." This principle is based on several Qur'anic verses and the following *hadith*: "Whoever witnesses evil should change it with his hand (physical action); if he cannot, then with his tongue (verbal objection); if he cannot, then with his heart, and the last is the weakest level of faith."[258] Gülen maintains that the first task the *hadith* enjoins, namely physical intervention, concerns governmental authority, rather than something that individuals should carry out.[259] He

---

[254] Ibid, p. 36.

[255] Gülen 1995b, pp. 251–52.

[256] Gülen 1998b, pp. 84–97; Sevindi 1997, p. 90.

[257] In reality, Gülen does not consider that marrying more than one woman as *sunnah* in terms of religious obligation. Rather, he thinks, this is a permission given in a particular period (Sevindi 1997, p. 90.). Personally, I understand this statement as his endeavor to rank everything according to its significance and to give priorities in religion their due. If a thing of first priority is in danger, things of lesser importance should not distract people. Gülen's following remarks clarify this point very well: "Time puts some things forward, and pushes back others. Because of some (religious) rules that increase in importance, other rules may be abandoned. (For example) there is no fasting in a time of war; prayers are shortened during travel. If ever polygamy puts a blemish on Islam or drives (people) away from Islam, no Muslim has the right to cause this" (Ibid, pp. 91–92).

[258] Muslim, *imān*, p. 20.

[259] Gülen 2010a, pp. 156–159.

asserts that "the authority for intervention by hand is the state."[260] This detail is critical for rejecting potential anarchy in society – to prevent chaos in society, and having only the state as the rightful authority that can punish violators of rules. Likewise, the declaration of war for a purpose, utilizing this approach, is the business of the state. Therefore, individuals or groups cannot initiate jihad nor punish people based on their own decisions.

6. CONCLUSION

In this study, I have attempted to summarize Fethullah Gülen's thoughts on *hadith* and the *sunnah* and highlight some aspects of his discourse. As readily seen, not only does Gülen narrate *hadith* in his preaching and lectures delivered to the public but he also comments on them and teaches subjects related to them.

As with the Qur'an, the attitudes of contemporary Muslim thinkers and scholars toward the *sunnah* differ. In the variety of approaches available, it is possible to see both those who try to minimize or completely ignore the theological and jurisprudential effectiveness of the *sunnah*, and those who assess it as a purely blind imitation of the Prophet. As a result, the authenticity and religious authority of the *sunnah* has become one of the most debated subjects in the Muslim world. When the authenticity of *hadith* known as reliable, and effectiveness of them as a religious source, are being debated, we see Gülen very tightly attached to the classical viewpoint. In his view, as in classical Sunni understanding, the *hadith* is treated as the secondary authority after the Qur'an. Likewise, when commenting on *hadith*, he takes pains not to contradict the classical standpoint in theological issues such as the incorporeality of God and the impeccability of the Prophets.

For the rest, especially in legal matters, he develops a modern interpretative methodology. Two important points stand out in his methodology: First, he recognizes the historical and cultural background of the Prophet's actions and statements and distinguishes between personal and universal characteristics of the *sunnah*. Second, he emphasizes the "spirit" of the *sunnah* which has priority, in his understanding, to be observed. It seems that the major reason leading him to follow this methodology is his zeal to (i) find solutions for the problems that Muslims encounter in the modern age,

---

[260] Gülen 2004b, p. 187.

and (ii) eliminate causes of accusations against Islam, such as the extreme interpretation of jihad that seeks to justify unjust violence. Indeed, through this methodology, he is able to introduce the *sunnah* as a more practical life-style and a more productive source. He can also offer a coherent interpretation employing general Islamic principles.

In brief, Gülen, who stands between the classical and the modern, adopts a moderate approach. He recognizes the authority of the *sunnah* on the one hand, and interprets this source to meet the needs of contemporary Muslims on the other. I believe that Gülen's methodology of interpretation, with its religious and social consequences, deserves further study. Here, we should not forget that his influential personality as a spiritual leader makes his scholarly ideas popular.

CHAPTER THREE

A Classical Scholar with a Modern Outlook: Fethullah Gülen and His Legal Thought[261]

İsmail Acar

1. INTRODUCTION

In this chapter, I attempt to situate the legal methodology of Fethullah Gülen within contemporary Islamic legal and intellectual discourse. In doing so, I will seek to answer questions about how he engages with Islamic teachings and texts to produce his juristic interpretation of the modern human condition and social circumstances. Thus, I argue that Gülen transforms contemporary Islamic thinking intellectually through his active engagement with Islamic learning and the current questions that Muslim societies face; he produces responses (*fatwa*) and independent juristic interpretations (*ijtihad*) by examining primary sources of Islamic law and current circumstances.

Why does Gülen create his juristic interpretation about current problems of Muslim communities within a classical scholar's (*'ālim*) perspective? Is he a qualified jurist, *mujtahid,* who has the competence to form his own judgments through the usage of juristic interpretation?[262] Or, is he only a regular pious Muslim who affects millions by piety? This chapter seeks to answer these questions through examining his educational background, his qualifications for *ijtihad*, his methodology, and sample examples from his responses and juristic interpretations.

---

[261] An earlier version of this chapter was presented at the ACU Melbourne campus as a lecture and at Georgetown University *Islam in the Age of Global Challenges: Alternative Perspectives of the Gülen Movement,* as a conference paper.

[262] According to Faruk Beşer, a professor of Islamic law at Sakarya University, Gülen is a *mujtahid.* For further details see Beşer 2006, pp. 15–22.

2. EDUCATIONAL BACKGROUND AND EXPERIENCE

While Gülen was thoroughly educated in Islamic institutions of the Ottoman tradition, the *madrasah,* a school for theological studies, he also studied modern thought and literature privately. He lived in an instructive environment and obtained essential knowledge in the core sources of Islam beginning from a very young age in his hometown, Erzurum, Turkey. He memorized the Qur'an, and became a *hāfiz,* when he was twelve. As well as being exposed to an intellectual environment, he experienced the *Naqshībandī* order, one of the major Sufi paths in Anatolia, through the *Naqshī* Sufi master Muhammed Lütfi Efendi, aka Alvarlı Efe, (d. 1954), in his early teenage years. Nourished from the organized Sufi path in his early years, he later on established his independent ascetic style by adopting the classical observances of a Muslim scholar, but without rejecting the benefits of modernity, in complete devotion to prayer, noticeably much more than an ordinary Muslim would do, but wearing ironed pants.[263]

Although he was attending local circles to learn classical Islamic texts in Arabic, he was struggling to read French texts with the help of a dictionary on his own.[264] Learning French was not expected from a student in his situation. He was looking for something different from the circumstances that he lived in. This enthusiastic approach led Gülen to receive classes in Islamic law and jurisprudence from one of the last *Hanafī* scholars of the classical Ottoman tradition, Mufti Osman Bektaş (d. 1986).

During this core education in Islamic studies, Gülen developed some initial experience in critical thinking. Based on his careful observation of the surrounding scholarly environment, meticulous study of his assigned texts in study circles, and individual readings, he began scholarly and critical thought at an early period in his education. One of his classmates in those years, Sadi Kayhan, states, "He was criticizing false convictions even though these were

---

263 Wearing ironed pants was considered a sign of modernity – in the sense of an assumed rejection of local Sufi tradition – at that time. Very few people, officers and high level administrators – who represented the secular way of life – were wearing such kinds of pants. Moreover Sufis, at that time, were wearing crushed pants and they considered this a part of ascetic life, in a way denying what is worldly. One of his Sufi friends asked Gülen to wear crushed pants instead of ironed ones. Gülen mentions this anecdote and adds "I have not understood yet, why they considered wearing crushed pants as ascetic behavior" (http://tr.fgulen.com/content/view/3157/157).

264 http://tr.fgulen.com/content/view/7970/129/.

widely accepted by people."[265] We will touch more on the details of his educational milieu in the next section, his qualifications for *ijtihad*.

By the end of his teenage years he had completed his education and had departed from a classical environment to a modern milieu; moving from Erzurum to Edirne, one of the European provinces of Turkey. In his new surroundings he was exposed to Western and modern ways of life inside Turkey. Not only has he experienced the relatively Western life of Turkey, but also that of the United States of America as he moved there in 1999. Gülen currently lives in a retreat centre in the state of Pennsylvania.

All these experiences from traditional institutions to modern societies equipped him as a scholar with a thorough knowledge of centuries-long legacy of Islamic disciplines who at the same time is familiar with modern needs and can provide new interpretations without deviating from core values of Islamic tradition.[266] He continues to study major classical Islamic texts page-by-page with his students or alone. He has achieved a balanced level of classical and modern perceptions for carrying out his juristic interpretation at a point of moderation, a well-known term for the middle way, in Islamic tradition.[267] He produced his juristic views within this perspective.

3. GÜLEN'S QUALIFICATION AS A *MUJTAHID*

The required qualifications for *ijtihad* are not mentioned in the Qur'an and the *sunnah*. Muslim scholars do not have a consensus, *ijma'*, on these requirements. Jurists and scholars throughout the history of Islamic jurisprudence regulated their own *ijtihad* rules and requirements. Therefore, Muslim

---

[265] http://tr.fgulen.com/content/view/169/133/. In one of his interviews Gülen stated, "In later years, around the age of eighteen to twenty, I inclined more toward books on jurisprudence and philosophy. I also read about Darwinism and relevant subjects. Some books led me to other books, and it continued like this. When I was in the army for my obligatory service, I had a very wise commander. He had a deep knowledge of Sufism. He had read both Eastern Islamic and Western classics. He advised me to read Western classics. This caused me to read many famous Western writers such as Rousseau, Balzac, Dostoyevski, Pushkin, Tolstoy, the Existentialists, and others" (Can 1995). "Meanwhile, he continued his 'modern' education in science and philosophy, literature and history. While gaining a deep comprehension of the main principles of modern sciences from physics to chemistry, biology, and astronomy, he read the works of such existentialist philosophers as Camus, Sartre, and Marcuse. He also was introduced to other Eastern, Islamic and non-Islamic, and Western philosophies." http://en.fgulen.com/fethullah-gulen-biography/751-years-of-education

[266] Beşer 2006, pp. 26–30.

[267] Kuru 2003, p. 117.

scholars who were interested in juristic interpretation created accounts on the required qualifications for *mujtahid*. The earliest complete published account for qualifications of a *mujtahid* was found in *al-Mu'tamad fi usul al-fiqh* by Abu Husayn Ali al-Basri (d. 436/1044).[268] The most detailed one is an account by Ghazzali (d. 505/1111) in his *usul* book, *al-Mustasfā*.[269] Later jurists' writings on this issue did not differ significantly from the established Sunni legal doctrine pronounced by Ghazzali:

i.   Knowing 500 verses needed in law; committing them to memory is not a prerequisite.

ii.   Knowing the way to relevant *hadith* literature; he needs only to maintain a reliable copy of Abu Dawud's or Bayhaqi's collection rather than memorize their contents.

iii.   Knowing the substance of *furu'* works (peripheral subjects) and the points subject to *ijma'*, so that he does not deviate from the established laws.

iv.   Knowing the methods by which legal evidence is derived from the texts.

v.   Knowing the Arabic language; complete mastery of its principles is not a prerequisite.

vi.   Knowing the rules governing the doctrine of abrogation.

vii.   Investigating the authenticity of *hadith*.[270]

Gülen's writings and speeches show that he has higher qualifications to make *ijtihad* than the regularly required credentials listed above. I will examine his qualifications according to Ghazzali's treaty:

(i. vi.) He knows more than the required 500 Qur'anic verses needed in law; he knows all the Qur'an by heart, *hāfiz*, with their meanings related to abrogation, *naskh* and occasions of revelation, *asbāb al-nuzūl*. Moreover, he has examined the major classical commentaries on the Qur'an page-by-page with his students, or alone.[271]

(ii. vii.) He has almost memorized *hadith* narratives in six major *hadith* collections, *kutub al-sitta*. He states, "I can understand *hadith* texts

---

268 Dates are After Hijrah (Islamic calendar) / Common Era.

269 For more information on *ijtihad* and its requirements see Hallaq 1984, pp. 5–7.

270 I have made arrangements by combining some points of the requirements. For the original translation from Ghazzali see Hallaq 1984, p. 6.

271 For further details see Albayrak's chapter in this volume.

whether it is in the six major *hadith* collections or not." Apart from the body of a *hadith* text, he knows chain of the transmitters, *isnad*, and *hadith* narrators, *rijal*,[272] and can quote their biographies one by one. He frequently gives references from the history of the Prophet and his Companions in his speeches and writing. He knows the names of the Companions, their relationship with each other, their contribution, and any weakness in the branch of *hadith*.[273]

(iii. iv.) As has been mentioned above, Gülen studied Islamic jurisprudence and Islamic law beginning from his teenage years and examined the majority of classical Islamic legal texts. In addition, since 1985 Gülen began re-reading classical Islamic literature in Arabic with divinity school graduates. He examined the *furuʿ*, from *fiqh* literature: Abu al-Husayn al-Quduri (d. 428/1037) *al-Mukhtasar*; Abu al-Hasan Burhan al-Dīn al-Marghinani (d. 593/1197) *al-Hidaya Sharh al-Bidaya*; Abu al-Fadl Majd al-Din al-Mawsili (d. 683/1284) *al-Ikhtiyar li taʿlil al-Mukhtar*; Muhammad b. Ibrāhīm al-Halabī (d. 956/1594) *Multaqa al-Abhur*; Wahba Mustafa al-Zuhaylī (1932–) *al-Fiqh al-Islami wa Adillatuhu*; in Islamic jurisprudence, *usul*: Abu Ishaq Shatibi (d. 790/1388) *al-Muwafaqāt*; Muhammad b. Farāmuz b 'Ali, known as Mullah Husraw (d. 885/1480) *Mir'āt al-Usul*; Mehmed Seyyid Bey (d. 1873–1925) *al-Madkhal*.[274] What he has engaged in is a classical type of reading and examining of whole books with a new perspective: analytical and critical reading of classical texts. Students read the portion that they have prepared before, and Gülen comments on the subject when necessary. Apart from examining Islamic law texts in group study, he re-reads early Islamic legal texts individually. The last one that he examined is Abu Zayd 'Isa al-Dabbusi (d. 430/1039) *Ta'sīs al-Nazar*.[275]

(v.) Gülen also began Arabic lessons in his teenage years and memorized Arabic grammar in classical Ottoman style, from *Amthila* to *Izhār* and *Molla Jāmī*. Later he used Mustafa Ghalayani's *Jami' al-Durus al-Arabiyya*, the commentary on Ibn Mālik's *Alfiya*, Ibn Aqil's commentary as a medium of instruction in his Arabic language teaching. He feels more confident in

---

[272] Hikmet 2008, pp. 133–34.

[273] For further details see Çalış's chapter in this volume.

[274] Interview with Ergün Çapan, one of the students who participated in one of Gülen's circles for almost a decade and who contributes to this volume with an article. Also, see http://tr.fgulen.com/content/view/7970/129/.

[275] Ibid.

Arabic letters and prefers using them in writing and reading, an Ottoman tradition. He reads classical Islamic texts fluently observing grammatical rules of classical Arabic. He has the capacity to interpret verses from the Qur'an, the *hadith*, and legal or any classical texts in their original languages without a dictionary.[276] Gülen also knows Persian at an academic level. He interprets major disciplines of classical Islamic literature, *tafsīr, hadith, fiqh, kalam, sīrah* within their authentic languages and produces new interpretations via sermons, speeches, books and articles.

With all these qualifications, Gülen has the capacity to be a *mujtahid*, but he deliberately regards himself as a regular pious Muslim because of his humility. Moreover, Gülen has conceded that he is not a *mujtahid* as Faruk Beşer mentions in his book, *Fethullah Gülen Hocaefendi'nin Fıkhını Anlamak*. This is a humble response and should not be understood as an absolute rejection by Gülen, for such an humility is inherently found in the nature of Islam, and perhaps is best represented by Sufis. In Islamic tradition, especially among religious scholars who were trained in Sufi tradition, it is common not to declare their scholarly qualifications. In the history of Islamic law, very few jurists declared that they were *mujtahid*. Jalal al-Din al-Suyuti (d. 911/1505), an Egyptian jurist, was one of the few. Therefore, Gülen's reply should be considered within this tradition, and his rejection does not prevent him from juristic interpretation when needed.

Since the 1970s he has responded to people's inquiries in "question and answer" sessions before late evening prayer. At the time, people were coming to the mosque to ask him various questions. They sat in the mosque in the same way they did in formal Friday sermons and wrote down their questions before the sessions started. These questions were placed on the table before Gülen's arrival. When the congregation took their place in the mosque and the questions were placed on his desk Gülen read the questions out aloud and answered them in order. It was like an organized lecture.

This question and answer method still goes on with limited audiences in the retreat centre in Pennsylvania following afternoon prayers. His students record these conversations in audio or video formats and transform them into written materials, books, and articles.[277] Some of his speeches in

---

[276] Ibid.

[277] For further information about Gülen's informal speeches see: http://www.herkul.org/bamteli/index.php.

question-answer format have been translated into English and published as *Questions & Answers about Islam, I–II.* These two volumes are mostly related to theological, social, and moral issues. Gülen's legal responses are being edited by Ahmet Kurucan, one of his earliest students, who has a PhD in Islamic law.[278] Because of this ongoing editing and translation of legal issues, we depend mostly on this unpublished work and a few other published books on legal matters.

4. GÜLEN'S METHODOLOGY IN *FATWA* AND *IJTIHAD*

In *ijtihad* methodology, Gülen mainly holds the Hanafi-Maturidi traditional line. It is obvious that the Hanafi legal school uses reason more than other Sunni counterparts. The Maturidiyya School of theology follows a line of thought which is between the Ash'ariyya and the Mu'tazilite schools by defending theological orthodoxy with rational methods, a moderate position.[279] Gülen stays within this perspective as much as he can while he is responding to questions about the contemporary issues of Muslims. Moreover, Gülen firmly emphasizes the need to follow a particular tradition in his juristic interpretation. Jerome D. Maryon states that Gülen builds on foundations from Abu Mansur al-Maturidi (d. 333/944) to Said Nursi (d. 1960), affording ample exegesis of Qur'anic prescriptions for moral duty: following the straight path, *al-sirat al-mustaqim.*[280]

Although Nursi was coming from a Shafi'i–Ash'ari traditional background, he offered unconventional responses to the problems of modern society that appeared to be in tune with the conditions of modern society. He re-interpreted some current issues using reason rather than following the classical way, provided by earlier Shafi'i scholars. For example, Nursi gives an opinion on discussion around verse 5:51, "O you who believe! Take not the Jews and the Christians for your friends and protectors!" and comments, in particular, on the term *awliya* (friends and protectors) with an analogy. He asks first, "Can a Muslim love a Christian or Jew?" and then answers his question with an example of a man married to a woman of the People of the

---

[278] Ahmet Kurucan checked all of Gülen's answers to questions from the 1970s up to the present and selected legal responses and legal interpretations. He is still working on the project.

[279] Madelung 2008.

[280] According to Maryon, Gülen was influenced by Said Nursi in spirituality and theology. For further information see Maryon 2007, p. 68; Nursi 1996, p. 1944.

Book: "Of course, he should love her." This indicates how Nursi combined reality and sacred texts with reason in his interpretation.

Similarly, while Gülen considers contemporary circumstances and reads current situations very carefully in his interpretations, he emphasizes the relevance of the times and the era of the Prophet and considers that time as providing concise examples for Muslims up to the Day of Judgment. "Since everything up to the Day of Judgment—not in macro plan, but in micro plan—has been exercised as signs during the Golden Era, and we can find something for our time."[281] For example, if a Muslim would like to extract blood from his body for health reasons, as in blood donation, knowing that the Prophet also did so, it is not required that he follow the historical method of the Prophet. It can be done by modern techniques and follow the Prophetic *sunnah*.[282] I think this re-interpretation could be extended to using a toothbrush instead of a *miswāk*, a stick of wood made into fibers at one end, used as a toothbrush by the Prophet. However, Gülen states that "there could be some extra benefits of using the *miswāk*" beyond the currently used toothbrush and toothpaste method.[283]

Since the eighteenth century, Muslim scholars have talked about new interpretations and understandings. Beginning with Shah Wali Allah of Delhi (d. 1762) to Fazlur Rahman (d. 1988); from Muhammad 'Abduh (d. 1905) to Hasan Hanafi (1935–) Islamic law has been examined to produce new solutions for responding to current circumstances and needs. Rahman was a critical figure, who stated that "formative period jurists had missed a crucial characteristic of Islamic revelation, and the development of the Islamic worldview [was] to be made possible only by reexamining Islamic tradition in light of the overall spirit of the Qur'an."[284] However, Gülen does not go further than the last three (sometimes five) centuries of Islamic history, and does not criticize the jurists from the period of formation as Rahman does. Gülen is full of respect to the classical period of juristic formulations and its institutions.

Furthermore, Gülen defends a new type of revivalism in Islamic jurisprudence. He emphasizes that all juristic interpretation based on custom and

---

[281] Gülen 1995a, p. 234.
[282] Gülen 1995b, p. 298.
[283] http://www.sonsuznur.net/content/view/318/1/1/5/.
[284] Sonn 1991, pp. 214–15.

tradition should be re-examined again to create new alternatives to current issues. This action requires examining whole juristic formulations based on juristic opinions, *ijtihad* with a new perspective. I categorize his conditions for this revision in three subtitles: (i) a new text on Islamic jurisprudence should be created by examining all legal literature (ii) existing juristic opinions based on customs and traditions should be criticized or at least re-checked bearing in mind contemporary circumstances (iii) all these should be done by a qualified committee, *shura*.[285]

While Gülen encourages the creation of new juristic opinions according to contemporary circumstances and conditions within certain respects, he insists on a qualified committee or *shura* to do this task. He considers a qualified committee can work in the current political system.[286] Although Abul A'la Mawdūdī (d. 1979) states Western democracy is incompatible with Islam because the Islamic concept of *shura* cannot allow for a "general election,"[287] Gülen states "it is wrong to see Islam and democracy as opposites."[288] However, Gülen stays away from the political arena as much as he can and seeks renewal beyond it:

> Islam does not propose a certain unchangeable form of government or attempt to shape it. Islam has never offered nor established a theocracy in its name. Instead, Islam establishes fundamental principles that orient a government's general character. So, politics can be a factor neither in shaping Islam nor directing Muslims' acts and attitudes in Islam's name.[289]

Gülen focuses on basic Islamic principles, i.e., belief, worship, morality, and behavior rather than politics to create his juristic interpretation for urgent and inevitable problems based on public interest, *maslahah*. For example, if a person receives interest through a salary payment by the state

---

[285] Gülen 2004c, p. 140; Gülen expands the meaning of *shura* from the political advisory group whom the Muslim ruler consults to a qualified committee – and I prefer this one to "consultation" in a political context – "Clearly consultation does not take priority over Divine Commands as a source of legislation. It is itself enabled by Divine Commands, and though it may be the basis for some laws and principles; consultation is restricted as it depends on true legislative sources. Those matters on which there is a clear divine decree remain outside the intervention of human beings and people may only turn to consultation in order to ascertain its full meaning" (Gülen 2005d, p. 49).

[286] Gülen 2005d, p. 49.

[287] Rahman 1981, p. 292.

[288] Sarıtoprak and Ünal 2005, p. 451.

[289] http://www.foreignpolicy.com/story/cms.php?story_id=4408.

and this is not within his control and free will to reject, he can use this money to make tax re-payments to the state.[290] Gülen responds to these kinds of questions with new juristic interpretations.

Gülen does his *ijtihad* without criticizing other juristic interpretations and indulging in the debate of "closing the gate of *ijtihad*," (*insidad bab al-ijtihad*) among Hanafi scholars.[291] Mostly, he keeps silent and argues that the saying "the gate of *ijtihad* is closed" is an extreme point of view. However, he mentions a number of obstacles standing in *ijtihad* for current jurists, especially Turkish ones: inadequate education in Islamic studies, lack of linguistic ability to understand the primary sources, and other terminological barriers.[292] On this point his views are very similar to those of Nursi who states, "The door to *ijtihad* is open, but six obstacles block it."[293] For Nursi, issues concerning the detailed subjects of law were not an immediate concern in a twentieth-century context. And, also there is a lack of devoted Muslim scholars who can cope with contemporary major challenges and so legal interpretations are postponed.

Likewise, according to Gülen, if a contemporary scholar is able to eliminate all these obstacles he should do what is necessary for contemporary needs. If a qualified scholar tries to adopt previous ideas regardless of current circumstances, he cannot enlighten the community and inevitably makes mistakes. Gülen is against blind imitation, *taqlīd*, and considers it a catastrophe: "Examine the imitators' books and you can find eighty mistakes in thirty pages. This is a catastrophe on behalf of knowledge, *ilm*."[294] A parallel approach to his idea is found in one of the late-Ottoman Hanafi jurist's writing, Ibn 'Abidin (d. 1262/1836). He quotes from another Hanafi jurist Ibn Nujaym (d. 970/1562), who says that later imitators repeated some early small mistakes and so compounded the error. For example, the issue of "hiring for Qur'anic teaching" is mentioned in one of the commentaries of al-Quduri, *al-Siraj al-Wahhaj wa al-Jawhara* by Abu Bakr al-Haddad (d. 800/1397) as a preferred opinion, *al-mufta bih*, against "hiring for Qur'anic recitation," and the former was extended to "hiring for worship, *tā'ah*."

---

290 Kurucan, unpublished book, pp. 88, 101, 325.
291 For further debates about closing the gate of *ijtihad* see Hallaq 1984; Karamali and Dunne 1994, pp. 238–57; al-Alwani 1991, pp. 129–42; Kamali 1996, pp. 3–33.
292 Gülen 1995a, p. 293.
293 Nursi 2010, pp. 499–504.
294 Gülen 1995a, pp. 226–27.

Concerning this point, hiring for pilgrimage, *hajj*, is derived from this understanding. However, there is a consensus on the falsehood of hiring for worship from the three founder imams of the Hanafi School, Abu Hanifa (d. 150/767), Abu Yusuf (d. 181/798), and Imam Muhammad (d. 189/805). In reality, "hiring for Qur'anic teaching was issued in a certain situation," and it should be considered within this framework. But, imitators could not see the reasoning, *illah*, and they combined it with "hiring for worship," *ibādah*, and that is repeatedly stated in later legal texts.[295]

Gülen gives an example of a small mistake which became widespread among Turkish Muslims because of blind imitation. Ottoman Muslims were very respectful of Islamic values but they produced their own versions of some customs. One of them concerns the width of space between the legs of a Muslim during worship service. Later Ottoman scholars stated that it should be four fingers while standing for regular worship, *salah*. All legal text and *hadith* collections mention the importance of standing side by side neatly aligned with others through shoulders, knees, and legs in a line of congregational prayer. There should be no gap between one person's leg and the leg of the person standing next to him in the congregation. This can only be done by a person standing with legs at shoulder-width, so that there is no gap between his leg and the leg of the person who is standing beside him. However, out of their customary respectful interpretation, Ottoman Muslims decided that the width of two legs during worship should be four fingers. But this distance between two legs is narrower than the distance described in legal texts and *hadith* narratives. Also, the persons who are praying cannot bring their legs close to each other if the customs insist on a four finger space between their feet. This false custom became a norm in later Turkish legal texts. Ömer Nasuhi Bilmen (d. 1971), in his *Büyük İslam İlmihali*, mentions this four-finger distance as a Prophetic *sunnah*. However, there is no *hadith* narrative and legal interpretation from the formative period of Islamic law about it. In this point, Gülen personally follows the *hadith* narratives and earlier Hanafi legal texts, and many Turkish Muslims who respect Gülen's *fatwa* and *ijtihad* follow him on this issue.[296]

In Gülen's writings and speeches it is obvious that he avoids open and disrespectful criticism of scholars of Islam, even if he does not agree with them.

---

[295] Ibn Abidin, pp. 14–15.
[296] Kurucan, unpublished book, pp. 446–47.

In critical analysis, he only mentions the name of a scholar when and if it is necessary. For example, he makes a comparison between Imam Shafi'i (d. 204/820) and Imam Abu Hanifa on the subject of "halal meat" consumption. He prefers Abu Hanifa's opinion of not allowing the eating of meat of unlawfully slaughtered animals. He insists on legitimate slaughtering, *dhabiha*.[297] However, Shafi'i allows eating any allowable and edible animal products by saying "in the name of God" when beginning to eat, irrespective of how the animal is slaughtered. Gülen examines both Abu Hanifa's and Shafi'i's evidence and finally states, "I like Imam Shafi'i, but he is in error on this point."[298]

Gülen would like to follow Abu Hanifa's methodology, but he pays more attention to public interest, *maslahah* than being a Hanafi. For the sake of supporting a community, sometimes in debated points, he may prefer Shafi'i's interpretation on a peripheral subject, *furu'*, by following the logic of the Hanafī School. Performing two consecutive prayers in immediate succession, *jam'u salatayn* – noon and afternoon or evening and night together – is mentioned in *hadith* collections, but Hanafi jurists do not allow such combinations of prayers with the exception of combining prayers during pilgrimage, *hajj*. Gülen firmly follows this rule, but seems to allow for people who really cannot find the time to perform their prayers because of their job circumstances. Again he emphasizes that one should perform the regular prayer each time, and only allows performing two consecutive prayers in immediate succession in very strict conditions.[299]

Gülen also formulates juristic interpretations according to his understanding of ethical and legal issues. While he deliberately tries to stay within Hanafī jurisprudence; he combines ethics and law together, and creates his own juristic opinions regarding these two concepts. Ethics and law were not considered together for some time in the Hanafī legal school; therefore, it led to some dry legal formulations without any consideration of ethics, which was condemned by other legal schools. Gülen is clearly against this type of legal interpretation which is called *hiyal* or legal devices. Legal devices are acceptable according to the founder of Hanafi jurists, Abu Hanifa and Imam Muhammad al-Shaybani: "Among Sunni schools of law, only the Hanafis are known for their systematic use of *hiyal*, which they developed

---

[297] Gülen 1995a, p. 292.
[298] Beşer 2006, p. 80.
[299] Ibid, p. 43; Kurucan, unpublished book, p. 113.

into a special field of jurisprudence, called "*makharij* (sin. *makhraj*)," i.e. "exits, to escape from unlawful to the lawful."[300] Gülen criticizes these kinds of legal devices and states as an example, "It is not lawful to give charity, *zakat*, to a debtor and take it back counting it towards the debt. This would be lawful in the strict sense, but it is not ethical behavior."[301] He does not mention Abu Hanifa or Muhammad al-Shaybani, but he creates his new juristic interpretation alongside their counter-statement through legal devices.[302] Gülen approaches the issue more from ethical perspectives than legal ones, or at least he combines the two.

In relation to his views on ethics, Gülen adds one more qualification to the requirement for *ijtihad*: sincerity and spiritual depth in the jurist and "togetherness of the heart and mind (*kalp-kafa bütünlüğü*)."[303] This is a subjective parameter and not possible to measure by objective criteria, but it is still a totally new requirement which comes from his mystical background.

Generally speaking, Gülen examines the sacred text carefully in creating his *fatwa* and *ijtihad* within a modern context. "Gülen has reinterpreted Islamic understanding in tune with contemporary times and has developed and put into practice a new Muslim discourse with respect to some traditionally sensitive issues."[304] He has developed a personal critical perspective that targets problems, not individuals. He criticizes wrong action, not the person; blind imitation, not imitators.

5. EXAMPLES FROM GÜLEN'S *FATWA* AND *IJTIHAD*

As mentioned, Gülen has responded to many questions about new issues concerning the Muslim community in public lectures and sermons. He did not write a separate book on his responses and juristic interpretations. His *ijtihad* and *fatwā* are mainly found in his generic book *Fasıldan Fasıla*.

We cannot examine all of his *fatwa* and *ijtihad*, rather we will choose examples from three major branches of Islamic law: transactions, *mu'amalah*; worship, *ibādah* and punishments, *'uqabah*. Although he does not consider

---

[300] Horii 2002, p. 315.

[301] Beşer 2006, pp. 30, 59.

[302] al-Shaybani 1930, p. 78.

[303] Kurucan, "Fethullah Gülen ve Fıkıh," unpublished article, 8; http://tr.fgulen.com/content/view/9849/85/.

[304] Yılmaz 2003, p. 209.

himself a pure jurist, he has the required qualifications, more than enough as I have explained above. Therefore, he feels a responsibility to make juristic interpretations.

5.1. TRANSACTIONS

His approach is clearly apparent in his contribution to the religious and public debate of Turkey regarding the headscarf. While the issue still haunts public and religious discourse in Turkey, Gülen's approach offers alternative readings of Islamic dress code regarding the headscarf. Yet, he avoids sanctioning his opinion as the only possible alternative to the issue. In the heyday of the debate in 1995, a journalist asked Gülen for his opinion regarding the headscarf issue in one of his interviews. "How important is it for a Muslim woman to cover her head?" Gülen's response to this question is as follows:

> This issue is not as important as the essentials of faith and the pillars of Islam. It is a matter of secondary importance (*furuʿ*) in *fiqh*. Faith in God was revealed to our Prophet in Mecca, and then came the daily prescribed prayers. Such command as giving alms, fasting, and pilgrimage came in Medina. In the sixteenth or seventeenth year of Muhammad's Prophethood (peace be upon him), Muslim women's heads were still not covered (in the prescribed way). It was not included in the pillars of Islam or the essentials of faith. Those issues to which Islam gives priority should, out of our own devotion, be given priority while becoming a Muslim and communicating Islam to others.[305]

As seen above, Gülen approaches legal issues from a wide and holistic perspective. In this conversation, Gülen used the term *tafarru'at* which means secondary or peripheral, to explain the place of the veil in Islam in comparison to the pillars and principles of Islam. He itemized and created a category regarding requirements for worship and belief for Muslims alongside other requirements to make clearer the level of the requirement to wear the veil. At that time in Turkey (and currently) the veil was not allowed in universities and female students were compelled either to interrupt their education or to stop wearing the veil. Gülen examined the topic in all circumstances and provided his response to help female students at universities: "This issue is not as important as the essentials of faith and the pillars of Islam. It's a matter of secondary importance." He intended to emphasize by this response that steadfast worship performed daily and dignified belief in

---

[305] Özkök 1995.

one's life comes first when one is a Muslim, then comes the veil. With this timely interpretation from an *ijtihad* insider, Gülen implied that attending their classes under such conditions would not make them unbelievers. With this implication, Gülen did not give a *fatwa* allowing female students to remove their headscarves; but he urged female students to think over their situation one's again when choosing their own way: education without wearing the veil or wearing the veil and interruption of their education. However, some conservative Muslims did not pay attention to Gülen's comparison and his holistic approach, and just focused on the term "secondary importance," *tafarru'at*. They took it out of its context and interpreted it as "unimportant details," *teferruat*, a term used in the Turkish language.[306] This misunderstanding fuelled debates about Gülen and his juristic opinions. However, this did not stop him from generating new interpretations in his classical, yet modern approach.

New technological inventions in modern times create new issues to be addressed. Artificial fertilization is one of the contemporary solutions for couples who cannot have a baby through natural conception. However, it is a new issue and should be examined by Muslim jurists who should create an *ijtihad* on it. Gülen emphasizes the importance of the lineage and its legitimacy in Islam and then issues his *ijtihad* for couples who have no chance of conception naturally. "In this circumstance, only the insemination of sperm from a husband to his wife's egg is legal. However, it is open to misuse."[307] Moreover, he adds that spouses who are involved in this medical treatment and the medical team who applies this method should be very careful not to make any mistakes. Permission for artificial fertilization was provided by many scholars in Turkey; Gülen was one of the first to declare it permissible.

Gülen states that marriage is one of the most important foundations of the Muslim community, and healthy generations depend on the careful maintenance of marriage and related issues. With the help of technological developments candidates who intend to marry should enquire as to whether they are likely to have difficulties in their relationship because of their partners. If there is likely to be a major health problem in a new marriage that leads to mortal disease in the offspring, these candidates are not allowed to marry even if all other requirements are met according to Islamic law. He provides a new inter-

---

[306] *Hakikat: Aylık İslām Dergisi*, March, 1995.
[307] Gülen 1995a, p. 214; Beşer 2006, pp. 63–64.

pretation based on public health and the health of later generations.[308] This is a new *ijtihad*. Thus, Islamic values can be upheld through application of contemporary medical developments about family genes.

Gülen interprets the issue of polygamy in Islamic family law as allowing permission in extreme situations only, not a right for men in all circumstances. It is just permission, not an order, and not a *sunnah* of the Prophet Muhammad, peace be upon him. Therefore, taking one spouse only would be the best choice for men, and it fits humanity:

> There is no record in the Qur'an or the *hadith* that it is *sunnah* to marry more than one woman by means of a religious ceremony. In the Chapter of Women (Surah Nisa), permission to marry more than one woman under special circumstances is mentioned only as a license or a special permission. However, marrying just one woman is encouraged to the degree of being mandatory. Thus, no one can consider marrying four women a matter of fulfilling a *sunnah*; they cannot claim to have fulfilled any religious law by doing so.[309]

Apart from the issue of marriage, in consideration of public interest, the *maslahah* principle, Gülen allows the study of a dead body for medical and educational purposes. He highlights the importance of human dignity first, and then allows such study on condition that if there is no alternative way and it is necessary, then "working on dead bodies" would be permitted.[310] Within this perspective, he also permits the performance of an autopsy for similar reasons. Again, he mentions that normally an autopsy is not allowed in Islam because of *hadith* narratives about the dead body and its dignity.[311] However, he makes a comparison between public interest and the dignity of a dead body, then states, "to find out the killer is more important than disturbing the dead body," therefore, an autopsy is allowed in a case where doing so allows us to find a killer.[312] This is a new *ijtihad* on a contemporary issue with a classical perspective. This approach shows that Gülen examines a text and context seriously to formulate his juristic interpretation.

Gülen is watchful in assessing current circumstances and pays regard to public opinion on new issues. He makes a comparison between the

---

[308] Gülen 1995b, p. 202.

[309] http://en.fgulen.com/about-fethullah-gulen/161-gulens-thoughts/1262-polygamy.

[310] Gülen 1995a, p. 289.

[311] Abu Dawud, *Sunan*, al-Janāiz, p. 64: The Messenger of Allah said: "Breaking a dead man's bone is like breaking it when he is alive."

[312] Gülen 1995a, p. 290.

Prophet's opinion about the extension of the Ka'bah to include the open part of it, hijr, and current issues of public interest. The Prophet Muhammad, peace be upon him, did not want to include the open part of the Ka'bah for the sake of public concern over the traditional Ka'bah. As a Prophet he could do that, but for the sake of public interest he did not build a new construction of the Ka'bah, which would be included in the open space. Gülen focuses on the real reason, *illah*, behind this action and declares that Muslim scholars need to learn a lesson from this incident. In neutral subjects, it is not lawful to do a permissible thing that would not be accepted by the community.[313]

Gülen uses reason rather than juristic interpretations of others in his *ijtihad* about feeding fish with pig products. One of the worms used in fish farms, among others, is produced from pigs, which raised question for Muslims. Gülen replied to this question with a new interpretation. "Using pig products in worm for fish, to feed fish in farms, does not make the fish unlawful, *haram*, since fish change the nature of pig products in their digestive systems."[314] This is a new issue and needed to be understood by contemporary scholars, so Gülen addressed it because of its urgency.

5.2. WORSHIP

Apart from technological improvements, globalization produces new issues for Muslims in every corner of the globe. Muslims in the northern part of Europe, Sweden and Norway, get confused over their night prayer time because of the length of the night in this region. The five daily prayers should be performed according to a certain position of the sun. As is obvious, the sun does not have the same position in all parts of the earth. Through proximity to the Arctic poles in Europe, the length of nights and days changes drastically. Muslims in this region cannot find a suitable time for their night prayer because night time is reduced. Therefore, it is a current question for Muslims of that region. What should they do to perform their night prayer? Gülen addressed this issue and created his *ijtihad* to respond to a question about the subject. In his answer to this question Gülen is basically saying that Islamic jurisprudence has answers for such questions

---

[313] Ibid, p. 218.
[314] Ibid, p. 227.

and in this specific situation he suggests to adopt the timetable of the nearest residential area where five daily prayers are performed properly. [315]

Gülen does not have a beard, and he accepts having a beard as the *sunnah* of the Prophet not an obligation, *fard*. He interprets having a beard as a personal choice and no one should be blamed if they do not conform, especially in the secular state of Turkey. He believes that there are many more important subjects than these details for Muslims:

> I see the robe, turban, beard, and loose trousers as details. Muslims should not drown in detail. Today many Muslims may be doing this. Choosing not to wear a turban, robe, or loose trousers should not be construed as weakening Muslim Turkish identity. From imams in mosques to members of Parliament, from governors to district officials, no one should be categorized as a sinner because of such things.[316]

The last two examples may sound strange for many Muslims, but Gülen is trying to remind us what is primary and secondary in Islam, thus setting priorities in its practice and representation. Gülen is very rigorous in his religious life but provides details on adaptations and arrangements which are not related to the core values of Islam. He creates an acceptable vision for living in peace and harmony in a modern society while maintaining an individual's own identity and beliefs. He pays utmost attention not to confine the perception of Islam to peripheral issues, thus he draws attentions to Islam's core values that are universally appealing.

5.3. PUNISHMENTS

Gülen is mostly silent on the last part of the legal literature, punishments. Generally speaking, he does not want to contradict sacred texts on this issue. He postpones new interpretations of the subject and leaves them to the qualified committee, the *shura*, believing that they are not urgent. However, if there is an urgent issue related to the subject he produces a juristic opinion on it. At the beginning of the 1980s, the Turkish community faced a chaotic and anarchic situation which it had not seen before. In those days as Muhammed Çetin states, "The racketeers had already murdered a number of their victims. In his sermons, Gülen spoke out and urged those being threatened by the rackets neither to yield to threats and violence, nor to react with violence and

---

[315] Gülen 1998b, pp. 134–35.
[316] Akman 1995.

exacerbate the situation. He urged them, instead, to report the crimes to the police and have the racketeers dealt with through the proper channels."[317]

He encourages Muslims to follow established rules and regulations and avoid any chaos and anarchy in their community in the name of Islam. Only legal authorities should have the right to punish wrongdoers, not individuals.[318] A famous *hadith* about preventing wrong actions by hand first, *awwalan bi yadika*, could be misinterpreted by some Muslims. They may try to punish wrongdoers individually on behalf of Islam and think, according to this *hadith*, that it is necessary.[319] Gülen emphasizes the stability of the community and asks Muslims to avoid such kinds of anarchy.

In addition, Gülen is against violence on behalf of Islam, and believes that "suicide bombing, whatever, wherever, whenever is absolutely forbidden in Islam and for those that commit such crimes, the logical prospect is eternal banishment."[320] It is a violation of basic Islamic principles and norms, humanity and sacredness of life. To stress this critical subject in the 1990s, he stated that children who were killed in suicide attacks in Israel or the recent military bombing in Gaza cannot be justified by Islamic law. These children are totally innocent regardless of their nationality and religious identity. He stated the same view in one of his latest interviews with *Foreign Policy* Magazine:

Islam abhors and absolutely condemns terrorism and any terrorist activity. I have repeatedly declared that it is impossible for a true Muslim to be a terrorist, nor can a terrorist be regarded as a true Muslim. Terrorism is one of the cardinal sins that the Qur'an threatens with hellfire.[321]

6. CONCLUSION

Fethullah Gülen has dedicated his life to deal with the current problems of Muslim communities. He has combined in his reading and teaching, classic

---

[317] Çetin 2010, p. 35.

[318] Kurucan, unpublished book, p. 50.

[319] "He who amongst you sees something abominable should modify it with the help of his hand; and if he has not strength enough to do it, then he should do it with his tongue, and if he has not strength enough to do it (even) then he should (abhor it) from his heart, and that is the least of faith.' (Muslim, *Sahih*, Kitab al-Iman, 1, p. 79). See also "Gülen as a Commentator on Hadith" in Halim Çalış's article in this volume.

[320] Wright 2007, p. 440.

[321] http://www.foreignpolicy.com/story/cms.php?story_id=4408.

and modern, old and new, east and west. He has kept the balance between being a Muslim scholar, *'ālim*, and living in modern circumstances when he migrated from Eastern Anatolia to the United States of America. This wide-ranging experience provides him with knowledge and understanding of both Islamic principles and the needs of contemporary society, and enables him to make new juristic interpretations.

Gülen has all of the required qualifications for *ijtihad* and *fatwa*, moreover, he can reply to the legal questions of Muslim communities. In his legal conversations, he demonstrates his expertise in classical texts and their modern formulations successfully. He has been in this position for more than three decades and has not had serious opposition about his *fatwa* and *ijtihad* from Muslim jurists and scholars, except for the headscarf issue at a critical period in the debate. However, his was a contextual response to help female students in colleges and universities, and it worked well.

Gülen comes from the Hanafi-Maturidi school, which uses reason relatively more than other Sunni counterparts within an orthodox approach. Moreover, he came to adopt a more tolerant view of society through his interaction with major Sufi orders of his time. The latter makes him a pious and humble Muslim who is full of respect for previous scholars and their formulations. However, this modesty does not prevent him from developing his juristic interpretations and critical thoughts.

Gülen defends a new type of revivalism in Islamic law by creating a new Islamic jurisprudence through re-examining all juristic formulations of Islam. To accomplish this huge project he suggests that a qualified committee, a *shura*, should deal with it. Although Gülen encourages a qualified committee, a *shura*, to reach a better solution, he produces his juristic interpretations and responses when he feels a new explanation is indispensable. Sometimes he prefers the interpretations of other legal schools, for example, the Shafi'i's, or he may form a new one free from his tradition like the interpretation on legal devices, *hiyal*.

He does not have a separate legal text, and does not form his *fatwa* and *ijtihad* in all areas of Islamic law. He replies to questions in circle discussions and sermons which are recorded and transformed into books. His purpose is not to create juristic opinions, but to answer the questions of Muslim communities. His ideas and interpretations are followed by many Muslims.

CHAPTER FOUR

Fethullah Gülen and His Theology of Social Responsibility[322]

Zeki Sarıtoprak

The aim of this chapter is to find an answer for the question of whether or not it is possible to talk about a contemporary Islamic theology of social responsibility. If so, who would be among the representatives of this contemporary theology? I argue that one contemporary Muslim scholar, Fethullah Gülen, could be considered among the most influential Muslim social theologians of our time. This chapter provides a brief background to the theological discourse in Islam as well as an Islamic theology of social responsibility and its possibility in our time.

The concept of a theology of social responsibility is not foreign to the nature of Islamic understanding of humankind's relationship with God, which is essential to the subject matter of theology. As Christian theologian H. Richard Niebuhr said, "The subject matter of theology is always man-

---

[322] In the Islamic theology, when an individual does a good action, or is encouraged to do a good action, he or she does not do it just because they are socially expected to do it, but for the sake of God. For example: to plant a tree in a place where there is no human being may not be considered to be a social responsibility, but from an Islamic theological perspective, it is a human duty because it is done for the sake of God. Though human beings will not benefit from the fruits of this tree, but the fact that birds, animals, insects, and even tiny creatures such as worms will benefit makes this action worth an award in the sight of God. For this reason, the phrase, "social responsibility" in my current paper will be used in the sense of accountability before God, the creation, and human beings. In this use, there is no secular connotation in this phrase which may indicate its disconnection with piety. In this paper, social responsibility includes the concept of *ridā*, or pleasing God, or doing for the sake of God only, with no expectation of personal advantages.

before-God ... (and) is implicit in all theological anthropology."[323] Similarly renowned Muslim sociologist, theologian, and historian Ibn Khaldun (d. 1406) divided responsibilities into two categories:

> Human responsibilities before God are two: those related to human actions and those related to heart. What is related to heart is faith, or Islamic creeds, which indicate what an individual should believe in and should not believe in; such as the essence of God, His attributes, things related to the afterlife, for instance resurrection, rewards, punishments, and destiny. The science that brings rational proofs for these beliefs is called the science of *kalam*.[324]

Early Muslim theologians and jurists, such as the great founders of three major schools of Islamic law, Maliki, Shafi'i, and Hanbali, have included "actions with limbs" in their definition of faith or *iman*. For them, "faith is belief with the heart, confession with the tongue, and action with limbs."[325] These three components of faith are shared by almost all Muslim theologians.[326] Although a lack of action may not be considered the same as a lack of faith, action is a great sign of the strength or weakness of one's faith. Therefore, it can be argued that the third component of this definition of faith, "action by the limbs," presents a foundation for an Islamic theology of social responsibility. Here it should be stated that the approach that I am proposing is different from that of the *Mu'tazilite*s who make action a sign of faith and inaction a lack of faith when they say, "The one who commits grave sins is no longer a Muslim." In the same way, they say that the one who does not fulfill religious obligations is no longer considered a believer. I argue the more mainstream Sunni approach that inaction can be a sign of *weak* faith, not a complete *lack* of faith. Many Qur'anic verses and sayings from the Prophet support this theology.

Historically, Muslim theologians developed intellectual and theoretical aspects of Islamic theology and left the action part of it to the science of *fiqh*, which deals with the believer's daily activities including daily prayers, social interactions, charities, marriages, trades, etc. Because the tradition of "actions by the limbs" did not find a chance to develop thoroughly within

---

[323] Niebuhr 1970, p. 141.

[324] Ibn Khaldun 1995. Retrieved from www.al-warraq.com on 11/05/2009, I.250. 436.

[325] Amir 1997, p. 56.

[326] Some Hanafis who exclude actions with limbs and include only belief with the heart and confession with the tongue, are an exception.

the scope of Islamic theology, historically what can be called a theology of social responsibility remained somewhat under the framework of Islamic jurisprudence or *fiqh*.[327] Until the twentieth century, Muslim theologians have not had a specific discussion of a theology of social responsibility, per se, although the concept was implied. Social theology had been developed by Ottoman intellectuals, Ziya Gökalp and Mehmed Şerafeddin, who were influenced by Western social sciences, namely sociologists Auguste Comte (d. 1857) and Emile Durkheim (d. 1917) and their theories of religion, and did not borrow from contemporary Christian social theology. Their approach, however, was centered on the idea of sociology, whereas an Islamic theology of social responsibility is centered on Qur'anic teaching. While the concept of a theology of social responsibility is more relevant to the teaching of Islam and centered in the Qur'an, as a specific field within Islamic theology, it did not develop thoroughly early on. This phenomenon can be traced to the powerful and encompassing nature of the science of *fiqh* among Muslim scholars which covered an Islamic theology of social responsibility for a long period of time. New studies may find some further reasons for this.

After this preliminary introduction to the subject, it is appropriate to comment on certain terminology and to provide a background on Islamic theology. Etymologically, the meaning of "theology," which is "reflection on God" or "talk about God," comes from the Greek words *theo* and *logia*, which mean "God" and "reflection." Any discourse that makes God the centre of discussion is considered theology. In this regard, the Islamic science of *kalam* can be translated as "Islamic theology" in modern English usage. The term *kalam* itself, like *theo* and *logia*, can also be translated as "talk" or "talk about God." "*Kalam* is a discipline in which God's essence, His attributes, and the conditions of contingents are discussed. This discussion is based on the principles of Islam with regard to a creature's beginning and end."[328] The phrase "principles of Islam" means to exclude the science of philosophy from *kalam*.

---

[327] Nevertheless, the science of *kalam* had developed a theology of Prophethood (*nubuwwah*) and leadership (*imamah*), which are also directly related to the social aspects of human life and are also related to the concept of a theology of social responsibility.

[328] See al-Tahanawi 1984.

Classical *kalam* has systematically discussed and centered on three main themes: *uluhiyyah* (divinity), *nubuwwah* (Prophethood), and *ma'ad* (the afterlife). These three are also the major themes of the Qur'an. After encountering various religious traditions, early scholars of *kalam* developed Islamic theological arguments on these and similar themes to respond to the challenges coming from pre-Islamic traditions, namely Zoroastrianism, Judaism, and Christianity. Despite the development of ideas in this early period, the Qur'an, with its dynamic nature, has remained a vivid source throughout Islamic history. It can be argued that each era has found a reference in the Qur'an for the needs of its specific circumstances.

Having a systematic discourse on God, Prophethood, and the afterlife, classical *kalam* has been merely theoretical and intellectual. Despite the above definition of faith, which is the main subject of *kalam*, in classical *kalam* the social aspect is almost absent. As mentioned above, the social and individual praxis of Islamic theology has become the subject of another Islamic science, known as *fiqh* or Islamic jurisprudence. Those who were studying this particular Islamic science would be known as *fuqaha* (jurists), while those who were studying *kalam* were known as *mutakallimun* (theologians). Interestingly, unlike the majority of early scholars of Islamic theology, Abu Hanifa, founder of the Hanafi school of Islamic law, named his brief manifesto of faith *fiqh al-akbar* (great jurisprudence or understanding), which connotes the science that has to do with practical aspects of theology, a meaning that may have been the author's intention. Most probably such a name comes from a Qur'anic verse which suggests that there should be a group of Muslims to do *fiqh* and be dedicated to it (9:122). In this verse, the Qur'an promotes learning and understanding of religion. Also, the Prophet mentioned the word *fiqh* when he said "if God wants to do good to someone He makes him a possessor of *fiqh* (deep understanding) in religion."[329] Action-oriented Islamic science, *fiqh*, has more references in the Scripture of Islam, while theoretical *kalam* is not at all referred to by name. *Kalam* is definitely a term developed later in the tradition.

Traditionally, the science of *kalam* would speak of God, while the science of *fiqh* would show how to worship such a God. These two sciences remain separate throughout Islamic history and some scholars of fiqh have

---

[329] Bukhari, *al-Jami' al-Sahih*, (hadith no. 65).

certain concerns about the validity of *kalam*-related discourse on Islamic themes. According to this claim, the existence of God and the afterlife does not need to be proven since any attempt to prove it shows doubt and any doubt will weaken the essence of faith. Also, since early *kalam* came from a heretical group, namely the Mu'tazilites, religious figures such as the prominent jurist and the founder of the Hanbali school of Islamic law, Ahmad Ibn Hanbal (d. 855), prohibited the study of the science of *kalam*, thinking that debating religious themes in such a philosophical manner was not compatible with the pristine teachings of the Prophet. Similarly, we have references that Abu Hanifa (d. 765), who arguably wrote the first book of *kalam*, prohibited his son from studying *kalam* because the Mu'tazilite theologians arrogantly discussed *kalam*-related themes.

In the first half of the tenth century, the intellectual world of Islam had an unprecedented development in the "Sunnitization" of the Islamic science of *kalam*. In this era Muslim intellectuals witnessed the emergence of two major figures, namely Abu Hassan al-Ash'ari (d. 936), who was originally a Mu'tazilite and later adopted the Sunni position after a vision of the Prophet who commanded him to support the true religion, and his contemporary Abu Mansur al-Maturidi (d. 944). The acceptance of *kalam* in the Sunni tradition made a considerable contribution to the sophistication of its arguments and to its survival until the present. Therefore, the Islamic science of *kalam* remains a powerful entity among all Islamic sciences. Despite this, in some countries the study of *kalam* is unwelcome due to its philosophical argumentation, which is considered to be against the teaching of the Qur'an by puritanical literalist approaches.

After this preliminary background, it is now appropriate to elaborate on the topic of an Islamic theology of social responsibility and its application in our time. Western scholars have used the term social gospel extensively, and later scholars, such as Dermot A. Lane in his book *Foundations for a Social Theology*, used this term to indicate the importance of praxis in theology. Therefore the challenging question is whether we can speak about a new concept of a theology of social responsibility in *kalam*. Although there were many attempts to renew the use of *kalam* in the twentieth century, scholars such as Abdullatif Harputi, Musa Kazım, İzmirli İsmail Hakkı and more, have developed arguments on how contemporary *kalam* can respond to the challenges of our time but with no connection to the social aspects of *kalam*.

Therefore praxis was neither emphasized in classical *kalam* nor among contemporary renewers of *kalam*. In fact, prominent Muslim historian and scholar of Islamic law, Ahmad Cevdet Pasha, criticized those who were not interested in the practice of Islamic principles.[330]

It should be noted that my approach here is different from the approach of scholars mentioned above, who made the social sciences the source of religion, such as when Mehmed Şerafeddin said, "social gathering creates sacredness." This chapter prefers to focus on praxis, which constitutes one of the elements of the definition of faith. Accordingly, unlike what Mehmed Şerafeddin suggested, this chapter proposes that social gathering around the Ka'bah does not make the Ka'bah sacred; rather divine revelation is what makes the Ka'bah important for believers and makes them gather around it. Actions and sacredness are inter-related, but the Qur'anic approach guides action that is based on the requirements of divine revelation and constitutes the third component of the definition of faith. As Cevdet Pasha rightly put it, "we should urge a more practical theology based on life and contemporary needs."[331]

Here the question comes to mind of who could be a representative of a theology of social responsibility. As we stated above, we will examine Gülen's contribution to the notion of Islamic theology of social responsibility. Although *kalam* presented a deep understanding of the intellectual quality of a human being, it neglected to deal with the ultimate transformation of humankind from a simple, biological creature to a creature whose spiritual level is even higher than that of angels. In fact, Gülen provides a framework for such a transformation through his socio-theological contribution. Traditionally Islamic *kalam*'s main task has been to defend the Islamic creed against intellectual attacks. For Gülen, this defense itself is not sufficient for such a transformation; however, it is still an important task.

Therefore at this juncture, it is appropriate to focus on two points. The first point is that the classical systematic science of *kalam* has served Islam thoroughly for a long period of time. Under new conditions, Muslim theologians need to renew *kalam* and filter out the Greek elements of classical *kalam* that are no longer valid in our time. The second point is that since praxis has not been the subject of classical *kalam*, it seems to be essential to include this

---

330 For the details of this, see Özvarlı 2007, pp. 317–30.
331 Ibid, pp. 317–30.

dimension in a renewed study of *kalam*. It can be argued that such an inclusion will make *kalam* more encompassing and more compatible with the overall teaching of the Qur'an. In this regard, *kalam* will not only respond to the challenges that come from a Western critical approach to religion, but will also provide a solid ground for some social activists. Fethullah Gülen, with his social endeavors, represents this aspect of the science of *kalam*.

It can be argued that scholars in the late Ottoman period, such as Bediüzzaman Said Nursi and Muhammed Hamdi Yazır, have left a legacy for Gülen and his endeavors through their writings. Nursi's teaching constitutes a paradigm for Gülen and his theology of social responsibility. The principles mentioned in Nursi's monumental work Risale-i Nur constituted a theoretical foundation for Gülen's understanding of what I call a theology of social responsibility. There is no doubt that Gülen is among those who are inspired by these scholars and their works. He successfully managed to build upon their intellectual inquiries. At the beginning of the twentieth century, Nursi spoke of the three enemies of Muslims as ignorance, poverty, and disunity, and provided certain intellectual arguments on how to defeat these enemies. Gülen, who came decades after Nursi, put those theories into practice by encouraging wealthy people to break down ignorance by establishing schools and educational institutions and environments, such as student dormitories. Gülen even expanded this plan by providing educational opportunities not only for Muslims but for non-Muslims as well. Therefore, it can be argued that Gülen's strength comes from his utmost conviction that without practice and the engagement of social life, intellectual curiosity and intellectual endeavors on their own will not be successful. Gülen promotes the premises of Islamic theology through his practical institutions. This may contribute to the reconceptualization of Islamic theology to meet the challenges of our time. It should not be an exaggeration to assert that Gülen is one of the rare personalities throughout the history of Islam who has brought a large concept of institutionalization to Islamic activities and philanthropy. He believes that for Muslims to be successful in this moment in history, they must be socially active through institutions. Gülen reminds believers of their social responsibilities not only to their individual faith but also to the need for working for justice and peace in this world.

During his social interaction with the community, Gülen has observed the problems that members of the community face, and he continually attempts to find remedies for those problems. This is why scholars of social theology in the West consider the recognition and experience of social situations and problems through participative observation as the first stage of social theology. Gülen experienced this firsthand. Gülen provided an alternative for families to educate their children, from the then-disliked state schools in Turkey by encouraging the establishment of educational institutions capable of providing safe environments for learning. Therefore, his theology of social responsibility contains a collective approach to the spiritual and social problems of our time, through the lenses of many social sciences. Of course, Gülen's theology of social responsibility goes hand-in-hand with other contemporary social sciences, such as sociology, economics, and cultural anthropology, as well as ethics. Since Gülen's efforts have evolved into a social contract that houses millions of recipients, their philanthropic contributions fulfill an important stage in Gülen's theology of social responsibility.

For Gülen, the message of the Qur'an, the holy book of Islam, is essentially universal. In his analysis of social matters, the Qur'an is his "guidance" and "light." As a result of such guidance, he emphasizes the importance of piety together with social participation. The second verse of the second chapter in the Qur'an reads, "There is no doubt that this Qur'an is a guide for the pious" (2:2). Historically, all Muslim theologians have taken the Qur'an as their main reference, but considering the Qur'an as a reference for a theology of social responsibility, as Gülen does, comes from divine imperatives that guide actions which were not the main subject of debates among early scholars of *kalam*. Muslim mystics, admittedly on a limited scale, have been discussing this aspect of religion, at least what relates to the inner life of believers. Therefore, divine imperatives that guide actions, as strongly presented in the Qur'an, constitute the main pillars of Gülen's theology of social responsibility.

One of the most important aspects of Gülen's approach is his focus on the exemplary personality of the Prophet of Islam. That is to say, Gülen's theology of social responsibility finds its roots in the practices of the Prophet. Therefore, in Gülen's theology, practice as a relationship between God, human beings and the world, is essential. Unlike early classical scholars, Gülen's theology of social responsibility is deeply involved with themes that include both intellectuals and lay people and was expressed through his early sermons and preaching. His sermons, attended by thousands of people from every section of society, aimed to emphasize the principles of faith. He constantly elaborates that the obstacles that sever a connection between human beings and God should be overcome since the divine door to the mercy of God is open to everyone, as the famous sacred prophetic tradition (*hadith qudsi*) says, "My mercy exceeds my wrath."[332] Elaborating on the scope of social responsibility Gülen describes "the believer" as someone who has knowledge of self, as the *hadith* quote states, "the one who knows oneself will know God." Gülen uses the potentiality of human beings to remind them of their spiritual and social responsibility before God and their fellow humans. In other words, their responsibility before God requires their responsibility before their fellow human beings. Gülen states:

> A believer is someone who trusts a candidate of trust with a worthy future, who promises safety to his surroundings, and who has integrated colorful differences in harmony. Such a believer is a decent human being. With such a kind disposition, one is gentle and sensitive, both before people and before God to the extent that if the believer is threatened with death or faces various pressures and false accusations will never attempt to act crudely … The believer is an exemplary person, who opens one's heart to everyone.[333]

Gülen's endeavors are not aimed at combating his opponents or his oppressors; rather he wants to bring his message to everybody and every member of his community. He also strives to respond to the cries of others as a part of his theology of social responsibility before God:

> One loves everyone and everything for God's sake, breathes love, and always creates an aura of love around oneself. The believer hastens to stop cries and responds to grievances, treats pains with antidotes, and transforms the cries of people to laughter … the believer transforms the storms of fire into breezes of divine pleasure. One mourns to prevent people's mourning and sheds tears as much as the river of Oxus to prevent the tears of others. The believer evaluates oneself based on contributions to the well being of others. The focus of the believer is always on "we" rather than "I." Therefore, the believer is not selfish, but someone who thinks of others.[334]

In his description, the individual becomes an agent of "positive action" and nothing can prevent one from acting and contributing positively to the community. As indicated above, a theology of social responsibility in gener-

---

[332] Bukhari *al-Jam'i al-Sahih*, (Hadith no. 6998).
[333] Gülen, 2006d, pp. 2–5.
[334] Ibid.

al has a direct relationship with everyday life. Again, in the context of a theology of social responsibility, one can see the synthesis between everyday life
and piety. Whether one is aware of it or not, piety has a great impact on
everyday life. Gülen says:

> When such believers are unable to solve problems with reason and comprehen-
> sion, they refer to the bright climate of the Qur'an for the solution. They never
> feel hopeless or emptiness; they do not encounter constant darkness because they
> enjoy the beauty of life which is as sweet as the water of *Zamzam*. They live in
> thankfulness to their Lord and grow the seeds of their lives and multiply it by 7,
> 70, or even 700.[335]

Gülen, because of his personal piety and prayer, gives an inspired
approach to the real life of people in their daily routines and practices his
theology of social responsibility. The idea of the presence of God encompasses every aspect of Gülen's life. Every action should be for God's sake.
Human beings should love creatures because God is the creator. In Islam,
the entire face of the earth is considered to be a mosque; thus, prayer can be
performed in any place, and piety is not limited to the walls of the mosque.
Gülen's understanding of piety transcends mosques. It has to be clarified that
Gülen is not against the establishment of mosques but his focus is on a different element of life, and that is education. Such circumstances of piety
embedded in the practice of social life prepare a healthy environment for the
flow of Qur'anic inspiration.

Therefore, in Gülen's theology, active participation in social life
through institutions and individual piety guides individuals to perfection
and maturity, not only in their individual lives but in their social lives. What
makes Gülen different from early scholars who included Islamic spirituality
in the science of *kalam*, such as Ghazzali and Said Nursi, is his emphasis of
inclusion on social action within piety. Gülen is making an addition to the
foundations of the previous scholars by emphasizing the importance of
social life in his theology. For "faith" has more meanings than previous
scholars have stated; "*iman*" (faith), is derived from the root *a-m-n*, which
means to believe, to promise, to trust, to provide safety for others and to
be trusted. Also it means to believe in God, to confess faith, to have a deep

---

[335] Gülen 2000e, pp. 258–59.

level of faith in heart and conscience ... These are the linguistic meanings carried by this word, faith.[336]

Scholars of social theology in the West have a diagram with four stages: action, Scripture, reflection, and analysis of existing social realities. Considering these four stages, Gülen's theology of social responsibility is essentially action-oriented. His main source of inspiration is the Qur'an. His emphasis on piety is embedded in his tradition of prayer and reflection, and forgiveness. In *The Servant of the Most Compassionate*, Gülen refers to Qur'anic verses and Prophetic tradition, "Those who spend in ease and in adversity, those who control their anger, and those who are forgiving toward mankind, God loves those who do good deeds" (3:134). Another verse states, "The servants of God do not commit vulgarity when they pass by profane things, they pass with dignity" (25:72). A saying of the Prophet suggests, "when a woman who already committed adultery came to the Prophet and asked for punishment, the Prophet said: Go back home and repent and God will accept your repentance."[337]

Gülen has also developed analytical approaches to the social realities of our time and to how problems can be cured through positive actions. Therefore he is not denying social realities, but is constantly working to make a change in a positive direction. Gülen's recent attempts at interreligious cooperation are an example of such positive action. Therefore, as a Muslim scholar and a social theologian, Gülen contributes to the building of bridges and joint efforts between the adherents of various religious traditions, particularly Christians and Muslims.[338] Such cooperation that has been practiced in different parts of the Islamic world is destined to enrich the social life of believers and contributes to a better understanding among members of various faiths.

As Gülen's efforts towards dialogue are unique in the modern day, he also, unlike classical theologians, focuses on educational institutions rather than the establishment of mosques. For Gülen, long-standing institutions are the source of successful social change. He believes that people, particularly young generations, are in need of schools and educational opportunities. Also, mosques only serve Muslims, while schools serve all human beings, which is an important aspect of Gülen's theology of social responsibility to serve

---

[336] Ibid.

[337] Muslim, *al-Sahih*, (Hadith no. 3209).

[338] See Griffith and Sarıtoprak 2005, pp. 329–40.

humanity. In this direction he has inspired hundreds of schools to be built in more than 120 countries around the world. In these schools one can find students from every nationality. On education he says, "… everything that is necessary for life should be taught in schools, this includes classes by experienced doctors on health and on family-related issues, including the relationships between husbands and wives and the raising of children."[339] He believes that education is the most efficient way to defeat terrorism.[340]

Gülen-inspired activities are not limited to schools; one can find examples from every area of society including hospitals; philanthropic activities such as financial aid to victims of earthquakes in Indonesia and Pakistan, of floods in Bangladesh and New Orleans and of war in Iraq and the Balkans.

Finally, why is understanding Gülen's theology so important in our age? Gülen has successfully managed to combine the values of Islam with contemporary life through educational, social and public health institutions, a combination which has few precedents in the history of Islam. Gülen has also managed to influence thousands of volunteers to go to different corners of the world and participate in the development of the education of human beings. Therefore such vast endeavors should find their place within the framework of Islamic theology, what I call a theology of social responsibility. Gülen does not do this through force or offering great material benefits. On the contrary, he does this only through spiritual inspiration and in conveying a belief in thinking of others rather than of oneself, the essence of his theology of social responsibility. It may be too early to judge Gülen based on these activities within the framework of Islamic theology, but one can see, considering the scope of these large social endeavors, that historians of collective social action and theologians will judge Gülen more accurately in the future. One can observe that Gülen has successfully created a group identity that is concerned with the value of cooperation, which has been contributing to his social theological ideals. It seems to me that Gülen is an important phenomenon in our time. Not only is his theology of social responsibility worthy of further research, but his charismatic leadership and spiritual strength has been catching the attention of people around the world. My hope is that this humble contribution will lead to research on a larger scale on Gülen and his theology of social responsibility.

---

[339] Akman 2004.
[340] Ibid.

CHAPTER FIVE

Sufism and Fethullah Gülen

Mehmet Yavuz Şeker

1. INTRODUCTION

This article deals with Fethullah Gülen's approach to *tasawwuf* (the spiritual life of Islam). After providing general information relating to this path, we will highlight Fethullah Gülen's approach to and understanding of Sufism as an individual raised in contemporary Turkey with ideas and influence transcending its borders, as the subject of myriad studies and research, and as the figure after whose name university chairs have been established. Finally, detailed analysis will be provided about his unique four volume *tasawwuf* work *Kalbin Zümrüt Tepeleri* which is published in English as *Emerald Hills of the Heart: Key Concepts in the Practice of Sufism.*

Fethullah Gülen, like many Muslims, is an individual who has chosen Sufism as a way of life. Nonetheless, we have not come across any references in his writing or speech that he identifies himself with any Sufi order or similar organizations. However, through his perception of the world as well as his profound devotion to prayer, he stands out as an individual who himself exemplifies the deep spiritual life of Islam. Providing a synthesis fusing tradition and modernity, Gülen's outlook and preferences with regard to Sufism are invaluable in terms of generating significant ideas for people of our modern period.

2. GENERAL OVERVIEW OF SUFISM

In this section, we elaborate the aim of Sufism, its historical development, significant phases in this development and several key concepts in its terminology. Owing to the need to restrict considerably the subject matter to a single chapter, we delineate only the Sunni strand of this exhaustive topic. Our information and approaches are those favorably received by the vast majority of Muslims.

2.1 The aim of Sufism

In Islam, the unique individual by whose example a Muslim shapes his or her life is the Prophet Muhammad, peace be upon him. His outlook on life, his understanding and the life that he lived, have at all times—for Muslims who lived in that era and then for all those who followed—have been the key considerations that Muslims have focused on. Loving him and observing his example constitute the crucial path and primary means to attaining God's love and forgiveness. Owing to the elevated position of the Prophet in Islam, Muslims have equated modeling their conduct on his example as drawing near to God's pleasure, or Divine approval, and being removed from him as being removed from God's mercy and forgiveness.

A Muslim who aspires to live their religion—in direct proportion to their effort—who trains, betters and improves himself or herself and loves and follows the Prophet of God as much as possible is, according to the expression employed in the terminology of Sufism, one who has reached the level of *al-insan al-kamil* (the perfected human being). When discussing a Perfected Human Being, the first figure who comes to mind is the Prophet himself:

> If perfection lies in purifying the spirit and cleansing the carnal self with Divine revelation and inspiration, and in developing human faculties, overcoming bodily appetites and animal impulses, and attaining subsistence by the subsistence of His particular blessings in utmost submission and obedience to Him, so as to become thereby the most polished mirror to the Divine Names, Attributes, and Essential Qualities ... then the only one who was able to achieve all these without the least imperfection ... is the master of creation, upon him be the most perfect of blessings and salutations.[341]

The key elements emphasized in the citation above, including the purification of the soul, the cleansing of the self,[342] the enhancement of human faculties and realization of human potential, as well as the conquering of carnal desires, among similar considerations, constitute the subject stressed

---

[341] Gülen 2004f, p. 291.
[342] The term used in Sufi terminology to describe the self is *nafs*.

most by those who will subsequently be described using the Sufi expression "endeavoring Muslims."[343] At this point, it is useful to note the absolute trust and reliance that aspirants have on the Sufi truth that *nafs*, or the self, can only attain perfection when it has annihilated its characteristic features and been freed from its yoke.

In actual fact, the Sufi considers every right step taken towards God, in ascending towards Him, as a stair for every new step taken on the path of purifying *nafs*. In other words, every step that he or she takes in drawing nearer to God constitutes the first movement of the next step; one step functions as the herald of subsequent steps. Spiritual ascent is the direct result of cleansing *nafs*, of struggle, great effort, and asceticism.[344] Concerns such as self-purification and the cleansing of *nafs* are mentioned first and foremost in the Qur'an and are represented as the ultimate goal: "He is indeed prosperous who has grown it (human selfhood) in purity (away from self-aggrandizing rebellion against God); and he is indeed lost who has corrupted it."[345]

In addition to demonstrating a level of understanding greatly exceeding that of humanity by means of his heart and spiritual life, Muslims believe that the Prophet Muhammad, peace be upon him, also showed extraordinary capacity in overcoming bodily desires. The best behavior, conduct, words, actions and mannerisms that could possibly surface in any individual became manifest in him. The Prophet was presented by God Himself for consideration by all humanity, with the Divine call for people to try their utmost to live their lives in accordance with his example: "Say (to them, O Messenger): If you indeed love God, then follow me, so that God will love you and forgive your sins. God is All-Forgiving, All-Compassionate."[346]

This being the case, Muslims exerted themselves to bring their own lives into congruence with the life of the Prophet, aspiring to be just like him. This understanding, which would later enter Sufi terminology under the term *mujahadah*, or striving, revealed itself demonstrably in the lives of "endeavoring Muslims." This is the greatest goal in the eyes of aspirants

---

[343] *Ghayra* (endeavor) literally means exerting utmost effort and concern in preserving one's purity, honor, and esteem.

[344] Afifi 2004, p. 147.

[345] 91:9–10.

[346] 3:31.

turning to God and preferring togetherness with Him to everything else, so much so that this notion has taken its place in the Sufi lexicon.[347] According to Afifi, Sufism is not contingent on deeds or actions; or on the wearing of a mantle, or sitting on a prayer mat; it depends on the action of the heart and the inclination of the soul. Sufism is challenging *nafs* and extinguishing the evil tendencies contained within it, refraining from pretentious claims of possession of deeds, or states and stations of the spirit and being enveloped with spiritual attributes—that is, striving in all earnestness, notwithstanding difficulty, to adorn oneself with those noble spiritual attributes—and in addition meticulously observing the example of the Prophet of God, making every effort to realize the hidden dimensions of religious knowledge.[348]

2.2. The development of Sufism

Under the development of Sufism we will provide information pertaining to the three distinct phases that represent this progression. We will first highlight the "early phase," also known as the "*zuhd* period," and will examine it as the result of an effort to emulate the Prophet. We will then consider the "Sufism" and *tariqah* periods respectively and highlight their unique characteristics.

2.2.1. Early phase, the *zuhd* (asceticism) period

During formative period of Islam the term "Sufi" was not used to describe these individuals, nor was the term "Sufism" employed to describe the path they had set out on. This era was one in which ascetics showed no material or spiritual attachment to this world. There was then no need to distinguish between Muslims on account of their worship or their level of piety. There was also no need felt to establish norms or delineate boundaries with respect to worldly attachments or to maintain a sense of balance in regard to worldly pleasures. As indicated by Ibn Khaldun, "in the second century and thereafter, when worldly inclination and attachment by Muslims became widespread, norms and boundaries and the like needed to be established. Thus

---

[347] For instance, according to Junayd al-Baghdadi, Sufism is "your being together with God without entertaining an interest in anything else" (Al-Qushayri 1972, p. 127). According to Ali b. Sahl al-Isfahani, Sufism is (*tabarri*) removing oneself from all other than God and separating from those apart from him (Mulla Jami', p. 116). Shibli describes the Sufi as one who is always with God or in His presence, so that they see no one else and feel attachment to none other than God (Al-Hujwiri 1979, p. 39).

[348] Afifi 2004, p. 56.

the term Sufi emerged, and was particular to individuals who predisposed towards worship."[349]

Drawing attention to this fact, Zeki Sarıtoprak points to Hujwiri's definition: "During the time of the Companions of the Prophet and their successors, the name (Sufi) did not exist, but the reality of Sufism existed in everyone."[350] Sarıtoprak stresses that the reality of Sufi thought and practice is much more important than the name "Sufism."[351] In subsequent centuries, Muslims with a stronger religious disposition, who sought to understand the meaning and purpose of life, and live their lives accordingly, came to be known as Sufis. Their preference for coarse, woolen cloaks, representing a very austere and simple manner of dress for the time, meant that—in correspondence to the Arabic term *suf*, denoting wool—they were called Sufis. From another perspective, they attempted to comprehend, within the confines of their finite understanding, the "Absolutely Infinite One," and through observing His actions in the universe, aimed to fulfill the purpose of their creation.

Thus, the word "Sufi" was in use in the second Islamic century after the generation of the Companions and their successors. At this point in time, Sufism was characterized by spiritual people seeking to follow the footsteps of the Prophet and his Companions by imitating their lifestyles.[352] It is axiomatic that the Prophet and his Companions wove the pattern of their lives in this way. As such, it can be said that the Sufi path is the path on which the Prophet and his friends travelled, and the Sufi is the "endeavoring Muslim" who undertakes the task of emulating them. As a result, the name given to the time encompassing the first two centuries of Islam is *zuhd*, or period of asceticism. This period, in which no rule or principle outside the ambit of the primary sources of Islam existed and wherein great importance was given to worship, action and uprightness, is thus exemplified by the likes of great ascetics like Hassan al-Basri and Rabi'a al-'Adawiyyah.

2.2.2. The "Sufi" period

Over time, Sufism transformed from this austere understanding as *zuhd* to having a more complex form, having its own methodology, principles, ter-

---

[349] Ibid, p. 34.
[350] From Reynold A. Nicholson's translation of *Kashf al-Mahjub* and cited in Lings, 1993, p. 34.
[351] Sarıtoprak 2003, pp. 156–69.
[352] Gülen 2000f, p. xxiv.

minology and regulations. Concerned with such subject matter as identify-
ing illnesses plaguing *nafs* and treating these, conducting psychological
study, developing methods of *riyadah* (austerity) and *mujahadah* (striving),
and embedding these within specific rules and regulations, "Sufism" began
to take shape as the systematic discipline of spiritual life.

The progression of Sufism, on the whole, encompassed other further
phases succeeding the *zuhd* period. The first of these was named the "Sufism
period." One of the other salient characteristics of this period was, on the
one hand, the increased prominence given to spiritual states of learning,
knowledge of God, known as *ma'rifah*, and *wajd*, or spiritual ecstasy. On the
other hand, it can also be described as the phase during which asceticism,
deeds and worship were of secondary importance. Figures such as Ma'ruf al-
Karkhi (d. 200/815),[353] Bishr al-Khafi (d. 227/841), Dhu al-Nun al-Misri
(d. 245/859), Abu Yazid al-Bistami (d. 261/874) and Junayd al-Baghdadi
(d. 297/909) are illustrious Sufis of this period.

This period gave rise to two distinct currents in relation to and their
emphasis on rationality. From one point of view, there appeared distinguished
figures who, in addition to assigning utmost importance to knowledge, also
accepted spiritual discovery and inspiration which they placed in the same category. Harith b. Asad al-Muhasibi (d. 243/857), Abu Talib al-Makki (d.
386/996), al-Qushayri (d. 465/1072), Hujwiri (d. 470/1077) and Imam
Ghazzali (d. 505/1111) were among these figures. These individuals approached
Sufism as a discipline and, by means of compiling texts and generating ideas,
they demarcated the boundaries of Sufism.

A number of Sufis who persistently assigned lesser importance to the
mind, emphasizing yearning and spiritual ecstasy instead, also emerged in
this period. Hallaj (d. 309/922), Suhrawardi al-Halabi (d. 587/1198) and
Attar (d. 590/1194) among others, contemporaneous with the Sufi period
also took their place in the history of Sufism.

2.2.3. The *tariqah*[354] period

The third and final period in the development of Sufism is the *tariqah* period which generally accepted to begin in the eleventh century ce when its

---

[353] Dates are After Hijrah (Islamic calendar) / Common Era.
[354] Term used to denote the structured Sufi orders.

institutionalization first took place. In this period, *tariqah*s, the most influential of Sufi establishments, emerged and increasingly became an important element of social life. Abd al-Qadir Jilani (d. 561/1165), Muhy al-Din ibn al-A'rabi (d. 638/1240), Ahmad Rifai (d. 578/1182), Najm al-Din al-Kubra (d. 618/1221) and Baha al-Din Naqshiband (d. 791/1388) are among the notable figures who founded these Sufi orders.[355]

An important point in relation to the chronicle of the development of Sufism, the broad outline of which is encapsulated above, is propounded by Affifi. He maintains that the Sufi path in Islam was initiated by a group of individuals who possessed their own distinctive method of practice and experience of religion and spiritual struggle, or *mujahadah*; that is, they had defined their own *tariqah*. Yet Sufis did not lead systematic lives within the milieu of Sufi lodges (*zawiyah*) and refuges (*ribat*) until the end of the second Islamic century. Nonetheless, it did not take long for those people to organize regular congregations and meetings; they gathered around *shaykh*s, or spiritual masters, and provided committed audiences to their sermons. While at first the *masjid*s, or places of worship, provided the setting for such gatherings, these thereafter ensued in *dhikr*[356] circles. In time, a spiritual leader emerged at the head of each of these organized gatherings. Through the establishment of their own set of guidelines, each of these groups adopted their own unique method with respect to morality and spiritual training. As can be understood from this, one of the meanings of *tariqah* is the particular way of life adopted by the Sufi, through adherence to and in accordance with one of the distinguished spiritual masters within their congregation; in other words, it is the complete system of teaching, principles and practice differentiating each of these congregations from one another.

However, *tariqah* has another, more comprehensive meaning. The term implies the spiritual, inner life that the one who is on the path—the willing disciple (*murid*)—leads through any means, with or without affiliation with any particular Sufi assembly or adherence to a spiritual guide. In this sense *tariqah*, in the literal meaning of the term, is individualistic, as each aspirant on the path to reaching God has one's own individual life and inner realm that is experi-

---

[355] Selvi 1997, pp. 24–26.
[356] *Dhikr* refers to the recitation of God's Names, ritualized by Sufis who conducted such worship individually or in groups.

enced by one alone. Thus, as stated by one of the Gnostics of old, "the roads leading to God are as numerous as those who are on His path."[357]

3. CROSSROADS ENCOUNTERED ON THE SPIRITUAL JOURNEY OF THE SUFI

Once a Muslim comes to the realization that the purpose of their creation begins with reaching true belief in God, with belief developing into conviction, and conviction deepening with increasing knowledge of God, and knowledge of God flourishing in the form of love, and love turning into a deep yearning to be on the path that reaches Him—and understands the natural result of all of these to be spiritual pleasure and enlightenment—they consciously become a traveler on a path to reach God. The term used to denote this journey in Sufism is *sayr wa suluk* (journeying and initiation). The focal point of this journey is the human "heart."[358] In Sufi terminology, the heart (*qalb*) is the source of spiritual knowledge, Divine love and manifestation, as well as being the instrument of perception, consciousness, emotion, and willpower.

Ghazzali refers to the human heart as the place where God is known, and that humanity, owing to this great distinction, is elevated to the rank of the most esteemed of all creation. According to him, the heart resembles a mirror. It becomes tarnished with sins and is accordingly polished and gains luster with good deeds. The form and image of objects are successively reflected on its face. Moreover, he likens the heart to a dome encompassed by windows. Through these windows, there is a constant influx of perceptions, feelings, and emotions. Akin to a target, arrows take aim at the heart from all sides. It also resembles a pool. All channels and pipes that lead to it are poured forth into it. Hence, by virtue of its disposition, the heart is capable of receiving both Divine inspiration and satanic whisperings.[359]

The ultimate aim of one of traveling on the road to truth is to reach God's pleasure, or approval. The term employed to describe the Muslim who has this lofty aim and who consciously sets off on this journey is *salik* (initiate); the great effort the *salik* displays in overcoming the difficulties encoun-

---

[357] Afifi 2004, p. 146.
[358] As distinct from the connotation relating to its physical quality as the human body's most vital organ.
[359] Ghazzali 1967, p. 21.

tered on this demanding path is thus *mujahadah*. Furthermore, reaching the horizon of *al-insan al-kamil*, or the final level of spiritual perfection, is as much a yearning for the initiate as it is an ultimate goal. A life of suffering, or *chila*, awaits this traveler. Through *riyadah* (austerity), the Sufi employs methods of training the carnal self—as recommended throughout the ages— such as restraining the appetite, maintaining thirst, reducing sleep, speaking little, engaging in regular recitation of God's Names, restricting company with people to a minimum and, occasionally abstaining from the consumption of animal products. The reason for such trials, the least of which is the *arba'in* (forty days), is to curb carnal appetites, placing these under control, in order to experience glimpses of life at the level of the heart and spirit. This "traveler to the Truth," who allots time for virtually all forms of worship in his daily life, begins arriving at knowledge that arises in the conscience, termed *ma'rifah*. Also defined as knowledge of God, *ma'rifah* is indeed a great attainment and is intimately connected with certainty or conviction of belief in God's existence and unity, known as *yaqin*.

The initiate performs acts of worship in the complete consciousness of *ihsan* (perfect goodness), acting as if seeing Him and endeavoring to be sensitive to the truth that "even if you do not see Him, He certainly sees you."[360] *Muraqaba*, referring to living in the consciousness that one is under God's constant supervision, is very important for the initiate. Such a traveler to the Truth regularly evaluates his present state and engages in self-criticism (*muhasaba*) by analyzing his deeds and thoughts. Responding to goodness, beauty and bounty in his life with thankfulness, or *shukr*, he acknowledges these, through his conscience, as Divine gifts and turns toward God with feelings of gratitude. One acknowledges all evil, ugliness, and deviation as stemming from oneself and so attempts to purify oneself through sincere repentance (*tawbah*).

The initiate, determined to reach God, notwithstanding the challenges and trials that await him, encounters particular spiritual states (*hal*) and stations (*maqam*) along the way. These can be considered as terminals on the road. *Hal* is the more readily changeable of the two; *maqam*, in contrast to *hal*, is more enduring and remains stable. In addition, it is important to note that *hal* is considered as a Divine gift to the Sufi, whereas *maqam* depends

---

[360] Bukhari, *al- Sahih*, Iman, 37; Muslim, *al- Sahih*, Iman, 7; Abu Dawud, *Sunan*, 16.

on the Sufi's determined effort and exertion. From time to time, the traveler on the path to God experiences particular anxieties regarding worldly life. Being unable to do justice to the performance of worship, being tainted by actions that displease God and the uncertainty concerning one's end and the future result of all one's deeds and actions, subjects the devout believer to the state known as *khawf* (fear). Overwhelming the ego, this fear, while seemingly negative, in actual fact serves important functions, such as the establishment of balance, protection against feeling secure against deviation and being deceived as a result, as well as safeguarding against *shatahat* which will be described below. The traveler who feels stifled by *khawf* catches one's breath with *raja*. This state produces a stockpile of hope for him. God's eternal Mercy and the performance one displays in aspiring to be on the path leading to Him engender rays of hope within the heart of such a "friend of God." The ebb and flow of fear and hope throughout one's life causes one to oscillate between happiness and apprehension.

Increasingly, the initiate awakens to sensations and perceptions which are in proportion to his inner adornments, as well as being in proportion to exertion in his spiritual life. Every so often, these sensations and sentiments produce contractions within the inner world. As a result, he feels as if his spiritual prosperity has been exhausted and as though he is left exposed and in a void. Causing the heart to feel as though it is being squeezed in the palm of one's hand, this state is identified as *qabd* (contraction). There is also the spiritual state of *bast* (expansion) which provides spiritual solace and allows the Sufi to feel nearness to God. Overjoyed and in rapture, one feels as though one has developed wings and one "flies" toward God. Each of these signifies an intimate and secret relationship between the Sufi and God.

The Sufi, who makes progress in strengthening his willpower and patience, continues on this journey called *sayr ila Allah* without growing weary or losing interest. Far from experiencing weariness or languor, he more often than not feels great exuberance in his heart toward his Beloved. At times it reaches the point where one has no longing for anything beyond union with Him. While burning with such *ishtiyaq* as one nears the end of the journey, the Sufi, having annihilated his ego, discovers the spiritual sense of being united with God. One has, in effect, become annihilated in God's existence. Being closed off to everything other than Him, the Sufi is at this point honored with the rank of *fana fi Allah* (annihilation in God). Provided that one can maintain this togetherness, one is then elevated to the rank of *baqa bi Allah* (subsistence with God) through which one is overwhelmed by indescribable pleasure and elation. Once Abu Yazid al-Bistami relates:

> On one occasion I went to *hajj*. I saw the Ka'bah, but I did not see the Owner of the Ka'bah. When I went a second time, I saw both the Ka'bah and the Owner of the Ka'bah. When I went to *hajj* for the third time, I saw neither the Ka'bah, nor the Owner of the Ka'bah.[361]

Abu Yazid al-Bistami's experience during his first *hajj* is that which is mirrored by most people. Like all Muslims who go to *hajj*—witnessing the material aspect—Bistami sees the Ka'bah, but not God who is the Unseen. His state of mind during the second *hajj* represents his seeing God's signs, and manifestations of His Names everywhere that he looks. His spiritual state during his third *hajj* is an expression of his having purged his heart of everything other than God. This last state represents such annihilation in God and subsistence in Him that the Ka'bah and the Owner of the Ka'bah can no longer be distinguished from one another; the state known as *istighraq*, or the state of complete immersion and ecstasy does not permit any such severance.

According to Junayd al-Baghdadi, the essence of Sufism is that the servant should be removed from one's own self and unified with God, or experience self-annihilation in God. In other words, it is capturing the state depicted in a *hadith qudsi*[362] where God becomes a person's "eyes to see with ... ears to hear with ... hands to grasp with and ... feet to walk on."[363] When this state is acquired, the actual and ideal identity of the physical being is now enveloped as a result of subsistence in God. However, this state, with the traveler to the Truth being entranced and intoxicated, called *sakr*, is temporary. After this, the servant returns to his former normal state. This return to oneself again, denoted by the term *sahw*, is in contrast to *sakr*, more objective, safer and steadier. In time, everything begins to fall into place for the *salik* who moves back and forth between these states.

The end of this spiritual journey, which takes many years, is sometimes not reachable in this world. This should not be understood to mean that this

---

[361] Afifi 2004, p. 194.
[362] A Prophetic saying whose meaning was directly revealed by God; that is, the meaning belongs directly to God and the wording to the Prophet.
[363] Bukhari, *Riqaq*, p. 38.

person did not do justice to this journey. Such a journey is particular to each person who undertakes it and is very much based on spiritual potential. Nevertheless, the end is sometimes in sight for travelers on the path. The shoreline of the seemingly limitless ocean appears at long last. The traveler to the Truth tastes ultimate union. He is henceforth *wasil*, or one who has reached his destination. He has received replies to all his endeavors, is rewarded for his sincere devotion to God being conferred the rank of being a *wali*, or friend of God, and is bestowed the honor of a nearness to God, *qurbiya*, that is beyond conception. A final point in relation to the end of this journey pertains to *mushahadah* (observation). *Mushahadah* has been accepted among Sufis to be the final point of this spiritual journey. It is seeing with insight (*basirah*), or through the eye of the heart, beyond God's actions and Names in order to reach the horizon of recognizing the Owner of the actions and Names. The people who have been elevated to this level see gestures, motifs and signs belonging to Him in everything they observe. They ascribe meaning concerning Him to all creation. They spend their lives on this exalted horizon. An alternative to the roads travelled in order to reach God elucidated thus far, will be expounded in the second section.

4. FETHULLAH GÜLEN AND SUFISM

In this section, Fethullah Gülen's understanding and interpretation of Sufism as well as aspects of his daily life will be elucidated. It goes without saying that it is not possible to take account of the entirety of his statements on this subject. For this reason, we offer a summary of the persons and institutions that shaped his spirituality and influenced his conception of Sufism. In turn, the understanding of Sufism that he acquired over time as well as its expression in his practical life and discourse will be examined. Finally, a concise reading of his compilation, *Key Concepts in the Practice of Sufism I–II*, will be presented.

4.1. Factors influencing Gülen's understanding of Sufism

Gülen emerged from an environment in which the Sufi life was both exemplified in practice and taught in theory. Islamic scholars who took their place in the history of Sufism, appearing in its later periods, occupied his interest and attention continuously. The austere life of Said Nursi, in particular, left deep and indelible imprints on him. Under this heading, we will briefly touch on the family members, teachers and Sufi masters who had great influence on Gülen, and highlight the particular role and distinctive contribution of Bediüzzaman Said Nursi.

4.1.1. Family

Sufism is not an understanding and path that is outside the boundary of the Qur'an and the *sunnah*; on the contrary, it is a way of life developed for the purposes of living Islam at a much deeper level. While there have been a number of approaches and interpretations that have not been accepted or espoused by the majority of scholars, these have not taken root in common Islamic Sufi understanding. The situation in Turkey, and expressly in the East of Turkey, in the twentieth century has been no different. That is to say, here too people were envisioning an Islamic way of life and were endeavoring to be good Muslims. Erzurum, in which Gülen spent his childhood in the mid-twentieth century, was a very conservative city. As is the case currently, Erzurum was then a city with a strong attachment to religious values and was home to many other Sufis.

The family environment in which Gülen was brought up was a house of learning and edification; mother, father, grandfather, and grandmother were the educators in this house. His mother's devotion to the recitation of the Qur'an, his father's meticulousness in observing the requirements of the lawful and unlawful and his passion for worship, his grandfather's utmost sensitivity and commitment to religious and spiritual concerns and his grandmother's tears were the paramount determinants that would forever shape Gülen's spiritual life.

Two short, but quite significant anecdotes help concretize the topic: first is the occasion when Gülen, who has not yet reached adolescence, goes to bed with the intention of delaying the late evening prayer. He subsequently hears the supplications of his mother who was weeping while entreating God to give her child a deeper consciousness of faith because he wants to delay his prayer. By the same token, his father's muzzling of his animals when taking them through fields belonging to someone else in order to prevent them from eating what was not rightfully theirs, and the religious conscientiousness that he displayed in all matters, undoubtedly left deep-seated impressions on Gülen. He makes the following observations regarding his family upbringing and the degree of influence of key family members:

If we are to speak about a major influence on me, then before my father and my mother I became aware of my grandmother's presence. Her serenity and profundity, which resembled calm seas, left a great impression on me. I came to understand belief and connection with God through her. Perhaps she used to laugh in the past—she smiled often—however I never once saw her engage in laughter. She was very dignified. Secondly, my father's influence was no less significant. He lived prudently. He paid special attention to his daily prayers. He was also very tearful. He never spent his time wastefully … my father was a person who filled each and every minute of his time doing something beneficial and productive and gave particular importance to contemplation. He was completely uninterested in living aimlessly.[364]

Gülen also does not neglect to talk about his mother. On one occasion he says "even though I may have been unable to appreciate, with a child's limited perception, my mother's delicacy and passion in teaching the Qur'an, her flawlessness in worship and her spending her life in suffering and sorrow, I now completely comprehend the fact that these are among the most important influences on me."[365] Undoubtedly, there are other family members who exerted an influence on Gülen but dealing with every individual is beyond the scope of this chapter.

4.1.2. Social milieu

A number of noteworthy Sufis—contemporaries as well as those from the past—had an influence on Gülen. Furthermore, Gülen's ideas and approach to Sufism, as a synthesis of his learning from eminent Sufi figures as well as his own experience and insight, will be presented.

4.1.2.1. Muhammed Lütfi Efendi (1868/1956)

Apart from the influence of family on Gülen, the well-known Muhammed Lütfi Efendi, also known as Alvarlı Efe, holds a significant place. Gülen's mother, father, maternal aunt and uncle were individuals who lived in the ambience of this esteemed figure who represented the *Naqshi* order in the region. Gülen too, from a very young age, entered his sphere of influence. He would attend his sermons, receive his compliments and would be present at *dhikr* gatherings called *khatmi hajaqan*. When Lütfi Efendi passed away Gülen was sixteen years old. Gülen states that this individual was the

[364] Erdoğan 1997, pp. 21–22.
[365] Ibid, p. 26.

first to appeal to his consciousness and holds that his current awareness, perception and feelings are due to the insight and understanding that he gained at that time.[366]

Over the years, Gülen has never forgotten the depth of feeling that he experienced during his youth and remembers with appreciation the incidents that gave rise to such an awareness and perception. To this day, whenever it is appropriate, he talks about the sentiments that he experienced during these childhood years. On one occasion, when addressing a question directed to him regarding austerity, he recalled Alvarlı Efe. According to Gülen, the influence of this individual was such that despite his very old age, his sitting in a gathering on his heels for hours on end, never displaying a change of manner or demeanor, along with not talking too much, every so often invoking the name of God, is sufficient for one's heart to skip a beat and for the human spirit to quiver as though it has been struck by electricity.[367]

Alvarlı Efe, who was bestowed with such qualities as austerity, intensity of gaze and such profundity of belief that it became visible on his countenance, engendered such an effect when he uttered the name "Allah," (known as *lafz al-Jalal*), that this was etched in Gülen's memory and consciousness. Gülen did not retain the experience merely as knowledge; on the contrary, it turned out to be a key factor in the inclinations and dynamics of his heart.

It may well be said that Gülen, despite his young age, did not participate as a neutral observer in his environment, but was in an active position through which he could maintain a high degree of benefit. He was, in other words, a very proficient observer. It is useful to note at this point his lifetime preference for shedding tears over laughter, as an example of this subconscious accumulation of insight and life experience.

4.1.2.2. Salih Efendi

Another figure who influenced Gülen in his formative years was Salih Efendi. As mentioned by Gülen, this individual is a person of complete *tamkin*, *tayaqquz* and *tawadu'*. Denoting self-possession, vigilance and humility respectively, these terms determine the sum of Salih Efendi's character and manner. Gülen sees the impact of such individuals, who have attained

---

[366] Ibid, p. 28.
[367] Gülen focuses on austerity of Alvarlı Efe in his talk entitled *Ciddiyet ve Biz* (Austerity and Us), www.herkul.org, December, 2006.

wholeness in elevated conduct, on the people around them, to be more forceful than reading a book from cover to cover.[368]

He maintains that "dry" knowledge without action is meaningless. What is essential, even if knowledge is limited, is that it is reflected in a person's manner and conduct and that it is translated into action.

4.1.3. Prominent Sufis

Throughout his life, Gülen has not severed his great connection with the spiritual life of Islam. In contrast, illustrious personalities in the history of Sufism have always remained a subject of significant interest for him. He has, quite intuitively, fulfilled the task of learning about them and imparting this knowledge to others. The individuals who constitute the greatest examples for Gülen, which he strives to follow and gain knowledge, are the Companions of the Prophet of God. Presenting them as exemplars of conduct is one of the chief aims of his discussions and written works. As to those apart from the Companions, the leading personalities within the Sunni line of thought such as Abd al-Qadir Jilani (d. 561/1165), Shah Naqshiband (d. 791/1566), Imam Ghazzali (d. 505/1111), Imam al-Rabbani (d. 1034/1624), Ahmad Badawi (d. 675/1276), Hasan Shazali (d. 656/1258) and Abu al-Hasan al-Kharaqani (d. 425/1034), have served as signposts along the way for Gülen.

In addition to these individuals, Gülen was influenced by the works of Sufi scholars such as Harith al-Muhasibi (d. 298/909), Kalabazi (d. 380/990), Abu Nasr Sarraj al-Tusi (d. 378/988), Abu Talib al-Makki (d. 386/1006) and Abd al-Karim al-Qushayri (d. 477/1084); and, having also been exposed to the thoughts and ideas of Bishr al-Khafi (d. 227/841), Abu Sulayman al-Darani (d. 215/830), Junayd al-Baghdadi (d. 298/911), Dhu al-Nun (d. 245/860), Mawlana Jalal al-Din Rumi (d. 672/1273), Muhyi al-Din ibn al-A'rabi (d. 638/1240) and Muhammed Lütfi (d. 1375/1956), he has enriched his own thought.

In actual fact, Gülen speaks very highly of the leading Islamic scholars of the early generations of Islam, known as *salaf al-salihin*. His discussions about them and his portrayal of examples from their lives are all directed towards enabling current generations to lean towards a spiritual life and to

---

[368] Ibid.

establish a strong connection with God. As can be seen from the names that have been mentioned above, Gülen possesses a rich and extensive background in Sufism. This has, moreover, prevented his being limited to any one *tariqah* directly and has afforded him the opportunity to benefit, in the midst of great diversity and dynamism, from this vast legacy.

4.1.4. Bediüzzaman Said Nursi (d. 1960)

Bediüzzaman Said Nursi has a significant influence on Gülen's thoughts. Coming to know Bediüzzaman by means of his works and through his students, and having never seen him in person, Gülen has profound knowledge on his ideas and philosophy.

Bediüzzaman is an Islamic scholar who succeeded in reflecting the spiritual side of Islam with extraordinary earnestness and discipline during his life. Never describing himself as a *darwish* or Sufi, Bediüzzaman took the Qur'an and the Prophet's life as examples that he held in high regard and from which he received spiritual sustenance. Nevertheless, the turbulent conditions of the period in which he lived caused him to remark, "this time is not the time for *tariqah*." While saying this, he was presumably referring to the institutional, structural dimension of *tariqah*. As for the personal, individual dimension of *tariqah* or Sufism, this manifested itself in Bediüzzaman's life in a very vivid manner. Indeed before us stands a man of worship who had the Qur'an by his side, and who went through volumes of selected prayers three to four times the size of the Qur'an every two weeks, and a hero of service, who was ready at any moment to give himself up for the salvation of all humanity. In his depiction of Bediüzzaman, Gülen makes the following comment:

> His behavior was shaped by the two parts of his pure inner character: the first was a heroic person, a great soldier of conscience, a man of love and enthusiasm; the second was a far-sighted thinker, leading his contemporaries from the fore, a balanced intellectual putting forward outstanding plans and projects.[369]

Bediüzzaman, undoubtedly, is an Islamic scholar who has simultaneously realized thought, practice, and action in his life; he is one of the key sources of the interplay between these elements also readily observed in Gülen's life and discourse.

---

[369] Gülen 2005d, p. 48.

4.2. Gülen's spiritual life

Gülen has approached Sufi life from the aspect of the individual, personal domain; he has considered it to be an articulation of a person's belief in and connection with God. Gülen, maintaining that "Sufism is the spiritual life of Islam; while *tariqah* constitute this spiritual life in disciplined forms," has himself been able to formulate the spiritual aspect of Islam in his own personal life. However, this achievement has in no way taken the shape of a *tariqah*. It has, instead, manifested itself through a heightened sensibility, performing worship with great fervor and dedicating life in its totality to God, that are all expressive of a complete Islamic way of life. For this reason, he has not been concerned with words or form. He has neither seen himself as, nor approved of others characterizing him as a *shaykh*, Sufi or *darwish*. Moreover, concerns such as forming a close connection with God, grasping the essence of Islam, capturing the spirit of worship and ascending to the life of the heart, have never been omitted from his agenda.

If he so wished, Gülen could have transformed his current standing very easily to that of a *tariqah shaykh*, and could have enabled his environment to take on the organizational structure of the classical form of *tariqah*. For example, he could have allowed people to kiss his hand,[370] and by giving those around him specified daily recitations and supplications within the framework of a specific code, he could have readily engendered a *shaykh-murid*, or master-disciple relationship. However, he has not done this. Keeping Sufi considerations at the individual level, he has simply encouraged others, addressing everyone in general, to strengthen their belief in God. He advised them to be closer to their Creator and devote their lives to Him. He extols the virtues of spiritual life, but does not institutionalize this. In the position that he holds, he has always preferred to remain inspirer to a movement and guide to a community in the role of dedicated teacher and mentor.

Possessing a remarkable opportunity for worldly gain, while not displaying an inclination toward it; his success vis-à-vis modern societal relations, at the same time as preserving his traditional identity and his demonstration of willpower in living a life in accordance with pleasing only God,

---

[370] Kissing the hand is often observed among Sufis as a sign of submission to a spiritual guide.

Gülen can be described as an unmitigated "modern ascetic" and a "modern Sufi." In any case, for him *zuhd*, or asceticism, is "forsaking the world in the heart, not in practice"[371] and the measure for this is "feeling no joy at worldly things acquired or grief over worldly things missed."[372] As he himself emphatically maintains, worldly opportunities and wealth are not obstacles to *zuhd*, on condition that one does not lose command of these and provided that these do not give rise to heedlessness of God.

Along with the above-mentioned, Gülen has for many years been implementing principles which are prominent in traditional Sufi understanding and which are crucial to attaining a life of the heart. These involve the preservation of balance in eating and drinking, sleeping, speaking and in interactions with people.

4.3. Sufi manifestations in Gülen's practical life

Earnestness, love, sorrow, and worship are central to Gülen's life. His solemnity—seeing Sufism as a profession of earnestness, and maintaining that Sufism can under no circumstances harbor impudence—propels those around him constantly towards prudence and vigilance. In that matter, it is not easy to become familiar with Gülen. Casualness, familiarity, and insolence are elements that cannot be found in his presence. The problems of the people who are inspired from him, the conditions and circumstances of the Muslim world and indeed of all humanity, are all of great concern to him; such interest and concern are revealed in the form of spiritual anguish and sorrow.

These qualities are so active and effective in Gülen that all those in his presence unavoidably enter his field of influence and try to keep themselves constantly in check. Those who are aware of Gülen's life sometimes equate his experience of *ghurba* (separation) with the term "loneliness." They speak of his being lonely even when in the company of people. However, in actual fact, Gülen pursues a level of subsistence that is beyond this meaning— "living among the people, but constantly being with God." Perhaps it is this manner of being that some construe as "loneliness." Gülen rarely leaves the

---

[371] Gülen 2005e, p. 203.
[372] Gülen 2000f, p. 43.

place where he lives, and thus colors it with his presence. Such places become completely wrapped up in "otherworldliness."

In short, just as we have described Gülen as a modern ascetic and Sufi, we can certainly say that his personal place of residence, in terms of its purpose, serves like a modern Sufi lodge. Indeed, there is no doubt that Gülen cultivates a Sufi culture in his immediate personal surroundings, at least, and he describes this culture as the context where "(he) first opened (his) eyes, and galvanized (his) spirit."

4.4. Commitment to *irshad* (guidance) and becoming an heir of the Prophet

The era of the Prophet and his Companions has served as the ideal model for all subsequent ages to follow. All "endeavoring Muslims" from that time on have made as their greatest objective the bringing of their lives into conformity with the lives of the people of the "Age of Happiness."[373] The most salient feature of the Age of Happiness is the manner of living a "guidance-centered life," also referred to as the "Profession of the Companions." Gülen describes this as the basis for being a true Muslim; and when indicating that Divine deliverance is contingent upon the struggle and endeavor to deliver others, he reinforces the same point. This approach has prevailed in Gülen's way of life. Expressed differently, Gülen has woven the fabric of his life around this belief. For this reason, in Sufi understanding the emphasis is on living a life that is on par with the Companions. That is, establishing a very close connection with God on the one hand, and striving to enable others to establish a strong connection with their Creator on the other. Such a way of life has been described as "guidance-centered," or living as an "Heir of the Prophet." This is the message that Gülen epitomizes to the utmost degree and expresses to as many people as he can.

At this level of life, there is no move to reclusion and isolation from people. On the contrary, there is a "conscious association" with people. This is attempting to live with a sense of responsibility like that of the Companions, and striving to be a means to raising the level of life of others to new heights. In Gülen's preference for such a life is presumably the endeavor to

---

[373] In the Islamic context, the "Age of Happiness" denotes the era in which the Prophet lived and guided his community.

engender a connection between modern human beings and their religion, without isolating them from the opportunities and realities of modernity.

In addition, the central requirement of this path is never severing connection from God. Gülen's way of putting his own Sufi understanding into practice is to maintain his "conversation with the Beloved" even when he is among people, and refuse to commit even the slightest error which could injure this personal connection with God Almighty. This is his being "among the people, but with God," as mentioned earlier. At this juncture, it is worth mentioning Gülen's own words on this issue:

> Indeed, the hero of the heart is, as the Qur'an and the Messenger of God have told us, the person of truth, who sees, thinks, and acts with all the faculties of such a conscience; whose sitting and standing are mercy, whose words and speech are mildness and agreement, and whose manners are politeness and refinement. They are the people of heart and truth who reveal and teach others the secret of knowing and perceiving the creation from the inside, who can express the true meaning and purpose of creation. The ultimate goal of such devout people is vast and very important, namely to carry every soul to eternal life, to offer everyone the elixir of eternity, and by escaping completely from their self, their personal interests, and their concerns for the future, they are able to be either in the depths of their self and inner world, or to be in the objective world, or to be in their world of the heart or to be in the presence of their Creator, and to observe and retain such significant and diverse relations all at the same time. Despite their own physical and material needs or poverty, they are a keen volunteer and altruist, and are always occupied and preoccupied with planning the happiness of the people around them. They are always developing for the community in which they live projects of peace, prosperity, and welfare, like beautifully expanding patterns of embroidery. In the face of the sufferings and miseries experienced by their community and the whole of humanity, with a heart similar to one of God's messengers, they endure palpitations, exasperation, and pangs of conscience.[374]

Gülen describes two facets of the purpose of the creation of human beings. On one hand, there is recognizing and knowing God, discerning him through the conscience and being immersed in the signs and manifestations of His existence. This constitutes the choice to live a life aimed at forming an intimate connection with God at a personal, individual level and continually striving to strengthen this bond.

Affirming God's existence and enabling others to reach knowledge of Him constitutes the second facet of the ultimate purpose for creating

---

[374] Gülen 2005d, p. 84.

humanity. Without this, God's objective in creating humanity cannot attain complete fruition. With his forceful emphasis on this element, Gülen rescues Sufism from passivity. In other words, through reconciling the need and constant effort to develop oneself spiritually with thinking of others and the altruistic desire to "let others live," a complete Islamic understanding is realized and Sufism takes on a very dynamic form. In short, according to Gülen, the purpose of humanity's creation is to know and reveal God's existence. No other purpose is worthy of being an objective of creation.[375]

5. HIS BOOK ON ISLAMIC MYSTICISM: *EMERALD HILLS OF THE HEART: KEY CONCEPTS IN THE PRACTICE OF SUFISM*

As maintained by Gülen, the work that he dedicated a significant portion of his time is entitled *Key Concepts in the Practice of Sufism*, the original being published in Turkish in four volumes. In this work, key concepts in the terminology of Sufism such as *ikhlas* (sincerity), *ihsan* (perfect goodness), *mushahadah* (observation), s*ayr wa suluk* (journeying and initiation) and *hal-maqam* (state-station) are taken up in the structure of separate articles. The topics expounded upon in this work gain a new form by means of the writer's distinct style. In its approach to the subject matter, knowledge imparted "from the inside" holds as much importance as the information conveyed from external sources. Above and beyond a study of the myriad themes and the collation of key terms, one can say that the most pronounced characteristic of this work is the way in which the themes are directed by feeling and insight. Put differently, while *Key Concepts in the Practice of Sufism* is a succinct explication of classical Sunni Sufism, its achievement continues beyond this.

In this compilation, Gülen's grasp of the Turkish language as well as his proficiency in religious and Sufi matters is axiomatic. Indeed, his use of an expansive vocabulary on the one hand, and his command of the Sufi lexicon on the other, lends great appeal to this work. In *Key Concepts in the Practice of Sufism*, lengthy, intense and even hidden matters are presented to current generations in a manner appropriate to their understanding and comprehension. Moreover, there is also no absence of topics that are difficult to fully understand, even after several readings, indicating the multi-lay-

---

[375] Gülen 1999a, p. 21.

ered nature of the subject at hand and complexity of thought in its approach to the subject matter.

An important point to note at this juncture, with regard to the way in which themes are introduced in *Key Concepts in the Practice of Sufism*, is that in addition to being in conformity with the tradition of Sufism which has been transmitted through the ages, the elements conveyed between the lines ensure that aspiration and ardor emerge from the reader. And sure enough, in virtually everyone who engages in close examination of this work there is kindled the desire and enthusiasm to demonstrate the topics they read about in their own personal lives. This is what is believed to be one of the author's most important aims, if not the most important guiding principle, in writing this text.

Key Concepts in the Practice of Sufism, at the same time, presents to its readership another Nursi-referenced path. This path is an alternative to the paths hitherto described that pave the way to achieving a "life at the level of the heart and the spirit" and/or becoming a "perfected human being." One of the two topics that will be explained under this heading is the alternative path, referred to as the "path of *ajz* (helplessness), *faqr* (poverty), *shawq* (joyful zeal), and *shukr* (thankfulness). Subsequently, a small bouquet of the new interpretations, contributions, and angles brought to bear on Sufi thought by Gülen will be presented.

5.1. The path of *ajz*, *faqr*, *shawq*, and *shukr*

The aim of Sufis has been to enter a special relationship of closeness to God. This journey, which is geared towards this objective, on one hand features the endeavor to attain spiritual knowledge of God, referred to as *ma'rifah*, and on the other hand, the consideration of the human being by way of which Sufis have sought to understand themselves with all their positive and negative attributes. The nature of "knowing" suggested in the aphorism featuring heavily in Sufism, "The one who knows their own self, knows their Lord too," has been interpreted in the following two ways:

> The first is the kind of knowing that has at its centre opposing forces. According to this, to the degree that a person acknowledges their own neediness, they will see God as free from and beyond all needs. One who sees oneself as insignificant and without value, will exalt and glorify God. One who perceives their transience will have no doubt about God's Infinite nature. One who sees one's own poverty

comes to fully understand God's absolute wealth. The second interpretation is that
humanity has been created in a form that is indicative of the Divine Being with
traits that are indicative of the Divine Ones, and has been bestowed the rank of
God's vicegerent. Accordingly, whoever understands form also understands the
Owner of form. Ibn Arabi, by means of the *al-insan al-kamil* (the perfected human
being) theory, appropriated this meaning.[376]

Since the early centuries of Islam, Muslims have discovered diverse
paths and methods in their attempts to reach the pinnacle of what is human-
ly possible in closeness to God, or in rising to the consciousness of forever
living under God's power—attaining conviction of belief in God's existence,
increasing their love and respect for Him and refraining from being occupied with anything else other than Him—and they have implemented these
practices in their lives. The *Naqshibandi tariqah*, from among these, have
developed specific criteria determining a Muslim-stance before God Almighty,
described as an individual's renouncing the world, renouncing the Hereafter,
renouncing their own existence, and then renouncing the very act of renunciation itself—condemning it to complete oblivion. Said Nursi, however,
discovered the path which he describes as being shorter, sounder and more
assured; called the path of *ajz*, *faqr*, *shawq*, and *shukr*. And Gülen, broaden-
ing this road, has continued to introduce it to others.

Like other paths leading to God, this path can also enable human
beings to attain closeness to Him. Just as people who progress on other
roads can glimpse the horizon of the heart and the spirit, travelers on this
road can earn the elevated distinction of being a perfected human being.
Ajz, or helplessness, the first principle of this path means that human beings
recognize their own powerlessness. God has created humanity as dependent
and needy. Human beings are innately powerless to attain the majority of
their desires and expectations. The needs of their spiritual lives in particular, by nature, exceed even the bounty of the world. It is God Almighty
alone who is able to fulfill these needs and wants in their entirety. As a
result, helplessness is not one person's servility with regard to another person; it is the name given to the feeling engendered as a result of a person's
effort to fully discern their own condition as well as God Almighty's infinite power. Put differently, it is their perceiving, with respect to themselves,

---

[376] Afifi 2004, p. 166.

that they are nothing in the face of Eternity and their adjusting their stance in accordance to this.

Poverty (*faqr*) denotes a "lack of capital." When individuals reflect upon what they possess in comparison with God's power and wealth, they come to perceive their own nothingness and become fully conscious of God as everything. In short, human beings come to realize that the relationship between them and God Almighty can be described as a "nothing-everything" relationship. This realization enables them to attract and attain God's guardianship and protection. Giving up the notion of their personal particular power and strength, they seek refuge in His absolute power and might.

Shawq, or joyful zeal, should be understood in terms of the notion of "not falling into despair, not panicking, and not living with the trepidation of taking a wrong step or erring."[377] It is the name given to the act of continually keeping one's inner world, or "system of self-interrogation and self-control," alive and dynamic.[378]

Shukr, thankfulness, suggests the act of responding to the bounties bestowed by God. Being an action of the heart, *shukr* safeguards human beings from ingratitude and serves as the means of devotion and worship to the One who is the Bestower of these bounties. Affection and reflection have also been considered underlying principles of this path. Gülen summarizes the essentials thus:

> Helplessness, poverty, affection, reflection, zeal, and thankfulness are the basic elements of this way. Helplessness means being aware of one's inability to do many of the things that one wants to do, and poverty denotes the awareness of the fact that it is God who is the real Owner and Master of everything. Embracing everybody and everything because of Him is affection, while reflection is thinking deeply, analytically and systematically about and meditating on the outer and inner world, with a new excitement every day. Zeal is the great, ardent desire and yearning to reach God and to serve in His way. Always thanking God for His bounties and proceeding to Him in full consciousness of all His blessings during the journey is thankfulness.[379]

Said Nursi's belief in this path has undoubtedly played a vital role in Gülen embracing this way of life and presenting it to others. Indeed, so reliable and secure is this path that one can say that these principles lie hidden

---

[377] Ibid.
[378] Gülen 2004f, p. 281.
[379] Ibid, p. 276.

in practically all the paths and ideas that people have thus far put forward in order to approach God. If the fundamental purpose for human beings is to recognize their insignificance in the face of God Almighty and observe the Divine Names and Attributes that are ceaselessly exhibited on the countenance of the universe, the effectiveness of the aforementioned principles in enabling one to reach this aim defies all expression.

There seem to be "outward-facing" and "inward-looking" dimensions in Gülen's understanding of Sufism. The outward-facing aspect is directed towards preventing people from being annihilated by the modern world. There are Muslims who, being preoccupied with an outer shell and form, lose the essence of religion. The importance, therefore, of offering them a path that can prevent them from becoming peoples devoid of spirituality should not be overlooked. It appears that the opportunity for people in the modern world to attain life at the level of the heart and spirit via the tradition of seclusion, as practiced in the early period, has greatly reduced. Furthermore, Gülen believes that this way is a compelling alternative allowing the individual in contemporary society to experience a life lived at this spiritual level. Such an emphasis can also be understood as Gülen's taking a precautionary measure against the negative correlation between Islam and a hollow "right/wrong" or "do/don't" attitude, or the diminution of religious spirit and meaning.

A crucial consideration regarding the inward-looking dimension of this topic pertains to people who are engaged in serving God's cause, who are present in public life and are continually among people. It is essential that such people, who undertake the task of the moral and religious guidance of others, known as the profession of the Companions, shield themselves, seeking protection in a spiritual greenhouse against degeneration and corruption. As such, they will fulfill their duties in the strata of society, with God's permission, with a more acute awareness and a greater consciousness. Consequently, this path possesses the capacity to protect and offer sanctuary to such people.

5.2. New interpretations, contributions, and angles in Sufi thought

As far as can be seen, Gülen, by way of *Key Concepts in the Practice of Sufism*, has expressed in writing the life of the heart that he has been speaking about publicly for many years; as such, he makes tangible all that has been said thus far. He invites the people of his time, who are becoming increasingly bound with materialism, to another life beyond the limited, narrow one of their experience. He extols the merits of a life befitting the purpose of creation and inspires Muslims to live such a life, in order for them to attain an Islamic sensibility at this elevated degree. Whilst doing this, he clarifies that ordinary people can also participate in this endeavor. In the past, the task of guiding others could only be undertaken by those who had received special training and instruction. Gülen states:

> A *murshid* (guide) is one who pronounces his or her cause and ideals in virtually all spaces without entertaining any expectation and with a complete spirit of devotion, exerting the greatest possible effort and acting as a bridge between the one who attains and that which is attained.[380]

By this means, he conveys his conception of guidance as the task incumbent upon every discerning Muslim, as opposed to a select few. Another facet of Gülen's contribution to classical understanding can be seen through his thoughts on the subject of *tawbah* (repentance). In addition to the already recognized conditions of repentance, he introduces the notion of making amends for the past.[381] In his view, a Muslim incurs a loss and experiences spiritual descent with each sin that they commit. A person who errs should feel remorse because of his sin, resolve upon never repeating it, and turn to God in sincere repentance. Apart from fulfilling these conditions, he must compensate for that particular loss and weakness and in order to regain his position must display even a greater performance and commitment.

According to Gülen, the sainthood (*walayah*) acquired by means of the recommendations of the traditional path is "subjective" or "personal." This is the specialized meaning of sainthood in the sense of affiliation with a spiritual master, and that which is attained through such means as spending periods of time suffering, whereby the initiate keeps to the absolute minimum in meeting carnal needs such as eating, sleeping and speaking, and is preoccupied with reaching amazement and finding God. This kind of sainthood is conferred by God and is not open to everyone. It encompasses spiritual stations upon one who strives with great devotion and rigorously pursues this path, and has, within it, its own specific degrees. There is also the

---

[380] Gülen 2005b, p. 38.
[381] Gülen 2000f, p. 18.

sainthood accessible to all, referred to as "objective" sainthood. The preconditions of this form of sainthood are linked to belief in God and the carrying out of righteous acts.[382]

Whilst Gülen has broadened the road of Sufism by means of his new constructions and contributions, he has occasionally made a particular choice from among earlier interpretations and descriptions. For example, he points to the fact that *khawf*, which denotes fear, has two meanings, awe and reverence; in contrast to the perpetual thoughts of "fleeing" by those who choose awe, the possessors of reverence (respect for God) adopt the approach of taking refuge in Him. Subsequently, through the statement, "Despite knowing everything that could be known, the Prophet did not flee, did not wish to escape from his position and did not want a change in state. On the contrary, he still chose to seek refuge in God Almighty," Gülen expresses his preference for a "refuge-dimensional" approach.[383]

Gülen has also observed a distinction between the terms *mutasawwif* and "sufi." After indicating that he concurs with the interpretation of Shaykh al-Islam Mustafa Sabri Efendi, he suggests that it is more correct to refer to those who undertake philosophical endeavors and remain, for the most part, in the theoretical domain of Sufism as *mutasawwif*, and those who personally practice and embody its principles as Sufis.[384] As demonstrated with the examples above, Gülen does not endorse and adopt all existing ideas within a technical context; in contrast, he examines and questions these and brings to the fore new understandings and insights.

6. CONCLUSION

Gülen was raised in a family and social environment nested in Sufi spiritual life. Subsequently, he made a conscious and concerted effort to concern himself with Sufism, in the belief that this way is the essential preserve of Islam.

The Sufi masters that he follows and presents as model human beings have taken as their foundation the Qur'an and *sunnah* and have taken on board all the ideas that they have propounded—in line with these primary

---

[382] Talk given by Gülen under title of "Take a Look at Yourselves," www.herkul.org.
[383] Gülen 2005e, p. 219.
[384] Talk given by Gülen under title of "Take a Look at Yourselves," www.herkul.org.

sources—within the underlying tenets of Islam. Gülen's approach to Sufism is no different. Given that in a Muslim's life, no greater virtue than that of emulating the elevated example of the Prophet can be conceived, this great ideal has guided Gülen also. He has personally exemplified a life centered on the Qur'an and *sunnah* and has incessantly spoken of its great merits. In short, he has never tended toward providing personal interpretations of the insights and perceptions he has experienced in his spiritual life. On the contrary, he has intensified the color of the Sunni teachings and balanced elements within Sufism and has always maintained that any idea and discourse outside this understanding constitutes deviation.

Gülen believes that "spirituality" and "morality" lie at the essence of Islam, and that Sufism is "the path followed by an individual who (has) been able to free himself or herself from human vices and weaknesses in order to acquire angelic qualities and conduct pleasing to God."[385] The most important facet illustrated in Gülen's life and discourse—what he describes as the journey of endless endeavor to the Infinite One—is a person's trying to reach God Almighty and enabling others to reach Him also. He says that this notion is what lies at Sufism's core.

Gülen presents the path discovered by Said Nursi for those whose hearts and minds have become preoccupied with worldliness, and wants them to establish a close connection with the Lord. At the same time as recommending such a life to others, he has both implemented the approach of the Sufi tradition of old, and also fulfilled the norms and principles of the *ajz*, *faqr*, *shawq*, and *shukr* paths. In this way, as a modern Sufi, Gülen sustains what we have termed the "modern Sufi lodge" as his personal living space. If the masters who rightfully assume their place in the history of Sufism were alive today, they too would adopt a way of life akin to that exemplified by Gülen.

---

[385] Gülen 2000f, p. xiv.

CHAPTER SIX

GÜLEN'S TEACHING METHODOLOGY
IN HIS PRIVATE CIRCLE

Ergün Çapan

1. INTRODUCTION

History has witnessed great mind-builders who have constructed human civilization and led us down new pathways with their ideas and projects of universal scope. Just as many leaders have changed the course of history through their actions. Rare, however, are those who have been able to convert their atlas of thought into action and put forth an excellent model to be followed. In our time, Fethullah Gülen is one of the most prominent of those who have embraced all of humankind with thought and action. Symposiums and panel discussions organized in different parts of the world are dedicated to the exploration of his ideas and activities, and he has been the subject of a number of academic research projects.

In the large collection of books and articles he authored and in the talks, conferences, and interviews he has delivered, Fethullah Gülen presents himself as a scholar who holds in his possession a myriad of knowledge, wisdom, and culture. At the top of the list are his works on basic Islamic disciplines, both classic and modern, such as *tafsīr* (Qur'anic exegesis), *sīrah* (the Prophet's life and relations with non-Muslims), *fiqh* (jurisprudence), *tasawwuf* (Islamic mysticism), and *kalam* (systematic Islamic theology), which have been nourished and developed from the Qur'an and *Hadith* (Prophetic traditions), two basic sources of knowledge in Islam. Gülen's discourse also reveals his vast knowledge of humanities ranging from literature, history, sociology and East-West classics to philosophy and the history of science and thought.

From Gülen's books, articles, recorded speeches, and sermons as well as the interviews conducted with him, one can find evidence that he has investigated the works of Eastern thinkers like Rumi, Sadi, Hafiz, Mulla Jami, Firdawsi, and Anwari as well as many Western figures such as Shakespeare, Balzac, Voltaire, Rousseau, Kant, Zola, Goethe, Camus, and Sartre; that he has read from Bernard Russell to Pushkin, Tolstoy and many others; that he refers to a variety of sources like Bacon's method and Russell's mathematical logic; and that he has examined the works of important cornerstones of Western thought and cultural life like Pascal, Hegel, and Dante. At the same time, he has read and analyzed in depth the works of greats from classical Turkish literature like Fuzuli, Baki, Nef'i, Shaykh Galip, and Leyla Hanım and modern writers and poets like Namık Kemal, Şinasi, Tevfik Fikret, Mehmet Akif Ersoy, Yahya Kemal, Necip Fazıl, Nureddin Topçu, Cemil Meriç and Sezai Karakoç.

Before turning to the books and teaching method employed by Gülen in different fields of Islamic disciplines, I think it would be beneficial to mention basically what kind of education he received and which books he read during this period, as much as I have been able to determine. Dr. Ahmet Kurucan had partially touched on this subject in the preface to Fethullah Gülen's book entitled *Fasıldan Fasıla 1*, published in Turkish. His educational background certainly has a role in the list of books he continues to teach today. The names of some of these books were mentioned earlier by Professor Ibrahim Ghanim Bayyumi in the conference "Future of Reform in the Muslim World: Comparative Experiences with Fethullah Gülen's Movement in Turkey" (Cairo, October 19–21), who pointed out that Gülen's service model was based on the Qur'an and Sunnah (the Prophet's practice and traditions).

2. GÜLEN'S EARLIER EDUCATION

After Ottoman *madrasah*s (traditional schools) were closed down in 1924, teachers raised in that system continued to teach Arabic grammar and religious legal sciences in the classical *madrasah* education system in different places in Anatolia. Thus, Gülen received his earlier education in this *madra-*

sah educational system during his years in Erzurum, a province in eastern Turkey.

The works he studied during his training period in Erzurum can be categorized into two fields of study: The first are works related to Arabic grammar and rhetoric (*balagat*). The second are related to different Islamic disciplines.

In terms of morphology in Arabic grammar (word knowledge, word anatomy), he studied *Amthila*, *Bina*, *Maqsud*, *Izzi* and *Marah*; in regards to grammar and syntax, he studied *Awamil*, *Izhar*, *Kafiya*, and *Mulla Jami'*. Among the mentioned works, he memorized *Awamil* and *Kafiya*.

Regarding Islamic disciplines, he read *Multaqa al-Abhur* from the science of law, *Mir'at al-Usul* from the methodology of jurisprudence, *Talkhis* from the science of rhetoric, *Mukhtasar al-Ma'ani*, and the complete rhetoric book from, *Majma' al-Mutun*. He also studied Ūshi's *Bad al-Amali* in the commentary of Aliyy al-Qari and Qadi Baydawi's *Tawali al-Anwar* from the discipline of systematic theology. From among the books he read Gülen memorized the texts of *Talkhis* and *Bad' al-Amal*.

Among exegetical works, he studied *Jalalayn* and Qadi Baydawi's *Anwar al-Tanzil*, and in regard to the science of logic, he studied *Mughni al-Tullab* and Imam Busiri's *Qasida al-Burdah* with Kharbuti commentary.

The teaching method of the above mentioned books was as follows: *Amthila* was memorized by the student down to the finest point. *Bina*, *Maqsud*, and *Izzi* were first be read by the mentor in class and necessary explanations were made. The student both repeated the previous day's lesson to the teacher and presented the concepts in summary form. The sections and subsections in *Bina* and the forms and conjugation rules in *Maqsud* were fully memorized.

The teaching method of syntax books—*Awamil*, *Izhar*, *Kafiya*, and *Mulla Jami*—was the same. The student repeated the previous lesson to the mentor and presented a summary of its concepts. The texts of *Awamil* and *Kafiya* were memorized. *Izhar* would have to be known and presented as a concept.

After studying the grammar books, *Amthila*, *Bina*, *Maqsud* and *Izzi*, Gülen began syntax books. After finishing *Awamil* and *Izhar*, his teacher had him skip *Kafiya* and join the students studying *Mulla Jami*. Gülen memorized *Kafiya*, although he was exempt from it. His teacher did not think it was necessary for Gülen to study the books after *Mulla Jami*, thus introduced him to *Mukhtasar al-Ma'ani*, a book on rhetoric, while at the same time he asked Gülen to memorize the text of *Talkhis*. In the *madrasah* system of that day, a student studying an upper level book supervised those studying a lower level book. Thus, a student monitoring a lesson many times with other students would have also memorized it. In Gülen's words, he even knew the marginal notes and annotations.

Gülen studied with the method briefly mentioned above under very difficult conditions in Erzurum during his youth. Later on throughout his career, he taught curious and eager students in places where he was assigned to duty. The following books, mentioned in accordance with their classification, are what I have been able to record and learn from others; I cannot claim it to be a full list. Still, I hope this serves as initial material for broader research to be conducted in the future.

3. BOOKS TAUGHT BY GÜLEN

3.1. Exegesis (*tafsīr*)

The following are books in this field that were taught by Gülen who said, "Although almost every individual who knows its language can grasp something from the Qur'an, a true and comprehensive understanding of it can be achieved by those experts of exposition and commentary (*tafsīr* and *ta'wil*) who have attained the required and correct level of knowledge."[386]

1. *tafsīr al-Jalalayn*. This very short and eloquently written single-volume exegesis was begun by Jalal al-Din al-Mahalli (864/1459)[387] and completed by Jalal al-Din al-Suyuti (911/1505). This work is attributed to both authors in the title, which means "The *tafsīr* of Two Jalals."

2. Nasir al-Din Abd Allah b. Umar al-Baydawi's (864/1286) exegesis entitled *Anwar al-Tanzil wa Asrar al-Ta'wil* (2 volumes). This work is better known as the Baydawi's *tafsīr*. It is a famous, short, to-the-point exegesis that summarizes the views of commentators with an emphasis on the Qur'an's literary miraculousness and eloquence.

---

[386] Quoted from Gülen 2006e, p. xli.
[387] Dates are After Hijra (Islamic calendar) / Common Era.

3. Abu al-Fida Ibn Kathir's (774/1341) commentary entitled *Mukhtasar Tafsīr al-Qur'an al-Azim* (3 volumes), which was summarized by Muhammad Ali al-Sabuni. It is one of the most important *tafsīr* works, explaining the Qur'an by referring to the Qur'an and *hadith* and to what the Companions (Sahaba) and Successors (Tabi'un) were recorded to have said. Gülen taught this *tafsīr* several times to different groups of students over the years.

4. The introduction of Zamakhshari's (538/1143) exegesis entitled *al-Kashshaf an Haqa'iq al-Tanzil*.

5. Sayyid Qutub's (1966) *Fi Zilal al-Qur'an* (6 volumes). This is a *tafsīr* written with literary, sociological, and psychological depth that gives important measure in understanding the Qur'an. Often, Gülen could not contain his tears when he taught this work to his students. Nevertheless, he emphasized at times that he did not agree with some of viewpoints in Qutub's commentary, which he felt could have been caused by the very difficult conditions under which Qutub lived.

6. Muhammad Ali al-Sabuni's (contemporary) *Rawa'i al-Bayan Tafsīr Ayat al-Ahkam* (2 volumes). It is a legal exegesis, presenting a new method and arrangement of judgments from legal verses.

7. Bediüzzaman Said Nursi's (1960) *Isharat al-I'jaz fi Mazann al-Ijaz*. This original *tafsīr* comments on the Chapter Fatiha and Baqara up until verse 32. Gülen read this exegesis in its original edition in Arabic at different times with his students.

8. M. Elmalılı Hamdi Yazır's (1942) *Hak Dini Kur'an Dili* (9 volumes). Regarding this commentary Gülen said, "No commentary equal to [Yazır's], including the ones in Arabic, has been written; not even the *Mafatih al-Ghayb* (*Tafsīr al-Kabir*) of the great commentator Fakhr al-Din al-Razi, from whom Yazır himself quoted in his exegesis *Hak Dini Kur'an Dili* in great detail."[388] Formerly, he taught this commentary by having his students summarize it. Recently he included it again in his comparative *tafsīr* teaching sessions in addition to the following commentaries:

Imam Maturidi's *Ta'wilat al-Qur'an*, Zamakhshari's *al-Kashshaf*, Fakhr al-Din al-Razi's *Mafatih al-Ghayb*, Baydawi's *Anwar al-Tanzil wa Asrar al-Ta'wil*, Abu Hayyan's *Bahr al-Muhit*, Abu al-Suud's *Irshad Aql al-Salim ila*

---

[388] Gülen 2006c, p. 36.

Mazay al-Kitab al-Karim, Tantawi Jawhari's *al-Jawahir fi Tafsīr al-Qur'an al-Karim*, Sayyid Qutub's *Fi Zilal al-Qur'an*, Mulla Badr al-Din Sanjar's *Abda al-Bayan*, and Bediüzzaman Said Nursi's *Risale-i Nur*.

9. Ibn Bazish's (1145), *al-Iqna' fi al-qiraat al-Sab'a* (2 volumes). This work explains famous forms of Qur'anic recitation that are known through a reliable chain of narration. Strongly emphasizing at every opportunity that every Muslim must learn to recite the Qur'an at least to a degree that is acceptable for prayer, Gülen stresses that recitations and variant readings are an important wealth in the revelation-based Islamic culture and that this richness must be revived. He studied this book with his students so that the recitations would be known theoretically at least.

10. Imam Maturidi's (333/944), *Ta'wilat al-Qur'an*. This exegesis is comprised of the interpretations of Imam Maturidi, who is the most important imam in *aqidah* (Islamic creed) and *kalam* (theology) in mainstream Islam. As soon as this volume was mass-produced, Gülen immediately began to teach it to his students.

In addition to these exegetical works, Gülen taught Muhammad Abd al-Azim al-Zarqani's (1367) *Manahil al-Irfan* (2 volumes) in relation to methodology of exegesis. In addition to taking up matters of former exegetical method, this is a useful work with a new method and approach that answers many questions today.

3.2 *Hadith*

1. Several times Gülen taught Muhammad b. Ismail Bukhari's (194/810) collection known as *Sahih al-Bukhari*, which is known to be the most authentic work after the Qur'an. Gülen conducted Bukhari classes by having students sometimes read Bukhari's main text while at other times present his work in the light of various commentaries on it, which were:

- Qastallani's (923/1517), *Irshad al-Sari li Sharh Sahih al-Bukhari*. This book was also taught in Ottoman *madrasah*s. It contains essential knowledge about many names, terms, and various expressions in several prophetic traditions that are mentioned in Bukhari's work.

- Badr al-Din al-Ayni's (855/1451) *Umdat al-Qari fi Sharh Sahih al-Bukhari* (20 volumes). It is one of the most important commentaries on Bukhari. It is also the most voluminous commentary made on Bukhari in regard to narration and verification and the best arranged commentary in terms of investigation and analysis. Based on the Hanafi school of thought, this important commentary presents the views of different schools.

While studying Bukhari's text with his students, Gülen also followed this commentary. As far as I know, he studied *Umdat al-Qari* twice at different times with a different group of students.

- Ibn Hajar al-Asqalani's (852/1448) *Fath al-Bari fi Sharh Sahih al-Bukhari*. This work has been regarded as the best Bukhari commentary in terms of *hadith* knowledge, the beauty of its delivery, and the superiority of its statement of purpose. It is the most famous Bukhari commentary and comprises 14 volumes. With his students, Gülen read this commentary from beginning to end together with special reference to the chain of transmitters.

2. Abu al-Husayn Muslim b. al-Hajjaj's (261/874) *al-Musnad al-Sahih* (5 volumes) a *hadith* collection called *Sahih*. Its arrangement is perfect, and it is famous for its systematic presentation of different variations of *hadith*.

3. Abu Dawud al-Sijistani's (275/888) *Sunan* (4 volumes). *Sunan* is a generic name for select *hadith* books whose main characteristic is that they include judicial *hadith*s categorized according to legal issues. One of the most important *sunan*s is that of Abu Dawud. Gülen taught this book at different times with following commentaries:

a. Khalil Ahmad al-Saharnafuri's (1346/1927) *Badhl al-Majhud fi Hall Abi Dawud* (10 volumes) is a commentary which takes the Hanafi school as a basis and combines *hadith* and *fiqh* disciplines, studying matters related to *hadith* in a manner compatible with the classical *hadith* methodology. It was used as a textbook; the students read the *hadith*, and Gülen read related passages from commentary.

b. Mahmud Muhammed Khattab al-Subki's (1352/1933) *Manhal al-Azb al-Mawrud Sharh Sunan Abi Dawud* (10 volumes). This commentary of Abu Dawud covers views of different legal schools of thought. It is a very systematic and well arranged work. However, it remains only halfway completed. Gülen read Abu Dawud's *Sunan* with a group of students to a certain place by following this commentary.

4. Muhammad b. Isa b. Thawrah al-Tirmidhi's (279/892) *Sunan Tirmidhi* or *al-Jami'*. Gülen taught this *hadith* book together with the commentary of Muhammad Abd al-Rahman b. Abd al-Rahim al-Mubarakfuri (1353/1934) entitled *Tuhfat al-Ahwadhi* (10 volumes). From time to time

Mubarakfuri criticizes the approaches of the Hanafi school of thought. At Gülen's request, one student presented these sections in summary form or by reading from the text together with *I'lau al-Sunan* of Tahanawi, a well-grounded book on Hanafi legal thought.

5. Malik b. Anas, (179/795) *al-Muwatta* (2 volumes). It is one of the earliest classification works (*musannaf*) organized according to *fiqh* topics. This work is especially important, for it includes narrations that are *mawquf* and *maqtu'* in addition to some that are *marfu*.[389]

6. Ahmad b. Ali b. Shu'ayb al-Nasa'i, (303/915) *Sunan* (2 volumes). It is famous for its arrangement and for giving the slightest nuances in narrations and, most importantly, for giving extreme importance to the narrators and choosing the most reliable individuals according to the author's own criteria.

7. M. Ali Nasif (contemporary), *al-Taj al-Jami'* (5 volumes). Arranged according to legal chapters, this *hadith* book is a compilation of *hadith* selected by the author from the collections by Bukhari, Muslim, Abu Dawud, Tirmidhi, and Nasai. As for the topics he did not find in these five books, he selected from Ahmad b. Hanbal's *Musnad*, Imam Malik's *Muwatta*, Ibn Majah's *Sunan* and Hakim's *Mustadrak*. This book was taught by Gülen to several different groups.

8. Murtada al-Zabidi (1205/1790), *Uqud Jawahir al-Munifah* (2 volumes). This book critiques variations of *hadith* used in the Hanafi school of thought's legal deduction as found in *Kutub al-Sittah*. Gülen continuously recommends that this book should be read and taught.

9. Ali al-Muttaqi (975/1567), *Kanz al-Ummal* (16 volumes). Comprised of more than 46 thousand *hadith*, this work is one of the largest collections of *hadith* to date. Gülen once taught his students ten volumes of this work during the month of Ramadan and the remaining 6 volumes in the following 6 months.

10. Zakariya al-Nawawi's (676/1277) *Riyad al-Salihin min Kalam Sayyid al-Mursalin*. While teaching this work, Gülen focused on the most

---

[389] *Hadith*s are classified as *mawquf*, *maqtu'*, or *marfu* according to the top person recorded in the chain of transmission. *Hadith*s whose transmitters are recorded up to a Companion are *mawquf*; those that are attributed to a Successor are *maqtu'*; and if they can be traced back to the Prophet, they are called *marfu*.

comprehensive *hadiths* related to every subject and had his students memorize them. The *hadiths* marked for memorization number around 550.

11. Qadi Iyad (544/1149), *al-Shifa bi ta'rif huquq al-Mustafa* (2 volumes). This famous book introduces the diverse qualities of the Prophet and teaches us how to show respect and adopt good manners while remembering him.

12. Muhammad Fuad Abd al-Baqi (1388/1968), *al-Lu'lu wa al-Marjan* (2 volumes). This is a work comprised of *hadiths* that are agreed upon by Bukhari and Muslim and are regarded as the most reliable.

In addition to these works, Gülen taught Ahmad Muhammad Shakir's *'al-Ba'is al-khasis'*, which is Ibn Kathir's *Ikhtisar Ulum al-Hadith* enriched with footnotes. In addition, he indicated that the work of late Ottoman scholar Ahmad Naim, *Tecrid-i Sarih Mukaddimesi* (composed during early Turkish republican period), was very important, and he recommended strongly that his students read it.

3.3. Jurisprudence (*fiqh*)

"Ours is a centuries-long civilization of jurisprudence, and its methodology welcomes everyone into its orbit of thought, intelligence, logic, and reasoning."[390] This quote from Gülen emphasizes the important place this discipline holds. He pointed towards a horizon in the name of what needs to be done when he said, "The studies on the methodology of jurisprudence in our history are the most serious initial enterprise in respect to developing the most perfect legal system and the most flawless science of law that can address every century."[391] Gülen states that methodology of jurisprudence is not given enough importance; whereas, without knowing methodology it is not possible to escape from contradiction and obtain sound thought. He recommends that one should read at least thirty books written in this field. The following are works on jurisprudence and methodology of jurisprudence that Gülen taught over the many years of his teaching:

1. Quduri (d. 428/1037), *Mukhtasar* (1 volume). It is one of the basic books of Hanafi legal thought.

---

[390] Quoted from Gülen 1999b.
[391] Ibid.

2. Abu al-Fadl al-Mawsili, (683/1284) *al-Ikhtiyar li ta'lil al-Mukhtar*. This is a commentary of *Mukhtar*, which is one of the four basic texts of Hanafi legal thought. The work takes up proofs and causes of legal judgments in respect to methodology of jurisprudence. Gülen taught this book twice.

3. Abu al-Hasan Burhan al-Din al-Marghinani (593/1197), *al-Hidaya* (2 volumes). This is one of the most famous and important legal texts of the Hanafi school of thought. For centuries it was taught in Ottoman *madrasahs* as one of the cornerstone books in jurisprudence. Gülen taught this important legal text to various student groups three different times together with the famous commentary made on *al-Hidaya* written by Kamal Ibn al-Humam (861/1457) entitled *Fath al-Qadir*.

4. Ala' al-Din Ibn Abd Zadah, (1306/1889) *al-Hadiyyat al-Aliyyah*. A very concise book takes up matters related to branches of this discipline in the Hanafi school of thought.

5. Ibrahim b. Muhammad al-Halabi (956/1549), *Multaqa al-Abhur*. Arranged according to *qawl al-asahh* (the most authentic view) in the Hanafi school of thought, this work was used as a textbook and was taught for a long time in Ottoman traditional education.

6. Wahba Zuhayli (contemporary), *al-Fiqh al-Islami wa adillatuhu* (9 volumes). This work is an encyclopedic legal text written by a contemporary author according to well-grounded approaches of various mainstream Muslim schools of thought. Gülen taught this book up to the sixth volume.

7. Asad Muhammad Said Sagharji (contemporary), *al-Fiqh al-Hanafi wa adillatuhu* (3 volumes). This work tries to apply Hanafi legal thought to a new method.

8. Ali al-Qari (1606), *Fath bab al-inaya bi sharh al-nuqaya* (3 volumes). This magnificent book of Ali al-Qari, who is considered to be a complete authority in the fields of *tafsīr*, *hadith*, and *kalam*, compares proofs of the four schools with special emphasis on Hanafi legal thought. Gülen *teaches* this book in comparison with the following books: *al-Wiqayah* of Taj al-Shari'ah, *al-Muhit al-Burhani* of Burhan al-Din Maza, *Hidaya* of Marghinani, *Majma' al-Anhur* of Shaykhzada, *Hashiya Radd al-Mukhtar* of Ibn Abidin, and *Istılahat-ı Fıkhiyye Kamusu* of Ömer Nasuhi Bilmen.

3.4. Methodology of jurisprudence

Gülen taught the following works related to the methodology of jurisprudence:

1. Mulla Husraw (885/1480), *Mir'at al-Usul.* Part of the curriculum in Ottoman traditional schools for a long time, Gülen taught this methodology text, reinforcing his students' active participation of reporting to him each chapter.

2. Abd al-Karim Zaydan, *al-Wajiz.* Gülen taught this methodology book to his students by translating it sentence by sentence. He had the previous lesson summarized during each class.

3. Ibrahim al-Shatibi (790/), *al-Muwafaqat* (4 volumes). One of the top works in the discipline of methodology of jurisprudence, this book was read by students, translating it sentence by sentence and later on summarizing it from beginning to end.

4. Sayyid Bey, *Madkhal.* This methodology book written in the Ottoman language was read in Gülen's presence. He made explanations where needed and answered questions. He stated that he did not agree with the approach of Sayyid Bey on some topics like *maslahat* (public benefit or affair).

In addition to those mentioned, Gülen said he would like to teach Abd al-Aziz al-Bukhari's *Kashf al-Asrar*, which he read at different times.

3.5. Islamic mysticism (*tasawwuf*)

Pointing out the fact that Islamic disciplines complete each other like different faculties in a university, Gülen states that darwishes and Sufis in the field of *tasawwuf*, which he calls "Islam's heart and spiritual life," have contributed to this university in their own capacity: "Many legal scholars, traditionalists, and interpreters of the Qur'an produced important books based on the Qur'an and the Sunnah. The Sufis, following methods dating back to the time of the Prophet and his Companions, also compiled books on austerity and spiritual struggle against carnal desires and temptations, as well as states and stations of the spirit. They also recorded their own spiritual experiences, love, ardor, and rapture. The goal of such literature was to attract the attention of those whom they believed restricted their own practice and reflection to the 'outer' dimension of religion and to direct it to the 'inner' dimension of religious life."[392] Taking into consideration that they have written books related to the action of the heart based fully on experience, Gülen recommends that one of these works be taught in every class circle. In addition to the fields like exegesis, *hadith*, jurisprudence, and theology, he taught books explaining "Islam's heart and spiritual life" as much as opportunity allowed. The following are books he taught at different times related to this field:

1. Qushayri (514/1120), *al-Risala al-Qushayriyyah fi Ulum al-Tasawwuf.* This work from the early periods deals with the mystical dimension of Islam and Sufis in line with the Qur'an and Sunnah.

2. Imam Rabbani, *Maktubat* (2 volumes). One of the most important works that opens horizons in regard to Islamic disciplines in general, especially mysticism, Gülen dealt with this work with deliberateness and frequently shared his interpretations.

3. Harith al-Muhasibi (243/857), *al-Ri'aya li Huquq Allah.* This book includes very sensitive and important criteria for a Muslim's constantly taking himself to account and living a life on a straight path. Gülen recommends that this book be read at least once or twice.

4. Murtada al-Zabidi (1205/1791) *Ithaf Saadat al-Muttaqin* (14 volumes). This is a commentary on Imam Gazzali's famous *Ihya Ulum al-Din.* Gülen commended this author for his comprehensive knowledge and for his authority on *hadith* and other Islamic disciplines. He further indicated that this commentary added up to the value of *Ihya*. Gülen continues to use this book in his classes.

5. Abd al-Rahman al-Jami' (Mulla Jami') (898/1492), *Nafahat al-Uns.* This work covers mystical terms and biographies of great Sufis.

6. Abd al-Hakim Arwasi, *al-Riyad al-Tasawwufiyyah.* This is a book in the Ottoman language that discusses the history of Islamic mysticism in broad terms, including other related topics and biographies of great Sufi masters.

3.6. Arabic grammar

As far as I can determine, Gülen accommodated a student's level when teaching. During the early stages, he taught his students Arabic grammar from

---

[392] Gülen 2004e, p. xix.

classical works. Later on he taught from books published in modern times. The books he taught are as follows:

1. *Amthila.* Anonymous, this small book containing verb and noun forms and conjugations attempts to explain rules and regulations by means of examples. Memorized for centuries in the classical *madrasah* system, this small grammar book was memorized by Gülen's students.

2. *Bina.* Anonymous, this book explains 35 rules that facilitate word derivations. A basic grammar book in the Ottoman *madrasahs*, Gülen has students memorize it.

3. *Maqsud.* Anonymous. Taught in Ottoman *madrasahs*, this book on grammar examines the morphology of Arabic words. Gülen lectured (*taqrir*) on this work.

4. Izz al-Din Abd al-Wahhab b. Ibrahim al-Zinjani, (1257) *Izzi.* This famous work covers the topics of grammar, syntax, and vocabulary. Gülen also lectured on this work.

5. Imam Birgiwi (981/1573), *Awamil.* This concise book covers basic syntax topics, like words that affect the ends of other words, such as particles, prepositions, and case endings (*i'rab*). Gülen had his students memorize the text.

6. Imam Birgiwi's (981/1573) *Izhar al-Asrar fi al-Nahw* is a book on syntax or Arabic sentence structure. It is actually a commentary on the author's own work *Awamil.* It was taught as a textbook in Ottoman *madrasahs*. Gülen lectured on this book by making a very broad commentary on it, and he had the text memorized.

7. Ibn al-Hajib, (646/1249), *al-Kafiya.* Taught for centuries in Ottoman traditional schools, this book on syntax explains syntax rules with examples and goes into the philosophy of language from time to time. It is an advanced level textbook.

8. Abd al-Rahman al-Jami', (898/1492), *al-Fawaid al-Diyaiyyah.* This work is a commentary on *al-Kafiya.* It became famous under the commentator's nickname of Mulla Jami'. It was the last and most comprehensive book on syntax that was taught in *madrasahs* throughout the Islamic world, Ottoman *madrasahs* in particular. Gülen taught this book in his early period.

9. Ali Jarim-Mustafa Amin, *al-Nahw al-Wadih* (2 volumes). A very systematic grammar book that was prepared with a modern Arabic teach-

ing technique and which covers both grammar and syntax. Gülen taught this book many times.

10. Baha al-Din Abd Allah b. Aqil (729), *Sharh Ibn Aqil ala Alfiyat Ibn Malik*. This is one of the most important commentaries on Malik's *Alfiya* which explains Arabic grammar in a thousand verses. It was Gülen's goal to have his students memorize the *Alfiya* text when this book first began to be studied. In consecutive lessons, he listened to the verses each student had memorized from beginning to end. However, after they memorized 30–40 verses, memorization was put aside at the students' request because they were having difficulty with it. "Memories are blown," Gülen regretfully said. Briefly the book is read as follows: First the student reads the verse and translates it; then the verse's case endings are explained, followed by commentary.

11. Mustafa Ghalayini's *Jami' al-Durus al-Arabiyyah* is a grammar book written in recent times. Gülen taught this book twice by having his students read and translate it sentence by sentence, give meaning to the poems, show the point of proof in the poem, and do the exercises.

12. Muhammad Muhy al-Din Abd al-Hamid, *Mabadi al-Durus al-Arabiyyah*.

13. Mehmed Zihni Efendi (1846-1913), *al-Muntakhab wa al-Muqtadab fi Qawa'id al-Sarf wa al-Nahw*. This work was written in the Ottoman language and takes up Arabic grammar and syntax in a broad and comprehensive way with plentiful examples.

14. *Takallum* (3 volumes). Gülen prepared this book for practical Arabic speaking. He taught this to his students by explaining it to them and having them practice it.

In addition to teaching an Arabic grammar book in study groups, Gülen also taught a work related to rhetoric. Pointing out the importance of the knowledge of rhetoric in order to benefit from the Qur'an and Sunnah, Gülen indicated that this branch of knowledge was not well known and practiced, and he continually recommended it. The textbooks he taught in this field are as follows:

15. Khatib al-Qazwini(1338), *Talkhis al-Miftah*. This is an abridged book on the science of rhetoric which was taught in *madrasah*s until very recently. Gülen taught this book during his early teaching years.

16. Ahmad al-Hashimi, *Jawahir al-Balaghah fi al-Ma'ani wa al-Bayan wa al-Badi'*. Presenting the science of rhetoric in a method different from the classical one, this book provides plentiful examples and exercises. Students were taught this book by Gülen by reading and translating it sentence by sentence and by doing the exercises.

17. Ali Jarim-Mustafa Amin, *al-Balagha al-Wadiha*. This book explains topics of the science of rhetoric with a new method. It was also taught with the method used for the previous book. Gülen taught this book at different times to various student groups.

3.7. Systematic Islamic theology (*kalam*)

Gülen described the science of *kalam* (theology) as follows: "*Kalam* is the totality of disciplines that defends the Islamic system of faith with reason and narrative proofs, protects the integrity of believers' thought, eliminates doubts and apprehensions regarding religion that are put forth from time to time or that may come up in the future, and protects and maintains truths formerly called '*aqa'id al-haqqa al-islamiyyah*' (true Islamic creeds or faith) within the framework of the *Sunnah al-Saniyya*, the splendid practice of the Prophet."[393] He indicated that as one of the "basic sources of our cultural heritage," the discipline of theology should be evaluated within the framework of secondary sources of Islamic law.[394] He taught some works from this field and summarized others. In particular, he recommends teaching Maturidi *kalam*, whose works, Gülen thinks, have been neglected. The works he taught regarding *kalam* are as follows:

1. Saad al-Din al-Taftazani, *Sharh Aqa'id al-Nasafiyyah*. This is a famous work explaining Maturidi creed.

2. Bediüzzaman Said Nursi, *Risale-i Nur Collection*. Gülen taught this work, which treats theology subjects with a very different style and very rich perspective, and he had his students make presentations by summarizing it.

3. Mehmed Vehbi Efendi, *al-Aqa'id al-Khayriyyah*. The *kalam* section in this book, which is very detailed, was taught alongside the commentary on *Ihya Ulum al-Din* called *Ithaf al-Saada al-Muttaqin*.

---

[393] Gülen 2000g.
[394] Gülen 2010b, p. 101.

Among the books Gülen taught, some books are related to more than one field of basic Islamic disciplines. I have listed them below under the heading of "miscellaneous works."

3.8. Miscellaneous works

1. Hasan al-Banna (1949), *al-Rasail.*

2. Muhammad Zahid al-Kawthari (1952), *Maqalat.* A collection of Kawthari's articles published in different places at the beginning of the twentieth century that responds to different problems related to Islam, doubts meant to confuse people's minds, and the degeneration of ideas.

3. The Fourth Caliph and the Prophet's cousin, Ali (40/661), *Nahj al-Balaghah* (Compiler: Abu al-Hasan Sharif al-Radi). This work includes the sayings and sermons of Caliph Ali. While teaching this book, Gülen benefitted from Ibn Abi Hadid's (655/1257) *Sharh Nahj al-Balaghah* when needed.

4. Kharbuti, *Sharh Qasida al-Burdah.* This is a commentary on Imam Busiri's famous eulogy to the Prophet Muhammad, peace be upon him, which has been recited for centuries.

4. BOOKS THAT ARE SUMMARIZED

In addition to the books Gülen taught – even if he calls it holding discussion with his friends – he had the students in his study circles summarize other books. Explaining that there are many books that need to be read and that it is very difficult for a single person to read them all, Gülen recommended that every person who participated in the class present a summary that is not longer than one twentieth of the book or even smaller, and he implemented this method with his students. Thus Gülen enabled even the study circle to benefit from the power of collective consciousness. Among these books, we see many texts written in Turkish or translated into Turkish. Some of the books summarized are as follows: Yusuf Has Hacip's *Kutadgu Bilig*; Mustafa Sabri Efendi's *Mawqif al-Aql wa al-Ilm wa al-Alam min Rabb al-Alamin wa Rasulihi*; Suat Yıldırım's *Peygamberimiz'in Kur'an'ı Tefsiri*; Orhan Türkdoğan's *Alevilik-Bektaşilik*; Imam Maturidi's *Kitab al-Tawhid*; Jabiri's *Arap Aklının Oluşumu*; İsmail Fenni Ertuğrul's *Maddiyun Mezhebinin İzmihlali, Vahdet-i Vücud ve İbn Arabi*; İrfan Yılmaz's *Evrim Teorisi*; Shurnubi's *Hikem-i Ataiye-Şerhi*; Toshihiko's *İbn Arabi'nin Füsusundaki Anahtar Kavramlar*; N.S. Banarlı' *Türkçe'nin Sırları*; Mehmet Ali Işım's

Upaniṣatlar; M. Ajjaj al-Khatib's *al-Sunnatu Qabla al-Tadwin*; Alparslan Açıkgenç's *Bilgi Felsefesi*; Ahmed Cevdet Pasha's *Mecelle-i Ahkam-ı Adliye*; M. Tahir Ibn Ashur's *Maqasid al-Shariah al-Islamiyyah*; Izz al-Din b. Abd al-Salam's *Qawa'id al-Ahkam fi Masalih al-An'am*; Sayın Dalkıran's *Ahmet Feyzi Çorumi'nin el-Feyzü'r-Rabbani'si Işığında Osmanlı Devleti'nde Ehl-i Sünnet'in Şii Akidesine Tenkitleri*; and some editions of periodicals such as *Sızıntı, Yeni Ümit, Yağmur* and *Hira* magazines.

To conclude this section, Fethullah Gülen studied under the classical *madrasah* style, learning from scholars in his home area. Later the knowledge he acquired in a very short period of time was transformed into a very broad perspective that he taught various students in the places he went. As can be understood from the books he taught, he introduced his study groups to many books that are not in the classical *madrasah* method or today's educational system. In fact, from time to time Gülen taught as textbooks those publications that are otherwise used as reference books.

In this section, I have attempted to pass on as much as I could determine regarding the books on various Islamic disciplines taught by Fethullah Gülen. The following section will focus on his teaching method.

5. GÜLEN'S TEACHING METHOD

It is not very easy to reflect and contain in words the far reaching extent of what I prefer to call the "culture of presence" of Gülen's lesson and teaching method. Alongside his documented teaching method, his students personally experience and benefit from his presence; they witness the vastness of his horizons and enthusiasm and are colored by his influence. The degree to which one benefits from that atmosphere depends on a person's capacity, intention, concentration, and abilities. Considering this, I will describe Gülen's lesson and teaching method to the extent that I am aware of it.

In the lesson and teaching method of classical *madrasahs*—and various lesson groups today that, in a sense, we can call the continuation of these traditional institutions—classical books are usually studied. The teacher explains the lesson, the students listen, and then there is mutual exchange within the framework of questions and answers. Again, in this method in every class an abstract of the previous lesson is presented and then the new lesson begins. Also in the *madrasah* system, an assistant to the teacher or senior students facilitate student discussions of the lesson. In today's schools of theology, professors do not prefer to follow a classical work but present their own notes and compilations followed by questions and answers.

Fethullah Gülen, who received lessons from mentors trained in the *madrasah* educational system, has followed the practice of teaching according to the student's level during his teaching life of half a century. He lectures more during the initial periods of a student's instruction. According to the qualifications of a student in terms of a good command of the language and knowledge in related disciplines, he may be ready to present the lesson to Gülen. Before his presentation, the student studies the text with a senior student or students. As students present the text, Gülen intervenes from time to time commenting over the passage while respectfully crediting other scholars' approaches. Although Gülen humbly says, "I discuss books with my friends," undoubtedly there is a teacher-student relationship. It is also possible to understand Gülen's reference to "discussion" as a student's attention on the class, his further research and comparative analysis with different works, active participation, and asking questions that can lead to yet further inquiry and explanation. In addition, Gülen never leaves a question unanswered. As the Prophet remarked, "A good question is half of knowledge,"[395] asking an appropriate and good question is very important in regard to gaining benefit from the lesson.

Before describing Gülen's teaching methods according to each discipline, let us take a brief look at how he selects books and determine the teaching hours.

5.2 Selection of books

Gülen gives great importance to the feelings and inclinations of others in certain matters. He follows this method when choosing a book as well. He observes students' approach to a certain course and whether they embrace it whole-heartedly and want to do it, and he follows their feelings. In this respect, he takes their responses seriously and decides accordingly. When Gülen wants to teach his students a book in some field he usually says, "There are books on this subject with such characteristics; we can read one from among them that you prefer." Sometimes he mentions the qualities of a book he thinks are very important, thus drawing attention to it. For exam-

---

[395] Tabarani, *Mu'jam al-Kabir*, 25/7; Ajluni, *Kashf al-Khafa*, 1/179.

ple, he mentioned at different times that *Kanz al-Ummal* is one of the most comprehensive of *hadith* books and that it could be covered rather quickly as a textbook. Upon students' interest in the book that grew over time, he made it a textbook. Sometimes a book is chosen when students want to read a particular book like *al-Fiqh al-Islami wa adillatuhu*, and it overlaps with Gülen's choice.

5.3. Teaching hours

Lessons are generally held between the morning and noon prayers. Lessons were also held many times in the afternoon. During one period, lessons began after breakfast and continued until noon. In another period, it began after the morning prayer and continued following a break for breakfast. In addition, at one time the lesson began one hour before the morning prayer and continued until the prayer. In fact, *Tuhfat al-Ahwadhi* was studied in this way. The ten volumes of *Kanz al-Ummal* were finished during the month of Ramadan during which lessons were held after the morning, evening, and *tarawih* (special prayer during Ramadan) prayers and after *sahur* (pre-dawn meal before fasting starts) for approximately 7–8 hours a day.

5.4. Students' preparation

Before each class students are expected to have fully examined the passages by extensive use of dictionaries (particularly *Munjid, Mu'jam al-Wasit, Lisan al-Arab*, and *Taj al-Arus*) and other references on exegesis, legal texts, and commentaries. They pay utmost attention to read Arabic sentences and words grammatically correct in the text. Gülen is very sensitive to reading correctly, especially with verses from the Qur'an and *hadith* texts, as well as pronouncing accurately the names of the transmitters and narrators. His approach to this subject is: "One may read Arabic incorrectly, but do not read Qur'anic verses inaccurately."

During the presentation, Gülen listens and in places that need correction, he humbly mentions the correction in a very polite manner. If he feels the text needs verification, he dwells on it. At such times, he asks other references dealing with this matter to be brought in, and he explains the matter by referring to them. Or he asks that references be checked before the next lesson. When students inquire about a matter, Gülen first respectfully states the general view of scholars on the subject, and then he expresses his own interpretations, particularly addressing the present conditions. Some of the most attractive aspects of the lessons are these explanations and interpretations of Gülen, which are in a sense dependent on the student's curiosity, the quality of his questions, and the vastness of his vision. Gülen takes his addressees' level of comprehension and their capacities into consideration and goes as deep in a matter as he perceives their capacities can accommodate. By all means, Gülen tries to keep his students engaged with the class and actively participating. He encourages them to read more, to develop skills in dealing with challenges posed by intense texts and concepts, to introduce them to varying ideas, methods, disputes, and debates, to help them adopt a holistic approach to all sciences, and to teach them not to limit themselves to one field of expertise but to be familiar with other sciences at least at the level of encyclopedic entries. Studying in this manner first of all facilitates the mapping of knowledge in the student's mind, allowing him to assume a broader perspective on disciplines and thus retrieve knowledge when needed.

With this method, 40–50 pages of text can be read in a lesson of approximately 3–4 or 2–3 hours. Very important to this teaching technique is also Gülen's patience in listening to his students with few interruptions.

Gülen gives importance to reading analytically. Always reserving his deepest respects for former scholars, he approaches a text by testing it against the logic of revelation, the essentials of religion, the criteria of narration, and common sense, through which the knowledge generated in our time is filtered and new interpretations are reached.

Together with all of these, Gülen continually emphasizes that students should immerse themselves in what they read, deeply analyze it, and make it a source of life. Their studies should become a profound part of their nature, and they should voice their experiences speaking from the heart.

There is almost no book that was begun in Gülen's study circle that was not finished, unless there was a very compelling reason.

5.5. The beginning of a lesson

Lessons always begin with mentioning the name of God, praising and glorifying Him, and praying for and sending greetings to the Prophet. Some of the prayers recited before the class are as follows:

> "Our Lord, increase our knowledge, faith, certainty, trust, surrender, entrustment, reliability, tranquility, sincerity, loyalty, faithfulness, ingenuity, affection, decency,

chastity, intelligence, wisdom, memory, and our trust in You and our love and desire for meeting You. My God, we ask You for perfect and permanent health and well-being and a sound heart. Bestow your power and might on us. O most compassionate of the merciful."

"My God, open the doors of wisdom to us. Pour your mercy on us, O Possessor of Majesty and Honor. I believe in God who is Unique, One, Truth, and Manifest. He has no equal. I reject everything considered to be equal to His divinity and lordship. My Lord, make things easier, not more difficult. My Lord, complete this with goodness. We seek help only from Him."

When a new book is introduced, Gülen reads all of its sections, including the foreword and introduction as well as the copyright page.

6. TEACHING SPECIFIC SUBJECTS

In this section, we will focus on how Gülen teaches basic Islamic disciplines in his study circle. Although we have already mentioned some of the books he has taught, here we mainly deal with not what he has taught but how he has taught.

6.1. Teaching grammar

Gülen has taught almost every group of students a book related to the structure of Arabic grammar. The books taught were listed in the previous section. In particular, several times he taught Imam Birgiwi's grammar book entitled *Izhar* during his early teaching period to students of different levels using the lecture method. One of these classes especially was conducted like a very broad open commentary.

Gülen pays attention to students' work on vocabulary and grammar before the class. He is especially careful with the variations of word forms in the root, past, present, and other derivatives, as well as the new meanings verbs assume with different prepositions (*huruf al-jarr*). He insists on the accurate pronunciation of the names, translation of poems, and providing from these poems evidence for grammar rules. During the lesson they read, translate, and do the exercises, if available. A summary of the lesson is usually given by several students at the beginning of the following day's lesson.

In Gülen's words, today the science of rhetoric is not taught well enough to allow students to sufficiently benefit from the breadth of the Qur'an and Sunnah. He taught works on rhetoric using a method similar to the method used with grammar.

6.2. Using dictionaries

From time to time Gülen says, "I do not know about you, but I look up several words in the dictionary everyday." He wants students to gain the habit of frequently using the dictionary so they will learn the language correctly and memorize words with their nuances. For example, at one time, he corrected his students' usage of *k-dh-b* with references to dictionaries. The infinitive and noun form of the *k-dh-b* is known more as "*kidhb*" and is generally used as such. Gülen pointed out that the infinitive "*kadhib*" is more in line with classical Arabic because this word is used as "*kadhib*" in several verses in the Qur'an (Yusuf 12:18, An'am 6:21) and that, in addition, when the word's infinitives are given in dictionaries, it is given in first place.[396] He constantly has *al-Munjid* at his side during the lessons. When he needs to, he turns to reference books like *Lisan al-Arab, Taj al-Arus,* and *al-Nihaya fi Gharib al-Hadith.* To find the Turkish equivalent of an Arabic word, he uses dictionaries like Asım Efendi's *Qamus-u Okyanus* and *Akhtar Kabir* and has his students look up the words in them. For Persian words he uses dictionaries like *Farhangi Farisi.* He stated that he likes and frequently uses the 3-volume dictionary entitled *Misalli Büyük Türkçe Sözlük* for Turkish words.

6.3. *Hadith* and methodology of *hadith*

Gülen has certainly taught almost every group a book on *hadith.* In addition to teaching basic *hadith* books like *Kutub al-Sitta* regularly, as mentioned in the previous section, he also teaches some among them repeatedly (like Bukhari). Together with this, he fully covers during his teaching commentary and reference books like *Kanz al-Ummal, Umdat al-Qari,* and *Fath al-Bari.*

If a *hadith* is not sound or authentic—many have witnessed that Gülen immediately notices this—he investigates which book it originated from and the critiques of the *jarh* and *ta'dil* scholars who either refuted or rectified the narration.[397] Regarding narrators and *hadith,* he uses books like *Tahdhib al-Tahdhib, al-Kashif, Mizan al-I'tidal, Siyar Alam al-Nubala, Majma'u al-Zawaid,* and *al-Matalib al-A'liyah.* If it is a popularly known *hadith,* he recommends

---

[396] Ibn Manzur. *Lisan al-Arab*; Zabidi. *Taj al-Arus,* "k-dh-b."

[397] *Jarh* and *ta'dil* is critiquing a narrator's position as a narrator. While *jarh* refers to deficiencies in a narrator, like being known as a liar, fabricator, having a poor memory, etc., *ta'dil* affirms a narrator as acceptable based on his or her being trustworthy, having a strong memory, etc.

that books like *Kashf al-Khafa* and *al-Maqasid al-Hasanah* be consulted. He is sensitive on the subject of teaching primary sources about *hadith*s.

Umdat al-Qari fi Sharh al-Bukhari (20 volumes): He taught *Umdat al-Qari* twice at different times to different students. In the first class students read *hadith*s from Bukhari's text, and Gülen read from the commentary he deemed necessary and gave his views and led the discussion. He explained unfamiliar words in the *hadith*, intervened when necessary regarding the names of the narrators, and read the richness of meaning included in the *hadith* and judgments derived from the *hadith*.

Gülen gives great importance to the *hadith* narrator's name being pronounced correctly and to knowledge of evaluations made regarding their lives and persons. In his youth, he recorded biographies of the *hadith* narrators in his notebooks and memorized them. He dwelled in particular on these people in his *hadith* classes and made notes from books of translators and men of learning and added them to the information in the commentaries. Later he again taught Bukhari together with the *Umdat al-Qari* commentary to another group. Before coming to class, students prepared file cards for each narrator mentioned in the *hadith*s according to the system in Dhahabi's *al-Kashif* book on important persons. These file cards included the teachers and students of the narrator and those who took the *hadith* from him and the views of the *jarh* and *ta'dil* scholars on the *hadith*. The cards prepared by the student were read by Gülen after the *hadith* chain of narration (*sanad*) and text (*matn*) had been read in class.

Fath al-Bari fi Sharh Sahih al-Bukhari (14 volumes): Gülen taught this famous commentary on Bukhari from beginning to end with a different study group. The teaching method was basically the same as that followed earlier with Bukhari's *Umdat al-Qari* commentary, but a few additions were made. With Dhahabi's *al-Kashif* as a basis while reading *hadith* narrators, books like *Tahdhib al-Tahdhib*, *Siyar A'lam al-Nubala*, *Hilyat al-Awliya*, *Sifat al-Safwa*, and Ibn Sa'd's *Kitab al-Tabaqat* were also benefitted from. In order to enrich the information with things like the narrator's teachers, those who took narration from him, striking examples of virtue from his life, examples of *hadith*s reported by him, and the views of *jarh* and *ta'dil* scholars, a word file on the computer was created and shown on a screen during class. In addition to a short biography of the Companions in the chain of transmission, their asceticism, worship, piety, and devoted spirit were presented as exemplary messages for today. Examples were given of *hadith*s they transmitted and those who reported from them were mentioned.

Gülen made some short additions in some places while information regarding narrators and transmitters was being read. For example, the wife of the Prophet, Aisha's nickname is mentioned in some books as "Umm Abd Allah al-Faqiha (the jurist mother of Abd Allah)" [Abd Allah: God's servant]. Gülen added, *wa-hiya umm ibad Allah ajma'in*, "She is the mother of all of God's servants."

Today, in *hadith* studies not much attention is given to the chain of transmission and only the text is reported. Gülen's method of teaching the narrators together with the *hadith*s and his efforts to inculcate respect and affection for them are extremely important. When it was mentioned to some prominent scholars of the Arab world that Gülen has these distinguished people's names read along with the *hadith*, they were greatly impressed expressed their amazement and approval. They said, "This science has become obsolete even with us. Not many teach the *hadith* narrators. Gülen's giving this much importance to it in his teaching is very important for the revivification of this discipline."

Knowing the Companions and *hadith* narrators as a model of knowledge, wisdom, worship, and dedication, Gülen treats them as most precious guests in his heart and memory. Gülen has used every opportunity to introduce, teach about and make these people known and appreciated by anyone who listens to him and especially those attending his classes. He wants them to be a beautiful example to students in regard to their concern for knowledge and the depth of their service to God, their worship and piety and their seeking God's approval in their learning. Just as he holds up the prominent figures of our history—especially the Companions—in his sermons, talks, and books as a model to follow, he wants to engrave in the memory and sub-consciousness of the students the important virtues of the narrators.

Sunan Abi Dawud: Gülen has taught this book several times. He did this together with commentaries on the book entitled *Badhl al-Majhud* and *Manhal al-Azb al-Mawrud*. After the students read the *hadith*'s chain of transmission and text, they focused on explanations of words from the commentary, a critique of the narrator, commentary of the *hadith*, comparison of it with other *hadith*s, judgments (*ahkam*), and epigrams (*nukta*). Gülen gave his own interpretation from time to time in response to a question regarding it.

Sunan al-Tirmidhi: While teaching the *Tirmidhi* commentary *Tuhfat al-Ahwadhi* (10 volumes) to a group of students, Gülen asked one student to compare the section of the book that criticizes from time to time the proofs of the Hanafi school of thought's approaches with Tahanawi's book entitled *I'la al-Sunan*, which takes up the subject of Hanafi jurisprudence in a broad and well-grounded way. As another method of teaching *hadith*, Gülen chose the most comprehensive *hadith*s from every chapter while teaching *Riyad al-Salihin* and had students memorize them. He said, "Put these in your reservoir; you will see abundance from them." Gülen taught Ahmad Muhammad Shakir's *al-Bais al-Khasis* from *hadith* methodology by having students prepare before class and read in his presence. At the same time, the preface to the *Tuhfat al-Ahwadhi* commentary is also a broad *hadith* methodology. With his method of reading *hadith* books together with their commentaries, Gülen has actually been teaching *hadith* methodology by practicing it. Gülen states that in this field the late Ahmad Naim's *Tecrid-i Sarih Mukaddemesi* is a very good work.

6.4. Exegesis (*tafsīr*) and the methodology of exegesis

As they do in other disciplines, students are well-prepared before class for the texts which they read to Gülen. Gülen offers explanations in places he sees necessary or about which there is a question.

Among Turkish commentaries, Gülen gives great importance to the great scholar Elmalılı Hamdi Yazır's *Hak Dini Kur'an Dili*. Once, together with students, he summarized all of Elmalılı's exegesis to students in the study group. Each student read and summarized a part of the *tafsīr* equivalent to one page of the Qur'an and presented it in class. First the student recited the page of the Qur'an and then presented the summary he had prepared. During the presentation, Gülen shared his views regarding the recited verses with the students. The book *Kur'an'dan İdrake Yansıyanlar* is one of the fruits of this. Recently Gülen has begun to teach *Hak Dini Kur'an Dili* comparatively with other *tafsīr*s. Each student studies a different *tafsīr*, and in the class they present the differences between Elmalılı's work and the respective *tafsīr*. Gülen makes further comments when he feels necessary. *Tafsīr*s read in comparison with Elmalılı's are the following: Imam Maturidi's *Ta'wilat al-Qur'an*, Zamakhshari's *Kashshaf,* Fakhr al-Din al-Razi's *Mafatih al-Ghayb*, Baydawi's *Anwar al-Tanzil wa Asrar al-Ta'wil*, Abu Hayyan's *Bahr al-Muhit*, Abu al-Su'ud's *Irshad Aql al-Salim ila Mazay al-Qur'an al-Karim*, Tantawi Jawhari's *al-Jawahir al-Qur'an*, Sayyid Qutub's *Fi Zilal al-Qur'an*, and Mulla Badr al-Din Sanjar's *Abda' al-Bayan*.

Covering Elmalılı's entire *tafsīr* with this reading method takes a long time. The real aim is to encourage the comparative reading method by show-ing an example of it. Gülen recommends that almost all the Islamic sciences, *hadith* in particular, are studied using the same method.

6.5 Jurisprudence and the methodology of jurisprudence

In every study group, Gülen teaches a book related to jurisprudence along with *hadith*, exegesis, and grammar. He once stated the truth that "one can-not become a scholar without knowing jurisprudence." In general, legal texts in Gülen's class are covered by students' reading and translating every sen-tence or paragraph into Turkish. Together with this, some juristic books were only read in Arabic. In fact, Wahba Zuhayli's work, *al-Fiqh al-Islami wa adillatuhu,* was only read in Arabic and was not translated because its lan-guage is plain in comparison with classical *fiqh* books, and its style can be understood by today's readers.[398] While reading legal texts, Gülen advises students to refer to concisely stated legal judgments or approaches to other juristic books which take up the matter in a broader and well-founded way. He points out that it is necessary to know well the assertions of legal schools regarding which legal judgments (*fatawa*) have been made and that there has been neglect on this subject. He points to the differences in approach that occurred from time to time between the former and latter jurists. Although he is tied to the Hanafi school, he is extremely respectful of the other legal schools of thought. He states that the Hanafis have produced a broad body of jurisprudential collective works, and these texts are a result of extensive brainstorming, addressing not only historical facts, but also developing judg-ments on events that may take place; they were never fruitless works as some critics claim.

As always and especially during a lesson, he gives great importance to the respectful reading of the names of various Imams from different legal

---

[398] Gülen 1995b, pp. 21–24.

schools, expounders of the law, and jurists, like Imam A'zam Abu Hanifa, Imam Shafi'i, Imam Malik, Imam Ahmad b. Hanbal, and two great pupils of Abu Hanifa, namely Abu Yusuf and Muhammad al-Shaybani.

Gülen taught some classical legal texts together with their commentaries. While the students read the texts, he read what he thought was important and necessary from the commentaries and gave his ideas from time to time.

Gülen taught *al-Hidaya* by al-Marghinani with its commentary *Fath al-Qadir* by Al-Kamal ibn al-Humam, a work that holds a very important place in Hanafi legal system, three times to different study groups. Just as reading Elmalılı's *Hak Dini Kur'an Dili* with other commentaries comparatively, he teaches Aliyy al-Qari's *Fath Bab al-Inayah* in jurisprudence by comparing it with other legal texts. After *Fath Bab al-Inayah* is carefully translated, it is compared with other legal books. Different approaches and interpretations are noted and presented in summarized form. The legal texts that are addressed in the comparison are as follows: Sadr al-Sharia's *al-Wiqayah*, Burhan al-Din al-Mazah's *Muhit al-Burhani*, Marghinani's *al-Hidaya*, Shaykhzadah's *Majma' al-Anhur*, Ibn Abidin's *Hashiya Radd al-Mukhtar*, Ibn Abidinzadah's *al-Hadiyyah al-Ala'iyyah*, Wahba Zuhayli's *al-Fiqh al-Islami wa Adillatuhu*, *Diyanet İslam İlmihali* (the Islamic Catechism) prepared by a committee from the Turkish Presidency of Religious Affairs, and Asad Muhammad Said Sagharji's *al-Fiqh al-Hanafi wa Adillatuhu*.

6.6. Islamic mysticism (*tasawwuf*)

Gülen always includes a Sufi work explaining "Islam's life of heart and spirit" in each study group parallel to the other Islamic sciences. Students prepare and then read in his presence Sufi works like Qushayri's *al-Risala*, Harith al-Muhasibi's *al-Ri'ayah*, and Imam Rabbani's *Maktubat*. When appropriate in these lessons, Gülen emphasizes the most important dynamics that take a person to a higher level of heart and spiritual life. He also shares his ecstatic experiences on this subject.

According to Gülen, one of the illnesses of today is to take a position against the friends of God, pretending not to see their greatness and evaluating them as if they were ordinary people on our own level. Such a view is a terrible lapse of thought. Some say, "Imam A'zam Abu Hanifa, Imam Shafi'i, Ahmad b. Hanbal, Imam Malik, Imam Ghazzali, Imam Rabbani,

Shazili, and Abd al-Qadir Jilani were as ordinary as we are; the legendary stories regarding them are not really true." Although they want to belittle them, they are not successful and remain deprived of the spiritual light and prosperity of those great people, and the paths to greatness become closed to them. For people who try and pull Abd al-Qadir Jilani and Imam Rabbani down to their own level close down their own horizons by doing this. Because they consider themselves on a par with these giant figures of history, they cannot advance and find themselves at the end of the road. People who do not believe that the spirit and heart have their own degree of life and that there are great ones in that field will absolutely not be able to ascend to those degrees.

On the other hand, Gülen points out that mentioning the heart and spiritual life of those great men of spirit like Abd al-Qadir Jilani, Ahmad Rifai and Hasan Shazili but not trying to emulate them and being satisfied with their life stories only is another disaster. According to Gülen, what actually needs to be done is to learn what made these men great in the spiritual realm and to implement this in our own lives.

6.7. Respect for the former scholars (predecessor/*salaf*)

While teaching his students, Gülen is extremely respectful towards the interpretations and approaches of scholars from the time of the Age of Happiness to the present. He shows great respect towards the Companions, their Followers, those coming after the Followers, the imams of the schools of thought, and great men of spirit like Abd al-Qadir Jilani, Hasan Shazili, Ahmad Rifai, Shah-i Naqshiband, Imam Rabbani, and Bediüzzaman Said Nursi and to their interpretations and approaches. He frequently emphasizes that the interpretations and approaches must be very respectfully taken into consideration regardless of which Islamic discipline the scholars are from. Furthermore, paying utmost attention to the essentials of faith, he humbly voices his own views saying, "Ibn Kathir ('the son of abundance') had this view, but Ibn Qalil ('the son of little' referring to himself) has this approach," or "This poor soul has this interpretation or view."

He states that students in the class may have/should have interpretations and approaches towards scholars on an axis of respect and in a way that does not contradict the basic disciplines of religion, for everyone in a sense is an "*ibn al-zaman*" (child of his or her own time). Every era has assets which are open to interpretation and which can be interpreted according to the conditions of the current period. It is the responsibility of every Muslim to read the signs of the time well and, taking that asset, to put the values he believes in into practice. Meanwhile, it is very important not to take scholars lightly and disrespectfully ridicule them saying things like, "They did not understand this matter."

6.8. Book summarization

This method was explained in the previous section. The summarization and presentation of the book are conducted as follows: Gülen gives books and magazines he deems beneficial to his students and participants in the class. Each work is read carefully, summarized, and then presented in class. Books that are summarized are from different branches of the Islamic disciplines, literature, history, philosophy, and so on. During summarization, Gülen expresses his satisfaction of dissatisfaction with the author. Many students find this way of studying exceptionally fruitful.

6.9. Conclusion

Gülen studied in the tradition of the *madrasah* system and later, while maintaining his loyalty and respect for the past, he expanded it with new techniques.

His teaching method is oriented towards the student. He is always open to new and different methods. In addition to using computers and other forms of retrieving sources, he also gives great importance to students' being able to find relevant passages in books. Together with technology's facilitating the rapid access of information, what is essential is reading the book and taking notes when necessary. Another important point he emphasizes is that technology should be a backup source for accessing information, but depending too much on it, a student runs the risk of technology becoming an obstacle to the development of a person's aptitudes and capabilities.

Gülen has expressed by different means that remembering one's honorable ancestors and scholars with good words and one's approaching their efforts and interpretation with respect are a Muslim's moral and religious obligation. Gülen points out, many times accompanied by tears, that those people have surpassed their own times and that we are indebted to them. Gülen believes every age has its own benefits; thus, every individual of this age should make use of the inspirations God grants to our hearts and to reveal them always seeking endorsement from the essentials of the religion. This, according to him, is an expression of making the best of our willpower, appreciating the inspiration Allah gives to hearts and minds, and showing gratitude for the blessings we have received.

From time to time Gülen has said, "I have no rights over you. If I did I would ask in return that you teach students like this until you pass away." Regardless of how much his students grow up and become teachers, he encourages them never to give up learning and remain as students in this regard. As an example, he gives Nur al-Din al-Haythami, a lifelong student to Zayn al-Din al-Iraqi. From time to time he says humorously, "Angels take the souls of truth-seeking students by feeding them honey and cream without hurting them," thus encouraging them to remain as students with the desire to constantly learn. In short, according to Gülen, the essential purpose of teaching and learning is to carry our faith to the horizon of *marifat* (divine knowledge), to deepen our knowledge with love, and to soar above by gaining His pleasure with our voluntary and devoted spirit in the path of His blessed word, never pausing even for a moment.

BIBLIOGRAPHY

Afifi, Abu al-Ala. 2004. *al-Tasawwuf: al-Thawrah al-Ruhiyyah fi al-Islam* (in Turkish trans.) *Tasavvuf: İslamda Manevi Devrim*, Istanbul: Risale.

Akman, Nuriye. *Sabah*, 23–30 January 1995.

——. 2004. *Zaman*, 22 March.

Albayrak, İsmail. 2006. "The Historical Status of the Qur'an: Modern Discussion among Turkish Academics," *Islam and Christian-Muslim Relations*, 17.

al-Alwani, Taha Jabir. 1991. "Taqlid and Ijtihad," *The American Journal of Islamic Social Sciences*, 8.

Amir, Abu Abd Allah. 1997. *Mu'jam Alfaz al-Aqidah*, Riyadh: Maktabat al-Ubaykah Publications.

Aydüz, Davut. 2001. "Fethullah Gülen ve Kur'an'ı İdrake Açtığı Ufuk," in *Yeni Ümit* No: 54.

Baljon, J.M.S. 1961. *Modern Muslim Koran Interpretation* (1880–1960), Leiden: Brill.

Beşer, Faruk. 2006. *Fethullah Gülen Hocaefendi'nin Fıkhını Anlamak*, Istanbul: Ufuk Kitap.

Bukhari, Abu 'Abdullah Muhammad b. Isma'il. 1979. *Sahih al-Bukhari*, Istanbul: al-Maktabat al-Islamiyyah.

Bulaç, Ali. 2006. "The Most Recent Reviver in the 'Ulama Tradition," in Robert A. Hunt and Y. A. Aslandoğan (editors), *Muslim Citizens of the Globalized World: Contributions of the Gülen Movement*, NJ: The Light Inc.

Çalış, Halim. 2007. "Holy Sources of Human Dignity," *The Fountain*, 58.

Can, Eyüp. 1996. *Fethullah Gülen Hocaefendi ile Ufuk Turu*, Istanbul: AD Yayınları.

——. 1996. *Zaman*, 13–23 August 1995.

Canan, İbrahim. 2007. *Fethullah Gülen'in Sünnet Anlayışı*, Istanbul: Ufuk Kitap Yayınları.

Çapan, Ergün. 2002. "Kur'an'ın Tarihselliği ve Tarihselci Yaklaşım," *Yeni Ümit*, 15.

Çetin, Muhammed. 2010. *The Gülen Movement: Civic Service Without Borders*, NY: Blue Dome Press.

al-Dāraqutnī, Ali b. 'Umar. 1981. *al-Sifāt*, Madīna: Maktabat al-Dār, I.

Erdoğan, Latif. 1997. *Küçük Dünyam*. Istanbul: Milliyet Yayınları.

——. 2006. *Küçük Dünyam*, Istanbul: Ufuk Kitap Yayınları.

Ergene, M. Enes. 2005. *Geleneğin Modern Çağa Tanıklığı*, Izmir: Yeni Akademi
       Yayınları.

Ghazzali. 1967. *Ihya al-ʿUlum al-Din III*, Egypt.

Görgün, Tahsin. 1998. "Dil, Kavrayış ve Davranış: Kur'an'ın Vahyedilmesi ve İslam
       Toplumunun Ortaya Çıkışı Arasındaki Alakanın Tahliline Mukaddime," *III.
       Kur'an Haftası: Kur'an Sempozyumu January 13–14, 1997*, Ankara: Fecr
       Yayınları.

Griffith, Sidney and Zeki Sarıtoprak. 2005. "Fethullah Gülen and the People of the Book:
       A Voice from Turkey for Interfaith Dialogue," *The Muslim World*, 95/3.

Gülen, Fethullah. 1989. "Kur'an," *Yeni Ümit*, 2/6.

——. 1992a. "Kur'ān-ı Kerīm ve İlmi Hakikatler I" in *Yeni Ümit* 5/16.

——. 1992b. "Kur'ān-ı Kerīm ve İlmi Hakikatler II" in *Yeni Ümit* 5/17.

——. 1995a. *Fasıldan Fasıla I*, Izmir: Nil Yayınları.

——. 1995b. *Fasıldan Fasıla II*, Izmir: Nil Yayınları.

——. 1996a. *İnancın Gölgesinde I*, Izmir: Nil Yayınları.

——. 1996b. *İnancın Gölgesinde II*, Izmir: Nil Yayınları.

——. 1997a. *Fatiha Üzerine Mülahazalar*, Izmir: Nil Yayınları.

——. 1997b. *Fasıldan Fasıla III*, Izmir: Nil Yayınları.

——. 1998a. "Science and Religion," in *Knowledge and Responsibility: Islamic
       Perspectives on Science*, Izmir: Kaynak Publications.

——. 1998b. *Asrın Getirdiği Tereddütler I*, Izmir: Nil Yayınları.

——. 1998c. *Asrın Getirdiği Tereddütler II*, Izmir: Nil Yayınları.

——. 1998d. *Asrın Getirdiği Tereddütler IV*, Izmir: Nil Yayınları.

——. 1999a. *Prizma III*, Istanbul: Nil Yayınları.

——. 1999b. "Kültür Mirasımızın Temel Kaynakları," in *Yeni Ümit*, No 46.

——. 2000a. *Kur'an'dan İdrake Yansıyanlar I*, Istanbul: Feza Gazetecilik Yayınları.

——. 2000b. *Kur'an'dan İdrake Yansıyanlar II*, Istanbul: Feza Gazetecilik Yayınları.

——. 2000c. "Dar Bir Zaviyeden Düşünce Sistemimiz" in *Yeni Ümit*, 13/49.

——. 2000d. *Sonsuz Nur III: Sünnetin Tesbiti ve Teşrideki Yeri*, Izmir: Nil Yayınları.

——. 2000e. *Işığın Göründüğü Ufuk*, Istanbul: Nil Yayınları.

——. 2000f. *Key Concepts in the Practice of Sufism*, Virginia: The Fountain.

——. 2000g. "Kültür Mirasımızın Temel Kaynakları 2," *Yeni Ümit* No. 47.

——. 2001. *Asrın Getirdiği Tereddütler III*, Istanbul: Nil Yayınları.

——. 2002. *Prizma III*, Izmir: Nil Yayınları.

——. 2003. *Yaratılış Gerçeği ve Evrim*, Istanbul: Nil Yayınları.

——. 2004a. *Sohbet-i Canan*, Istanbul: Gazeteciler ve Yazarlar Vakfı.

——. 2004b. *Kırık Testi*, Istanbul: Gazeteciler ve Yazarlar Vakfı.

——. 2004c. *Fasıldan Fasıla IV*, Istanbul: Nil Yayınları.

——. 2004d. Interview with Nuriye Akman in *Zaman*. 22 March.

——. 2004e. *The Emerald Hills of the Heart. Key Concepts in the Practice of Sufism*, Vol. 1. NJ: Tughra Books.

——. 2004f. *The Emerald Hills of the Heart. Key Concepts in the Practice of Sufism*, Vol. 2. NJ: Tughra Books.

——. 2005a. *The Essentials of the Islamic Faith*, NJ: Tughra Books.

——. 2005b. *Kalbin Zümrüt Tepeleri III*, Istanbul: Nil Yayınları.

——. 2005c. "Kur'ān-ı Kerim ve Meāli Üzerine" in *Yeni Ümit* 17/68.

——. 2005d. *The Statue of Our Souls: Revival in Islamic Thought and Activism*, trans. by Muhammed Çetin, New Jersey: The Light Inc.

——. 2005e. *Kırık Testi 1*, Istanbul: Nil Yayınları.

——. 2006a. *Kalbin Zümrüt Tepeleri II*, Istanbul: Nil Yayınları.

——. 2006b. *Fasıldan Fasıla V*, Istanbul: Nil Yayınları.

——. 2006c. *İkindi Yağmurları*, Istanbul: Gazeteciler ve Yazarlar Vakfı.

——. 2006d. "Allah Karşısındaki Duruşuyla Mu'min" (Believer in the sense of responsible before God), *Sızıntı*, 28/327.

——. 2006e. "On the Qur'an and Its Interpretation," in Ali Ünal, *The Qur'an with Annotated Interpretation in Modern English*, NJ: Tughra Books.

——. 2007a. *Asrın Getirdiği Tereddütler III*, Istanbul: Nil Yayınları.

——. 2007b. *Kendi İklimimiz*, Istanbul: Nil Yayınları.

——. 2007c. *Prizma 2*, Istanbul: Nil Yayınları.

——. 2008a. *Kalbin Zümrüt Tepeleri IV*, Istanbul: Nil Yayınları.

——. 2008b. *Sonsuz Nur: İnsanlığın İftihar Tablosu I*, Istanbul: Nil Yayınları.

——. 2008c. *Prizma VI*, Istanbul: Nil Yayınları.

——. 2010. *Prizma I*, Istanbul: Nil Yayınları

——. 2010. *Kendi Dünyamıza Doğru*, Istanbul: Nil Yayınları.

Hakikat: Aylık İslām Dergisi, March, 1995.

Hallaq, Wael B. 1984. "Was the Gate of *Ijtihad* Closed?" *International Journal of Middle East Studies*, 16/1.

Hikmet, Ertuğrul. 2008. *Himmeti Milleti Olan İnsan: Fethullah Gülen*, Istanbul: Işık Yayınları.

Horii, Satoe. 2002. "Reconsideration of Legal Devices (Hiyal) in Islamic Jurisprudence: The Hanafis and Their 'Exits' (Makhārij)," *Islamic Law and Society*, 10/3.

Al-Hujwiri. 1979. *Kashf al-Mahjub* Tehran: n. pub.

Ibn Abidin, Muhammad Amin b. Umar. *Majmū'at Rasā'il*, Damascus: Matba'at Ma'rifah Suriyah, n.d.

Ibn Khaldun, Abd al-Rahman bin Muhammad. 1995. *al-Muqaddimah*, Beirut: al-Maktaba al-Asriyya. I.250. Retrieved from www.al-warraq.com

Ibn Manzur. *Lisan al-Arab*; Zabidi. *Taj al-Arus*, "k-z-b."

Juynboll, G. H. A. 1969. *The Authenticity of the Tradition Literature: Discussion in Modern Egypt*, Leiden: Brill.

Kamali, Mohammad Hashim. 1996. "Methodological Issues in Islamic Jurisprudence," *Arab Law Quarterly*, 11/1.

Kandemir, M. Yaşar. 1988. "Hadis," *Türkiye Diyanet Vakfı İslam Ansiklopedisi*, Ankara: Diyanet Vakfı Yayınları, XV.32.

Karamali, Ali, and Fiona Dunne. 1994. "The *Ijtihad* Controversy," *Arab Law Quarterly*, 9/3.

Kuru, Ahmet. 2003. "Fethullah Gülen's Search for a Middle Way Between Modernity and Muslim Tradition," in Hakan Yavuz and John Esposito (editors) *Turkish Islam and the Secular State: The Gülen Movement*, New York: Syracuse University Press.

Kurucan, Ahmet. 1995. "Introduction," in Gülen's *Fasıldan Fasıla I.*

—— (editor). *Soru-Cevaplar'da Fetvalar*, unpublished book.

——. "Fethullah Gülen ve Fıkıh," unpublished article

Madelung, W. 2008. "al- Māturīdī," *EI2*, Brill Online.

Maryon, Jerome D. 2007. "Balancing the Candle on the Right Path," in İhsan Yılmaz (editor) *Peaceful Coexistence: Fethullah Gülen's Initiatives in the Contemporary World*, London: Leeds Metropolitan University Press.

Motzki, Harald. 2001. "The Collection of the Qur'an: A Reconsideration of Western Views in Light of Recent Methodological Developments," *Der Islam*, 78.

Motzki, Harald (editor). "Introduction," in *Hadith: Origins and Developments*, Aldershot, Burlington, VT: Ashgate, Variorum, 2004.

Mulla Jami'. *Nafahat al-Uns*, Tehran, n.d.

Muslim, Abu al-Husayn al-Hajjāj al-Naysābūrī. *Sahih Muslim*, Beirut: Dāru ihyā al-turāth al-'Arabī, n.d.

Nicholson, Reynold A (translator). 1993. *Kashf al-Mahjub*. Cited in Lings.

Niebuhr, H. Richard. 1970. (unpublished lecture) "The position of Theology Today" cited in Libertus A. Hoedemaker, *The Theology of H. Richard Niebuhr*, Boston: Pilgrim Press.

Nursi, Bediüzzaman Said. 1996. *Kaynaklı, İndeksli, Lügatli Risale-i Nur Külliyatı* Istanbul: Nesil Yayınları, II.

——. 2006. *Sözler*, Istanbul: Şahdamar Yayınları.

——. 2001. *Şualar*, Istanbul: Yeni Asya Yayınları.

——. 2010. *The Words*. NJ: The Light, Inc.

Özkök, Ertuğrul. 1995. *Hürriyet*, 23–30 January.

Özvarlı, M. Sait. 2007. "Transferring Traditional Islamic Disciplines into Modern Social Sciences in Late Ottoman Thought: The Attempts of Ziya Gökalp and Mehmed Şerafeddin," *The Muslim World*, 97.

al-Qushayri. 1972. *al-Risalat al-Qushayriya fi 'Ulum al-Tasawwuf*, Cairo.

Rahbar, Daud. 1956. "Sir Sayyid Ahmad Khan's Principles of Exegesis: Translated from his Tahrīr fī Usūl al-Tafsīr I–II," *The Muslim World*, 46.

Rahman, Fazlur. 1979. *Islam*, Chicago: The University of Chicago Press.

——. 1981. "A Recent Controversy over the Interpretation of *Shura*," *History of Religions*, 20/4.

Robson, James. 2008. "Hadīth," *EI*, 2nd ed. Brill Online.

Sarıtoprak, Zeki.2003. "A Sufi in His Own Way," in Hakan Yavuz and John Esposito (editors), *Turkish Islam and the Secular State*, New York: Syracuse University Press.

Sarıtoprak, Zeki, and Ali Ünal. 2005. "An Interview with Fethullah Gülen," *The Muslim World*, 95.

Schacht, Joseph. 1967. *The Origins of Muhammadan Jurisprudence*, Oxford: Clarendon Press.

Selvi, Dilaver. 1997. *Kur'an ve Tasavvuf*, Istanbul: Şule Yayınları.

Sevindi, Nevval. 1997. *Fethullah Gülen'le New York Sohbeti*, Istanbul: Sabah Kitapları.

al-Shaybani. 1979. *al-Sunnah li ibn abī 'Asim*, Beirut: al-Maktabat al-Islāmī, I.

al-Shaybani, 1930. *al-Makharij fī al-Hiyal*, ed. by Jaseph Schacht, Leipzig: Ahmet Ihsan Publishing House.

Şimşek, Said. 2008. *Günümüz Tefsir Problemleri*, Konya: Kitap Dünyası Yayınları.

Sonn, Tamara. 1991. "Fazlur Rahman's Islamic Methodology," *The Muslim World*, 81/3–4.

Stern, S. M. (editor). 1967–71. Ignaz Goldziher in *Muslim Studies*, trans. by C. R. Barber and S. M. Stern, Chicago: University of Chicago Press, II.19.

Suyūtī. 1993. *al-Itqān fī Ulūm al-Qur'ān II*, Beirut: Dār Ibn Kathīr.

al-Tahanawi. 1984. *Kashshaf al-Istilahat al-Funun*, Istanbul: Kahraman Yayınları.

Tuncer, Faruk. "Fethullah Gülen's Methodology of Interpreting the Qur'an." This paper was presented at the Second International Conference on Islam in the Contemporary World: The Fethullah Gülen Movement in Thought and Practice, March 4–5, 2006, Southern Methodist University, Dallas, Texas, U.S.A. The paper is accessible at www.fethullahgulen.org.

Uludağ, Süleyman. 1988–. "Durretu'n-Nāsihīn," in *Türkiye Diyanet Vakfı İslam Ansiklopedisi*, Ankara: Diyanet Vakfı Yayınları, X.

Ünal, Ali. 2003. *M. Fethullah Gülen: Bir Portre Denemesi*, Istanbul: Nil Yayınları.

Ünal, Ali. 2006. *The Qur'an with Annotated Interpretation in Modern English*, NJ: The Light Inc.

Ünal, İsmail. 2001. *Fethullah Gülen'le Amerika'da Bir Ay*, Istanbul: Işık Yayınları.

Watt, Montgomery W. 1988. *Muhammad's Mecca: History in the Qur'an*, Edinburgh: Edinburgh University Press.

Wright, T. Steve. 2007. "Now More Than Ever: Making Non-Violent Change in a Globalised World," in Ihsan Yilmaz (editor), *Peaceful Coexistence: Fethullah Gülen's Initiatives in the Contemporary World*, London: Leeds Metropolitan University Press.

Yıldırım, Suat. 2003. "Fethullah Gülen Hocaefendi Hakkında," Introduction in Ali Ünal (editor). *M. Fethullah Gülen: Bir Portre Denemesi*, Istanbul: Nil Yayınları.

Yılmaz, Ihsan. 2003. "*Ijtihad* and *Taqlid* by Conduct: The Gülen Movement," in Hakan Yavuz and John Esposito (editors), *Turkish Islam and the Secular State*, New York: Syracuse University Press.

Zarkashī. 1990. *al-Burhan fī Ulum al-Qur'an I*, Beirut: Dār al-Ma'rifah.

INDEX